Jonson and the Contexts of His Time

Jonson and the Contexts of His Time

Robert C. Evans

Lewisburg
Bucknell University Press
London and Toronto: Associated University Presses

Associated University Presses
440 Forsgate Drive
Cranbury, NJ 08512

Associated University Presses
25 Sicilian Avenue
London WC1A 2QH, England

Associated University Presses
P.O.Box 338, Port Credit
Mississauga, Ontario
Canada L5G 4L8

The paper used in this publication meets the requirements of the American National Standard for Permanence of Paper for Printed Library Materials Z39.48–1984.

Library of Congress Cataloging-in-Publication Data

Evans, Robert C.
Jonson and the contexts of his time / Robert C. Evans.
p. cm.
Includes bibliographical references (p.) and index.
ISBN 0-8387-5268-3 (alk. paper)
1. Jonson, Ben, 1573?-1637—Criticism and interpretation.
2. Literature and history—England—History—17th Century.
3. Jonson, Ben, 1573?–1637—Contemporary England. I. Title.
PR2642.H5E93 1994
822'.3—dc20 92-56607
CIP

PRINTED IN THE UNITED STATES OF AMERICA

for Ruth

Contents

Preface

Although my introductory chapter discusses some of the assumptions on which this study is based, it may be useful here to sketch briefly the book's contents, organization, and chief concerns. Thus, although my opening chapter does raise certain large theoretical issues (especially those having to do with the so-called "new historicism"), the book as a whole focuses on very specific moments and circumstances in Ben Jonson's life and writings. Nonetheless, various themes do recur throughout the book, and the volume does have a certain shape.

Here as in some of my previous work on Jonson, I am chiefly interested in the *micropolitical* aspects of his writings. That is, I am interested mainly in his works as personal acts, assertions, or performances undertaken in specific social contexts. I am far less interested here in Jonson's *macropolitical* views—his "ideological" attitudes or positions on larger political issues. I have discussed such views at length in another book (*Jonson, Lipsius, and the Politics of Renaissance Stoicism*), but my main interest in this volume is with a kind of politics that strikes me as far more fundamental and inevitable, a kind that involves issues of power at a very personal level. It seems to me that issues such as these are largely inescapable, and that is why I find them so interesting and so continually "relevant." Jonson's specific attitudes toward, say, the Spanish marriage or Scottish courtiers are certainly significant and worth studying, but I suspect that he was at least as interested in his personal power and security as in the "larger" issues of the day. Indeed, to call them larger is already prejudicial, implying that personal politics is somehow petty and small. That, however, is a value judgment I try to avoid. In any case, it is one that strikes me as very limited, however attractive and personally consoling. Just as I have no interest in agreeing or disagreeing with Jonson's "macropolitical" views, and just as I have no interest in consciously pushing (or "subverting") any particular current ideology, so I have no interest in judging Jonson as a human being caught up in complicated issues of self-presentation, competition, and power.

To say that Jonson was necesssarily concerned with personal power is simply (but not entirely) to say that he was concerned with such questions as these: how will I survive? how will I manage to live the kind of life I wish to lead? how, in a very pragmatic sense, will I be able to practice the ideals most important to me? how may I achieve and maintain a simultaneous sense of personal worth and social acceptance? how much freedom or autonomy will I be able to exercise? how can I secure my future while living the kind of life I can respect? All of these, to one degree or another, are *social* questions; they did not exist, and could not be answered, in a vacuum. My book's basic assumption is that Jonson could not ignore the social dimensions of questions like these, that he could not neglect his relations with other people and the effects those relations might have on his life and writings.

Chapter 2 suggests why Jonson's relations with rivals and patrons were particularly significant. The first half of the chapter discusses one of his most important rivalries—the so-called poetomachia—and its significance to the early years of his career. In this section I focus particularly on how Jonson was satirized by Thomas Dekker and John Marston, rivals who attempted to embarrass him before the powerful people on whom his fortunes greatly depended. The chapter's second half then jumps from the beginning to the end of Jonson's career and emphasizes works he himself addressed to William Cavendish, Earl of Newcastle and one of his most significant later patrons. The emphasis on patronage and rivalry that characterizes Chapter 2 recurs in one way or another in all the subsequent chapters, which follow a roughly chronological scheme. Thus Chapter 3 examines the earliest and perhaps still the best of Jonson's great plays, *Volpone,* which was written several years after the end of the poetomachia. My concern here is with the possibility of personal satire of a different sort than one finds in the conflict with Dekker and Marston. The chapter explores new evidence suggesting that Jonson may have used his play to mock a powerful and well-known contemporary figure, the Jacobean moneylender Thomas Sutton. The chapter suggests that micropolitics may have been at least as important in the composition and reception of Jonson's dramatic works as they seem to have been in the case of his poems.

My concern in the three middle chapters, for instance, is to examine three significant works from the important middle portion of Jonson's career—that period in or shortly after 1616 when his monumental Folio and royal pension had established him as the most important English poet of his day. Chapter 4 explores a play produced that year, *The Devil is an Ass*, and attempts to suggest the very complicated political and social circumstances in which it was enmeshed. Chapter 5 attempts to show how the important masque entitled *Pleasure Reconciled to Virtue* (written late in 1617) offered a detailed response to another aristocratic entertainment produced earlier the same year by Robert White, a writer little known to literary historians but apparently then very much on Jonson's mind. Finally, Chapter 6 surveys Jonson's contentious relations with a far more significant and talented rival, Thomas Campion, and suggests that one of Jonson's most successful masques, *The Gypsies Metamorphos'd* (1621), may have been written partly in response to an earlier work by Campion on a similar theme. All three chapters attempt to show how issues of patronage and rivalry (which I have heretofore examined mainly in connection to Jonson's nondramatic poetry) could also impinge on his dramatic works. In addition, all three chapters attempt to supplement and modify the generally macropolitical (or nonpolitical) analyses of these works offered by other recent critics.

Chapters 7 and 8 focus on the closing years of Jonson's career. Chapter 7 explores his little-known friendship with Joseph Webbe, a grammarian and theorist of poetry and language whose ideas were quite controversial at the time. Webbe turned to Jonson as a kind of patron in fending off his own rivals, but the documents that detail their connection have never been previously quoted at any length, and their connection has never before been examined in any great detail. I hope that this chapter, like the three that precede it, may have some value simply as presentations of new historical evidence, aside from any interpretations I have offered. Yet I also hope that this chapter will suggest something about Jonson's social status, views of poetry, and connections with other learned men in the final decade of his life.

That decade is also the focus of my final chapter, which examines Jonson's relations with Sir Kenelm Digby and especially with Richard Weston—the Earl of Portland and one of the most powerful and controversial figures at the court of Charles I. Jonson's relations with Weston, and the poems that resulted from them, have not been examined in great detail before, but they provide fascinating evidence of his relations with the powerful at a time when his own power had begun to fade. One poem in particular suggests as clearly as any I know not only the importance of patronage to Jonson but also the complicated ways in which the patronage "system," so often discussed in the abstract, could operate in actuality. By discussing the details of Weston's circumstances as well as Jonson's, this chapter, I hope, will emphasize a point presupposed throughout this book: that micropolitics was an inescapable concern for Jonson's contemporaries no less than for Jonson himself.

Acknowledgments

One of the main purposes of this book is to offer new archival evidence about important aspects of Ben Jonson's life and writings. Thus I am indebted to a host of librarians in this country and in the United Kingdom who did so much to facilitate my research. I am particularly grateful for the love and support provided by the librarian to whom the book is dedicated. In addition, I wish to thank the staffs of the Folger, Huntington, Newberry, Yale, and Harvard libraries, and those of many libraries in Britain, especially those connected with the Bodleian, the Cambridge University Library, the Library of the University of London, and, of course, the indispensable BL.

My research could not have been undertaken without the generous support of fellowships from such institutions as the National Endowment for the Humanities, the American Philosophical Society, the American Council of Learned Societies, the Newberry Library, the Huntington Library, and the Folger Shakespeare Library. I would especially like to thank the Research Grant-in-Aid program at Auburn University at Montgomery.

Finally, I am grateful for the support of my friends and family, for the satisfactions provided by my students, for the encouragement of my teachers at Pittsburgh and Princeton, and for the stimulus provided by the many Jonsonians, living and dead, from whom I have learned.

Several essays in this book first appeared, in unrevised form, in various scholarly journals. These included *Comparative Drama*, the *Iowa State Journal of Research*, *Philological Quarterly*, *Renaissance and Reformation*, and *Renaissance Papers*. By allowing me to reprint these pieces, their editors have also afforded me the opportunity to update them and make them contribute to a larger argument. For that and for their various kindnesses I am very grateful. In particular I wish to thank John Stroupe and

Clifford Davidson for all their encouragement, support, and good humor. Not since Alvin Kernan and Earl Miner have I had two more thoughtful or attentive readers—always excepting, of course, that tireless proofreader who knows many of these essays backwards and forwards. In this as in everything, any errors are mine, not hers.

Jonson and the Contexts of His Time

1
Jonson and Historical Criticism

The title of this book emphasizes Jonson's *Contexts* because my central assumption is that no single or simple approach can encompass the full richness and complexity of Jonson's various writings. Thus the book presents a series of individual essays that examine particular works or issues from differing perspectives, but all the essays are united by the shared belief that the more we know about Jonson's contexts, the better we may understand his works as responses to them. The individual essays deal with the connections between the poet's writings and contemporary events, and also with Jonson's own relations with friends, rivals, and patrons. In these senses the present book builds on arguments outlined in an earlier study, *Ben Jonson and the Poetics of Patronage*, in which I stressed the crucial importance of such contexts for a better understanding of Jonson's life and art. That book dealt especially with his poetry, whereas this one more prominently emphasizes some of his works in other genres, particularly drama and the masques. I hope, if nothing else, that the book provides new information about certain specific facets of Jonson's writings and career.

My earlier book stressed the importance of Jonson's relations with his audience, particularly with patrons and rivals, and I see little reason to modify that emphasis substantially. For lack of a better term, I chose to stress the importance of *micropolitics* in Jonson's life, writings, and environment—by which I meant the importance of power relations on an individual level. I am less interested in competing ideologies or ideals than in competing individuals, although it is often impossible to make such neat distinctions stick. In any case, it is issues of personal power and personal security that intrigue me, and in Jonson's case these issues necessarily involve study of his links with patrons, rivals, and friends. In fact, as I hope the ensuing essays will show, the more we examine his works in detail, the more important such contexts become.

There are, of course, dangers inherent in this approach, as recent critics of the so-called "new historicism" have suggested. Since these dangers are significant, they seem worth discussing at some length. For instance, it is possible to misunderstand my earlier arguments by assuming that I read Jonson as completely dominated by his involvement in Renaissance patronage systems.[1] However, I do not see Jonson as so dominated, and I emphasize this point throughout my earlier book. Its first paragraph, for instance, says that to call Jonson a "'poet dependent on patronage' . . . stresses his *dependency* in a manner that fundamentally simplifies the complex nature of his relations with superiors" (9). I reiterated this point frequently, and in fact one of my purposes was (and is) to show how Jonson attempted to transform a social position that lent itself to domination into one in which he could hope to enjoy a measure of personal power. If that last sentence seems a bit fussy ("attempted . . . could hope . . . a measure"), that is because I do not see his situation as reducible to simple alternatives of freedom or submission. The temptation to resort to either/or explanations is one I wish to resist.[2]

Thus, although I earlier warned against taking Jonson simply as he presents himself, I also disavowed any depiction of him as a malignant competitor or as a literary prostitute. As I said, "Neither of these negative views does justice to the real complexity of his position" (35). I feel no great need to evaluate Jonson in moral terms; in fact, doing so strikes me as a bit presumptuous. Modern professors—with our tenure, comfortable salaries, retirement packages, medical insurance, present and future Social Security, and all the benefits of living in a modern liberal democracy—are not in much of a position to pass judgment on lives shaped by the conditions Jonson knew. Even if Jonson could be proven a moral reprobate (however defined), this would not necessarily detract from the *literary* value of his writing. Perhaps literary historians should attempt to function neither as apologists nor as prosecutors but simply as neutral investigators of the data at hand. In any case, as a critic I am chiefly interested in the richness and complexity of an author's writings, not in defending his personality.[3]

For this reason I do not share the assumption that recent readings of Jonson undermine his moral stature and consequently the value of his art. I do not equate Jonson's literary achievements with his personal qualities (although I greatly respect both). I feel impelled neither to attack nor to defend him. His artistic merit strikes me as obvious, and his life and writings as complex. My work simply attempts to unfold certain of his complexities. It notes various ambivalences, contradictions, ambiguities, and tensions in his life and works, but if these diminish his ethical and literary worth in others' eyes, that is because they make assumptions I do not share. As I have suggested, "the more we acknowledge the universality and inevitability of micropolitics and of individual self-interest, the more we may be able to scrutinize our own motives and behavior with a certain humility, even humor. The implications of such an approach to Jonson's poetry need not be cynical or amoral, and could in fact prove precisely the opposite" (14).[4] That is, the more we are willing to concede the difficulty of passing simple or easy moral judgment on other people, the more morally we may treat them.

I do not see Jonson either as a sycophant or as a flatterer. As I have stressed, the "more we know about the conditions that helped shape [his] works, the less likely we are to judge his character hastily. The more closely we examine the issues of independence and flattery in his works, the more problematic they seem" (86).[5] "The impulses to romanticize his situation by viewing him either as an oppressed crypto-democrat or as an unperturbed servant of God and country should both be resisted. So, by the same token, should any tendency toward automatic cynicism, whether this means viewing him as a toady or as a schemer. Both reactions may reflect more our own preoccupations than the complexities of his real position" (87–88). Instead, I have argued that

> Both the view that emphasizes [Jonson's] independence and the view that sees him as a toady tend to overlook the true complexity of his position. Both seem concerned to depict him in some moral light; both imply assumptions about the kind of independence he *should* have exercised and the ideals or behavior he either exemplified or failed to attain. Both tend to obscure the extent to which he necessarily served *himself*—the extent to which his works can be viewed in terms of personal strategy and tactics. Of course, emphasizing power relations cannot explain *everything* about his writings, and indeed, once we begin to think of literary works as instances of behavior, their implications can come to seem as complex—even as apparently contradictory—as human beings themselves. Emphasizing the strategic significance and aspects of Jonson's works is simply one approach worth pursuing further—one that can perhaps even prove more neutral, more objective, than some others because it

> requires us neither to promote the poet nor to denigrate him. Instead, it is an approach that sees power as an inevitable and inherently fascinating aspect of human relations. (37–38)

This passage, in fact, is relevant to a number of other possible charges. It might be alleged, for instance, that I see Jonson as a writer wholly concerned with self-promotion. Yet, as I have already suggested and will later suggest again, I wish to avoid a totalizing rhetoric, a language of simple, either/or distinctions.[6] On this particular point it would be more accurate to describe self-promotion (shorthand for such other terms as self-presentation, self-protection, self-assertion, self-definition) as a nearly inevitable *aspect* or *effect* of Jonson's works (30). To deny this would seem to suggest that he intended to denigrate himself in public, which seems inherently improbable. Although some readers may consider self-interest morally shameful, self-interest of some sort or at some level seems merely a fact of life. This would not surprise biologists or social psychologists. However, as I have stressed, "there is no need to associate poetic self-promotion—or indeed self-promotion of any kind—with conscious deception or cynical calculation. Other resources being equal, the best competitor in any power game is likely to be the person least conscious of the game as such, the one most sincerely committed to (and involved in) his role" (38).[7] As I have argued, an individual's social

> performance is likely to convince others precisely when it convinces himself; his absorption in his role gives him an advantage over the less committed, even though increasing his power may be the furthest thing from his mind. The analyst of power relations must be careful not to ascribe to the actor the analyst's own awareness of the tactical advantages of different self-presentations. The actor may or may not be aware (there are strong incentives to suppress or disguise such awareness), and if he is aware, the degree of his self-consciousness may vary. If the image he presents reflects his own self-image, then his need to have it accepted—thus his need to accept it himself and to promote most effectively its acceptance by others—becomes all the greater. And it is with the tactics he uses to promote that acceptance that the analyst (or critic) must be concerned. (38)

From this it should be clear that I do not think Jonson was totally ignorant of what he was doing as a poet. If I really believed he was, I could hardly also accuse him of being a flatterer or sycophant. The notion that some motives are unconscious is not especially startling, and in any case it seems likely that sometimes Jonson may have been conscious of how his poems served his self-interests, and sometimes he may not have been. The state of his mind *at any given moment* is obviously unknowable, and that is why I have emphasized a greater concern with the likely *effects* and *effectiveness* of his works. In general, our self-consciousness about self-interests seems likely to depend on external stimuli, especially other people.[8]

This comment, in fact, relates to another charge that has been leveled against the "new historicism." It has been claimed, for instance, that for new historicists

> Power becomes relational rather than substantive, something invested in networks of social interactions rather than invested indigenously in persons. "Power" is consequently possessed by no one, and yet it comes into existence through interaction among these individuals. The new historicism situates a contradictory conception of power at the center of its own analysis: others possess power, others do not possess power. (131)

Since this critique can be considered crucial, it deserves a full response. Although I cannot speak for new historicists, I *can* lay out my own reaction.

To the first quoted sentence I have no strong objection, although I would note the either/or tendency it reveals. The idea that power is largely relational rather than purely substantive strikes me as at least defensible, if not simply a matter of common sense.[9] No matter what attributes a person may "indigenously" possess, if those attributes are not regarded, rewarded, or valued by the community in which he lives, he is unlikely to win any real social power (affirmation, security, influence) as a result of them. Jonson's "greatness" as a poet is not (as is sometimes implied) an uncomplicated matter. Jonson performed very well certain tasks that powerful segments of his community valued. To locate the source of his power in his indigenous literary "greatness" simply begs various questions about his social contexts, which valued and in many ways encouraged the kinds of talents he may indeed have been born with and that he cultivated so well.

To take an extreme example, if Jonson had been born in a society in which poetry-writing was regarded as sick, deviant, or criminal, his "indigenous" potential would have mattered little. If as an Englishman he had used his indigenous power to extol the glory of the Pope or to commend Islam or Judaism over Christianity, we would probably have heard little from him. In fact, if he had simply been born a woman (a fifty-fifty chance), it is unlikely that we would today possess eleven fat volumes of her works and commentary. Or, to take a more modest example, it could be argued that Jonson's personal power rested partly on his creative labor. Yet many contemporaries accused him of being plodding and laborious, and many subsequent readers (influenced by Romantic assumptions about the nature and purposes of poetry) have agreed. The literary excellence that some critics see as the most crucial feature of Jonson's works is an attribute many readers, then and since, have questioned. The fact that many critics share a regard for Jonson's poetry says less about the poetry itself than about our tastes, training, and social conditioning. To claim that Jonson's literary excellence or indigenous talent was the source of his social power simplifies his situation, both as a writer and as a person.[11]

Having admitted to thinking that social power is largely relational, I would now deny the force of what is deduced from this premise: "'Power' is consequently possessed by no one and can be conferred by no one, and yet it comes into existence through interaction among . . . individuals." However, seeing power as relational hardly means denying that it exists or that anyone possesses it.[12] Once again, this charge suggests a tendency to totalize, to think in terms of sharply defined alternatives. Consider, for instance, the claim that embedded in the new historicism is the contradiction that "others possess power, others do not possess power." Drop the totalizing rhetoric, and the "contradiction" disappears: "others possess *some* power, others do not possess *all* power." This is a claim I can live with, and once again it seems easy to defend. By virtue of the way Jacobean society was organized, King James had *some* power, some influence, over others. But this, as my earlier book argued repeatedly, hardly means that he had *all* power. In relation to the Earl of Pembroke, the King had *some* power (in fact, *greater* power), but in relation to the King, Pembroke had some power of his own. In relation to Jonson, Pembroke had *some* power (in fact, *greater* power), but in relation to Pembroke, Jonson had some power of his own (a point true of his relations with nearly all his patrons). Jonson's power in relation to the King and the Earl depended partly on his "indigenous" talent, but also on such other factors as (1) his native ability to exploit that talent; (2) the opportunities he was given or was allowed to cultivate and demonstrate that talent; (3) how he presented his talent to his patrons and other readers; (4) his readers' attitudes toward such talents as he possessed; (5) his need to compete with other talented people.

Where some might see a contradiction in "relational" notions of power, I see at most a paradox, and not even really that.[13] Others *do* possess certain powers, and others do *not* possess certain other powers. And even the "powers" others possess are socially conditioned and defined. In all these respects and for all these reasons, power *is* relational (or at least it seems so to me), and thus power relations can be extremely complicated, messy, and multivalent. The "power" one possesses and confers is power possessed in a given social context at a given moment in time. James Stuart, born a commoner, would have possessed very little power; James Stuart, born to the Scottish throne, happened to possess a great deal. James Stuart, born to that throne but having different relations with Elizabeth I and Robert Cecil, would have had little power over Jonson's career. In the competitive world depicted in my earlier book, it makes little sense to speak of "the" source of "the" power a poet might seek to tap, but rather of various sources of various kinds of power, all depending on the social network for their acceptance and validation (and thus for the acceptance and validation of those who possessed and conferred such powers). In a system such as this, power is a matter of *negotiation*.[14]

Precisely because I do see power as largely relational, I am skeptical of any attempt to read Max Scheler's concept of *ressentiment* as the master-trope that underlies micropolitical analysis. *Ressentiment*, it has been said,

> invests all members [of society] with a sense of personal inadequacy and the consequent need to compensate for it. It is a characteristic of any hierarchical social structure in which sado/masochistic relations dominate. Each individual masochistically accepts the deflation of self imposed by those above him/her, and in turn relays this deflation sadistically to those below. [Thus] micropolitical analysis emphasizes the devaluation of the individual in a courtly context. This devaluation drives him/her to seek validation in the eyes of an alien Other who consequently takes on a radically divided function: it confers a sense of self on the subject, while being the object of the subject's envy and hatred. . . . The radical source of *ressentiment*, and of the "micropolitical" social structures that [are posited] as universal, is self-loathing. The person of *ressentiment* in Scheler's account always sees himself/herself through the eyes of an Other. This alien-

> ation of self from self nevertheless involves a corresponding projection of the self's self-loathing onto this Other, so that the denigrating glance of the Other has no content save that invested in it by the subject. *Ressentiment* in short is a form of narcissistic paranoia. (131)

This is very interesting, but it does not reflect my view of Jonson's personality and circumstances. In some respects Jonson did seem to feel socially disadvantaged (or inadequate), and in some respects he really was. For instance, a wealthier background might have given him greater autonomy and more time to cultivate his talents. The evidence that he was acutely sensitive about his social status, and that his antagonists tried to exploit his sensitivity, is so abundant that it need not be recounted here.[15] However, the fact that Jonson was sensitive about his status and tried to improve it hardly means that he felt totally inadequate; almost everything suggests the opposite: if any poet had an assertive ego, it was Jonson. (It goes without saying, however, that a sense of inadequacy and a tendency toward self-assertion are not necessarily contradictory.) To claim that Jonson felt socially inadequate or socially disadvantaged is hardly to suggest that he was consumed by "self-loathing." Here as throughout, the quoted passage on *ressentiment* quickly turns from relatively objective and knowable social circumstances to private psychology. (It might make more sense, instead, to emphasize the ways private psychology is shaped by social psychology, which is in turn shaped by objective social conditions.) The quoted passage seems to assume that a person's private self-opinion is enough to ensure his objective social security and status. Members of any "marginal" group know how questionable this assumption is. Yet it may be true to some extent: a person who is sure of himself—without seeming threateningly arrogant—is likely to seem powerful and prove attractive to others. However, it seems unlikely that a simple change in Jonson's self-perception would have altered fundamentally the social circumstances with which he had to cope.

Particularly questionable, however, is any notion that Jonson "masochistically accepts the deflation of self imposed by those above." In fact, Jonson seems to have resisted denigration in a wide variety of ways, as the very fury of his often self-defensive satire testifies. If the adverb "masochistically" implies that he somehow took pleasure in being degraded by others, I confess that I see little evidence of this. Moreover, the modified verb—"accepts"—attributes to him more autonomous power than a person in his position was likely to possess. It is as if Jonson could simply ignore the hostility of superiors and rivals. Abundant data, however, indicate that he did *not* ignore it, nor is it easy to see how he could. He might have responded differently, but even a different response would have been some response. Consistently, the passage on *ressentiment* attributes greater social independence to persons than I think is merited. It is as if Jonson could simply have decided to overlook personal attacks and affronts, as if they would have no real effect on his social standing and practical social power. One of the reasons that Jonson took the opinions of his superiors and antagonists so seriously, it seems, is precisely because he realized that those opinions might influence the attitudes of others. He seems to have understood that power *is* relational, and that no matter how healthy one's opinion of oneself, the opinions of others would inevitably affect one's objective social standing. The idea that one's real social power depends greatly on others' assessments and acceptance seems unremarkable, rather than needing explaining in terms of abnormal psychology.

Just as Jonson was probably not "masochistic," so he seems not to have been a sadist. Surely he did not enjoy inflicting pain on others, particularly on social inferiors. In fact, his relations with his "sons" and friends seem to have been among his most satisfying and consoling (although not, for that reason, without complexities). These relations provided some of the few and most pleasurable alternatives to the competitive life of a courtier/poet, particularly one whose status was so unprecedented.[16] If Jonson occasionally inflicted pain on others—especially rivals, but also "unworthy" superiors—that is probably not because he possessed a mean, sadistic streak or lacked true self-respect, but largely because he felt threatened. And to say that "he" felt threatened is simply shorthand for saying that the values and ideals that he tried to embody and promote seemed threatened as well. Any threat to *his* power was a small threat to theirs; it would handicap his ability to promote them. His personal power cannot easily be separated from his "impersonal" ideas and ideals.

Finally, from this it should be clear that just as I reject any notion of Jonson as a masochist or sadist, so I resist the idea that he was paranoid.[17] The old joke applies: even paranoids have enemies. Jonson, it seems to me, was not a paranoid, but he did have antagonists in abundance, and the threats he perceived, as well as the inherent insecurity of his social position, were not merely figments of his imagination. His vulnerability was largely and simply a social fact, not a projection of his fevered mind.[18] His insecurity was less a problem of personal psychology than a real problem rooted in the inherently relational nature of social power. Once again it seems worth remembering how easy it is for us, with our whole panoply of social security, to forget how brief, uncertain, and contingent life could seem to our ancestors. There is no need to see Jonson's defensiveness and aggressiveness as projections of "self-loathing." They may have been born partly from frustration with his circumstances, but that is hardly the same thing as self-contempt. Jonson was probably just as "normal" as most people, but he was also a man caught up in difficult and complicated circumstances.

There seems little need to judge Jonson, either psychologically or morally. Rather, it seems more useful to describe one's perception of his circumstances and responses. Jonson does not seem to have lacked any sense of identity except that bestowed by others, nor were the threatening opinions of others threatening only because he chose to feel threatened by them. We must resist simple definitiveness, in which complicated questions are reduced to matters of all-or-nothing. In fact, the master-trope of my earlier book is not so much *ressentiment* as paradox. I see Jonson's situation as variously paradoxical, and my analyses of his poems tend to emphasize explanations of the "both/and" rather than the "either/or" variety. For this reason, there seems little conflict between my approach to Jonson and most others. In fact, my book's final sentences read as follows:

> Since nearly every other approach implies something about the poet's presentation of himself to an audience, there would seem to be little difficulty in relating most other ways of reading Renaissance literature to a patronage perspective. Indeed, such an endeavor, by complicating and deepening our understanding of how a patronage poet like Jonson interacted with his audience, could only further enrich our understanding of his works themselves. (268)

It is to one of those works, the Sackville epistle, that I now wish to turn. Certainly this is one of Jonson's most significant reflections on patronage.[19] Discussing it here will allow me to deal with some significant issues, particularly the poem's relation to its main source, Seneca's *De Beneficiis*. In my opinion, the fact that Jonson drew some of his ideas from a prior source provides no magic key to a simpler understanding of his own poem, as if Seneca's attempt to propound answers to difficult questions had eliminated the difficulties for good.[20] In any case, I find the epistle itself quite complex in its own right. Simply because the poem seems (or attempts) to situate itself outside the world of personal politics hardly means that it has no micropolitical functions or effects. In fact, the very attempt to seem distanced from such politics was attractive and thus could prove beneficial both to Jonson and to his poem.

The long opening section of the poem raises many fundamental issues:

IF, *Sackvile,* all that have the power to doe
Great and good turns, as wel could time them too,
And knew their how, and where: we should have, then,
Lesse list of proud, hard, or ingratefull Men.
For benefits are ow'd with the same mind
As they are done, and such returnes they find:
You then, whose will not only, but desire
To succour my necessities, tooke fire,
Not at my prayers, but your sense; which laid
The way to meet, what others would upbraid;
And in the Act did so my blush prevent,
As I did feele it done, as soone as meant:
You cannot doubt, but I, who freely know
This Good from you, as freely will it owe;
And though my fortune humble me, to take
The smallest courtesies with thankes, I make
Yet choyce from whom I take them; and would shame
To have such doe me good, I durst not name:
They are the Noblest benefits, and sinke
Deepest in Man, of which when he doth thinke,
The memorie delights him more, from whom
Then what he hath receiv'd. Gifts stinke from some,
They are so long a comming, and so hard;
Where any Deed is forc't, the Grace is mard.[21]

The Sackville epistle seems very much concerned to assert and demonstrate Jonson's own dignity as a recipient. Although Sackville himself obviously enjoyed in many respects greater influence than the poet he patronized, Jonson uses his work to claim and to illustrate his own power in the very act of acknowledging (or "owing") his indebtedness. The poem presents Sackville as a model patron, but also Jonson as a model recipient. In both senses it implicitly addresses two very important segments of Jonson's audience: other or potential patrons, and real or potential rivals.

Although arguably the poem's derivation from a classical source renders its tone somewhat conventional or impersonal, this very derivativeness sanctions and objectifies its rhetoric, making it seem more disinterested and for that reason (paradoxically) potentially more effective as an instrument of self-assertion.[22] In fact, the epistle illustrates many claims made in the Preface to my book on Jonson and patronage, where I detail the ways a Renaissance poet could exploit the connections between his own work and a classical source. By drawing so strongly on Seneca, Jonson (1) compliments Sackville by assuming that he will note the connection; (2) demonstrates his own learning; (3) demonstrates his ability to imitate without being slavishly imitative; (4) attempts to insulate himself from the appearance of flattery by drawing on conventional wisdom; (5) implies a link between himself and those readers learned enough to appreciate his allusiveness; (6) sanctions his voice by giving it a kind of timeless, impersonal authority; (7) appropriates a valued text and moral tradition for personal use; (8) calls attention to a recognized standard against which his own claims can be authenticated and judged; (9) distinguishes himself from less learned competitors; (10) renews and extends an important cultural legacy; (11) implies his selfless reverence for the thought and ideals of a widely admired predecessor; and (12) dignifies and depersonalizes an obligation that might otherwise seem somewhat uncomfortable. Such a list could easily be extended, but by now the point is clear: the relations between Jonson's poem and its "source" are hardly simple or straightforward. In these ways and in others, Jonson's use of Seneca could be called self-serving, although it is hard to see why this should seem morally reprehensible. To deny such connections between poem and source would indeed mean failing to take Seneca's essay seriously. Viewing the poem merely as a versified transcript of *De Beneficiis* would, I think, immensely simplify a complex connection.

Potentially, "all" persons have the power to "doe / Great and good turns" in a moral sense (1–2), but it was a simple fact of life—and one the poem abundantly ackowledges—that only a few people, such as Sackville, were positioned to do "Great and good turns" in a practical, pragmatic sense. Although Jonson can distinguish himself from "proud, hard, and ingratefull" recipients (4), and although his own poem, by magnifying Sackville's reputation, partly pays the debt Jonson owes, the poet could hardly return the material favors he had received. His poem, then, attempts to make a literal (and literary) virtue out of the real "necessities" (8) of his indebtedness and dependence. The epistle enhances Sackville's public dignity while also asserting and defending Jonson's. Although Jonson uses the poem to call attention on more than one occasion to his humility, and although in this way and in others he distances himself from the egotistical ingratitude of other recipients, his poem also displays (in several senses of that word) a healthy pride and self-respect. It presents Jonson as humble, but not humiliated by his need to take favors from Sackville. Indeed, part of its paradoxical quality is that Jonson takes a kind of pride in his very humility. He presents it as a model others should emulate.[23]

By enacting the socially sanctioned role of the properly grateful recipient, Jonson illustrates his willingess to subject his ego to his culture's larger values and ideals, yet to do so is also to promote his own social security and acceptance (particularly by Sackville). Although explicitly addressed to Sackville, the poem implicitly and inevitably (by its very public nature) also addresses that wider audience of patrons, friends, rivals, and other powerful people that Jonson could not afford to ignore. In one respect it celebrates an unusual private relationship, but in another it exalts that relationship as a worthy public model. In still another respect, the poem functions as a kind of advertisement, as a bid for Sackville's continued patronage and for future patronage from others. And, in yet one more respect, the poem functions partly as a self-defense, for Jonson had repeatedly been charged with the very faults of ingratitude, egotism, and selfish ambition from which the poem seeks to distance him. Seeing the work simply as a versified restatement of moral commonplaces means dealing with only one level of its very rich significance. A micropolitical reading of the sort just outlined perhaps does greater justice to both its social and aesthetic complexity.

Such complexity can be seen even in the particular words Jonson chooses. Take, for instance, the repeated adverb "freely": "You cannot doubt, but I, who freely know / This Good from you, as freely will it owe" (13–14). Jonson "freely know[s]" Sackville's "Good" (itself a pun) in the sense that he comfortably but also willingly realizes it, and perhaps also in the sense that he realizes that it comes to him willingly or freely. He "freely will it owe" in the sense that he will owe it without feeling burdened by it, and also in the sense that he will acknowledge it openly and willingly. Yet the lines are more complex still, for there is a sense in which Jonson's "free" expression of thanks is itself in part a response to the same social norms, conventions, and expectations that the poem so skillfully articulates. Failure to respond as he does (in behavior if not in writing) might have threatened Jonson's standing with Sackville in particular and with other persons (and patrons) generally. Thus the very freedom of response the poem exalts can be seen partly as a submission to the cultural mores which Jonson attempts to speak for and enforce. To say this is simply to say that Jonson, like anyone, could not be completely autonomous. His "freedom" was conditioned, conditional—because relative, relational.

Jonson's attempt to equate his own dignity with Sackville's affects the poem in ways both large and small. For instance, at one point Sackville is praised for his instantaneous generosity: his "Act did so my blush prevent, / As I did feele it done, as soone as meant" (11–12). The blush was "prevented" not only by being obviated but also by being forestalled; Sackville's act "came before" (*prae* + *venire*) the blush could (or needed to) occur. By the same token, however, when Jonson vows that he "will" freely acknowledge Sackville's generosity, this very claim performs what it seems to promise. Sackville's rapid generosity is matched by Jonson's rapid thanks. Yet even though his gratitude in one sense is spontaneous and immediate, it is also embedded in, and serves as the impetus for, an extraordinarily elaborate and self-conscious exercise in public etiquette. There is nothing very simple about this poem.[24]

The epistle's public nature is always worth recalling. Remembering that others would read this work complicates our sense of its rhetorical functions. Later, for instance, Jonson attacks patrons who exploit dependents to enhance their public image. He condemns the giver "that doth sound a Trumpet, and doth call / His Groomes to witnesse" (35–36). Yet as the poem's existence testifies, what bothers Jonson is not publicity itself, but how, why, and by whom it is practiced. The poem implies that the patron who celebrates his own gift-giving thereby demeans both the recipient and himself. In Jonson's poem, the recipient controls the publicity; the poet himself acts as a trumpet, calling others to witness his relation with Sackville. His trumpeting of his patron's generosity benefits them both, especially since the poem is addressed not to such utter dependents as "Groomes"—from whom the poet clearly wishes to distinguish himself—but to the writer's (and his patron's) superiors and peers. Jonson's poem gives the recipient greater control over how both the relation and the gift would be understood and interpreted publicly, and it was this more than any single relation or gift that would affect his social power.

Of course, there were risks even in writing such a poem. One was the risk of seeming too *much* to "Trumpet" the poet, of calling too much attention to his own act of thanks. Jonson anticipates this charge of egotism—one he constantly faced—by implicitly distinguishing himself from the sort of recipient "that will receive / Nought but in corners; and is loath to leave / Lest Ayre, or Print, but flies it: Such men would / Run from the Conscience of it, if they could" (43–46). The very existence and public nature of his own poem distance Jonson from such ingratitude; by the logic implied here, the work's extreme length testifies not to any desire to flaunt his own skills and thoughts but to the depth and freedom of his thanks. Moreover, as already indicated, the epistle's conventionality protects it from seeming too rooted in one man's ego. Yet the poem's very elaborateness could open its author to another charge—the accusation of flattery. This is one that Jonson again denies (155), and in general he is careful to distinguish himself both from recipients whose thanks are hypocritcally profuse (53–55) and from those who "Give thankes by stealth, and whispering in the eare" (49). Although addressed to a patron, the epistle for that very reason is also much concerned to differentiate the writer from potential competitors.

In two fascinating passages, dependents are compared to dogs. The first alludes to recipients who speak "worst of those, from whom they went / But then, fist-fill'd, to put me off the sent" (51–52). Such clients condemn their benefactors not only to hide their indebtedness but also to discourage the poet from pursuing the same quarry, from competing for a likely source of patronage. The competitive context openly alluded to here arguably underlies the entire poem. But while the poet's rivals compete by denying what they owe, Jonson competes by "freely" confessing his debts so as to benefit both himself and his patron. The poem demonstrates both the natural interest of patrons in being thanked and Jonson's skillful ability to thank them.

A second reference to dogs condemns patrons who seek to profit by asking "Like Money-brokers, after Names, and hire / Their bounties forth, to him that last was made, / Or stands to be'[i]n Commission o' the blade" (62–64).

Still, still, the hunters of false fame apply
Their thoughts and meanes to making loude the cry;
But one is bitten by the Dog he fed,
And hurt seeks Cure, the Surgeon bids take bread,
And spunge-like with it dry up the blood quite:
Then give it to the Hound that did him bite;
Pardon, sayes he, that were a way to see
All the Towne-curs take each their snatch at me. (65–72)

The links between this and the earlier passage are intriguing. Earlier the writer was likened to a dog put "off the sent" by wary competitors, whereas here those rivals themselves are dogs who bite the hands that feed them. The similar language suggests the parallel situations of Jonson and his competitors, their actual, practical dependence on superiors. It was precisely these objective parallels that made it so important for Jonson to distinguish himself from his rivals, and much of the Sackville epistle is concerned to do just that. Yet by calling his patrons' attention to such treachery, Jonson exploits his superiors' insecurity, showing them how unreliable their dependents could be, and, by implication and contrast, how different he is.

Jonson's disdain for the curs with whom he had to compete is rivalled by his contempt for the patrons who almost cooperated in their own exploitation, who fell for tactics that struck the poet as nauseatingly obvious. As my earlier book stresses, what bothers Jonson almost more than his rivals themselves is their success. Indeed, without the support of powerful benefactors, such rivals would be inconsequential and could largely be ignored. Jonson condemns patrons who "seeke not wants to succour" (61)—phrasing that not only puns on "wants" ("once") but that also strikingly recalls his earlier praise of Sackville for desiring "To succour my necessities" (8). The buried echo enhances the sense that Jonson saw as direct and personal competitors the treacherous recipients he later attacks in relatively impersonal terms. At one point he calls them "Pyrats"—those who take what rightfully belongs to others (81). By depicting them this way, he makes it easier for their supporters to reject them. Public ethics and private self-interest equally demand that patrons repudiate clients who exploit them.

Jonson seems frustrated, in part, by the prospect that his genuine needs might be ignored in favor of the mere desires of competitors. Because they are less needy and possess "Names" and other "bounties" (62–63), the rivals he attacks are in real and practical ways more powerful than he. They seem to have more to offer their benefactors, and this is why the patrons themselves, driven by a need for social power, even seek out such "dependents" (on whom in fact they ironically depend). Although Jonson initially depicts false recipients as simple sponges with little to offer in return (cf. 47–58), it soon emerges that they can confer many practical benefits on their benefactors. This makes them more threatening competitors, and two tasks of this poem are to make associating with them seem a liability to their patrons, thus making association with men like Jonson seem even more attractive.

After attacking false patrons and false clients at length, Jonson again asserts his own modesty: "I have the lyst of mine owne faults to know, / Looke to and cure. Hee's not a man hath none, / But like to be, that every day mends one, / And feeles it; Else he tarries by the Beast" (114–17). However, even his acknowledgment of what he shares with his targets distinguishes him from them. His very willingness to confess faults contrasts *his* morality with their blind egotism. Moreover, Jonson no sooner admits his failings than he generalizes them: "He's not a man hath none." Indeed, there even seems something virtuous and commendable about Jonson's willingess to admit his vices publicly and pledge to correct them. What might have seemed merely self-critical becomes an attractive part of his public self-presentation. To fail to admit faults, to fail to try to improve, is to "tarr[y] by the Beast": not only to behave like an animal (as in the earlier references to dogs), but perhaps also to repudiate goodness in an almost demonic way.[25] Subsequent lines make the ability to distinguish good from bad seem natural, inevitable, easy (118–22). This makes the viciousness of those condemned seem all the more culpable and irrational.

Although Jonson makes recognizing goodness seem easy, he makes attaining it seem to require effort and continuous self-scrutiny. Of course, those who distinguish virtue from its counterfeit—a group including good readers generally, Sackville in particular, but also (implicitly) the poet—"cannot choose which you will be" (154). Paradoxically, Sackville is praised for an attribute that at first seems indigenous and inevitable. Addressing him, Jonson claims that "You know (without my flatt'ring you) too much / For me to be your Indice" (155–56). This tactic is typical: frequently Jonson credits patrons with full knowledge of the very precepts he so fully and carefully expounds.

Although the poem is addressed to Sackville, ostensibly he doesn't need it. He already embodies the virtues it commends. Poet and patron become partners in an effort largely aimed at others. Yet the poem, of course, is in fact aimed at Sackville, and Jonson acknowledges the possibility that his patron may ultimately prove morally (and pragmatically) unreliable. To maintain the poet's respect, Sackville must maintain his goodness ("Keep you such"—156). Significantly yet realistically, near its end the poem raises prospects of uncertainty and instability, of a collapse of the clear distinctions it has labored to construct. Even Sackville may apparently prove unreliable.

Given this possibility, the poem's last words seem especially significant. Although emphasizing the mutuality of benefactor and dependent, they finally stress the poet's own role as a model recipient. Jonson anticipates a time when both "*Donnor's* or *Donnee's*, to their practise shall / Find you to reckon nothing, me owe all" (163–64). These lines are variously paradoxical. Thus, Jonson exploits rhetorical oppositions (between "*Donnor*" and "*Donnee*," between "nothing" and "all," between "reckon[ing]" and "ow[ing]") to suggest a deeper and more fundamental concord between benefactor and recipient. The poet stresses his indebtedness, yet by doing so he presents himself as exemplary; he "owes" in the double sense (implied throughout) of being obligated and of acknowledging that obligation freely. The three final, monosyllabic words end the poem emphatically and shift its focus finally to Jonson himself: "me owe all." It is a brief confession of indebtedness that the whole poem elaborates, a confession of obligation that also reasserts a power to some degree independent even of a man as good as Sackville seems to be.

Even an analysis as lengthy as this must ignore many local details that enhance the epistle's power, such as the wordplay on "Great" and "ingratefull" (2; 4) or the ironic pun on "streightned" in describing the growth of "Dwarfes of Honour" (152; 147). Yet my analysis will, I hope, suggest why and how the epistle strikes me as an extremely complicated poem. I do not say "extraordinarily complicated," because this work seems exceptional more in its length than in its complexity. As both this book and my earlier one try to show, Jonson's poetry frequently raises problems of the sort this poem confronts. That it does not—cannot—easily or entirely resolve such problems strikes me as one of the fascinations of Jonson's art. Any critical method that can help us see the fuller richness of his work—without feeling the need to simplify, take sides, or choose between obvious alternatives—seems worth pursuing further.

Each of the following essays highlights a different specific aspect of Jonson's career or a different specific context of his writings, yet all share the basic assumption that detailed study of historical contexts can help us better appreciate Jonson's works not simply as historical documents but also, as in the poem to Sackville, as complicated works of art.

2
Rivals and Patrons: Early and Late

Among the contexts most important to Jonson—as to most people—were his relations with others. Among the persons most important to him, patrons, rivals, and friends were exceptionally crucial. As the last chapter has argued, his relations with his superiors, antagonists, and allies could determine not only his objective standing in society, but also, to some extent, his subjective sense of self-worth and self-fulfillment. With the support of patrons and friends, Jonson could feel some sense of social security and thus some hope of achieving his most heartfelt and important goals. Without such support—or in the face of active threats—the very meaning and purpose of his life might seem ambiguous or unattainable. Jonson was very much a social poet—a writer caught up in and responsive to the social contexts of his day. By scrutinizing some of those contexts and his responses to them, we can come to a fuller appreciation of both his life and his art.

One of the most interesting events of his life—his early involvement in the war of the theaters, termed by Thomas Dekker the "poetomachia"—sheds some light on the contexts in which Jonson operated. For instance, the attacks on Jonson by Dekker and John Marston in their famous theatrical onslaught, *Satiromastix*, seem much more closely tied to questions of patronage than has perhaps been previously stressed. The play can be seen as a conscious attempt to embarrass Jonson in front of the most influential and important segment of his audience at a critical juncture in his progress as a poet. Looking at the play from the perspective of patronage helps emphasize how crucial and representative an event the poetomachia was, how much it typified many of the tensions and challenges Jonson faced throughout his career as a writer dependent on patronage.[1]

Moreover, looking at *Satiromastix* in this way also suggests new insights into the thematic unities and structural sophistication of the play itself. Usually dismissed as a hastily prepared hodgepodge of personal satire and romantic tragicomedy, the play has rarely been given much credit for exhibiting artistic skill. Its main plot—about a king's abuse of power, betrayal of trust, and lecherous designs on the virginal innocence of the beautiful Caelestine—would seem at first to have little in common with the work's nominal subplot, which in fact comprises most of the play's bulk.[2] It is easy to assume, as most critics have assumed, that the two plots were quickly cobbled together in response to demands extraneous to any concern with thematic coherence or artistic design.[3] But in fact significant similarities and meaningful contrasts between the two actions do exist; moreover, these connections are numerous and highly suggestive, and are reinforced and emphasized through pairings of scenes and through parallels in phrasing, in stage action, and in relations between characters. In the satiric subplot, a poet named Horace (closely patterned after Jonson) abuses his social power, betrays the trust of his friends and superiors, and prostitutes his heavenly gift of poetic talent in ways that strikingly suggest the similar motives and behavior of the king. For these reasons, questions of patronage and social power are important to a fuller understanding not only of the play's biographical context, but also of the text itself.

The plot of *Satiromastix* can be quickly summarized. The play opens with preparations for the wedding of Sir Walter Terrill to Caelestine, the virtuous daughter of Sir Quintilian Shorthose. Guests at the wedding include Crispinus and Demetrius Fannius (appealing stand-ins for Dekker and Marston), as well as the widowed Mistriss Miniver, who quickly attracts the comic and competing attentions of Shorthose, of Sir Rees ap Vaughan (a Welshman with a broad and funny accent), and of Sir Adam Prickshaft (whose most notable feature is his prominent bald head). Horace the poet (modeled after Jonson) has been commissioned to write verses for the affair, and the second scene satirizes his methods of composition, his arrogant self-regard, his social duplicity, and his unctuous relationship with a sycophantic admirer named Asinius Bubo. Another important character, Captain Tucca, is anything but an admirer of Horace, and much of the play is given over to the soldier's bombastic threats and to the poet's sneaking retaliations. Meanwhile, Horace is employed by Vaughan to write love letters on his behalf to Mistress Miniver, as well as to compose a poetic attack on bald heads—an attack soon answered in a poem by Demetrius praising baldness. Juxtaposed with such farce, the main plot grows suddenly serious when King William Rufus, invited to the wedding, develops a lustful infatuation for Caelestine. He dares Terrill to test her innocence, pressuring him to agree to send her that evening to the court, where the King secretly hopes to seduce her. Terrill recognizes the King's motives but feels bound by his oath to comply. Caelestine, wanting to obey her husband but determined to preserve her purity, drinks a potion (prepared by her father) that apparently kills her. Her body is borne to the court, where Rufus—confronted with the horrible results of his corrupt designs—condemns himself and sincerely repents of his vice. No sooner does he do this than Caelestine revives: the potion was not poison after all. Meanwhile, Horace and Bubo have also been borne into the court to stand trial for all their duplicitous offenses. At first the poet refuses to admit any guilt, but after being painfully crowned with a wreath of nettles, he soon confesses to a long list of charges and vows to change his ways. At the very end, Tucca—to everyone's surprise—abruptly wins the widow, and the play concludes with a dance.

Much of the action of *Satiromastix* clearly seems symbolic, and indeed Dekker effectively blends realistic detail, sharp satire, and broad comedy with elements more obviously emblematic. At the beginning of the play, for instance, two gentlewomen strew flowers on the ground in preparation for the wedding celebration, all the while making jokes about the bride losing her maidenhead (1.1.1–58). From one perspective the flowers, soon to be trampled underfoot, do symbolize Caelestine's forthcoming sexual initiation, but in light of the threat she later faces, the imagery of lovely flowers being crushed takes on a more disturbing significance. As her very name suggests, Caelestine symbolizes beauty and virtue of an almost heavenly perfection, and the King's attempt to abuse her corresponds on many levels with Horace's perversion of poetry. The opening preparations for the wedding suggest an ideal of social harmony that both the King and Horace help to undermine, while the true love that exists between Terrill and his bride makes an effective counterpoint not only to the calculating, humorous courtship of the widow Miniver by Prickshaft and Vaughan, but also to the selfish scheming of the king and the poet.

Not until the very end of the play do we witness as much concord and freedom from tension as we do in the opening scene, and it seems significant that the two chief threats to that harmony—Horace and King Rufus—are mentioned almost in the same breath by the man who trusts them both and whom they both deceive. Terrill happily reports to the assembled celebrants that the King has decided to "grace our marriage" by attending in person; he then immediately instructs his friend Sir Walter Blunt to check with Horace to make sure that the commissioned "nuptiall songs" have been completed on time (1.1.151–64). The juxtaposition stresses the theme of patronage, simultaneously reminding us of Terrill's subordinate position to the King, of the pride he takes in knowing that his superior will honor his wedding, of Horace's subordinate position to Terrill, and of the fact that Horace's words will be spoken before the greatest patron in the land. At the same time, the pairing of Horace and the King here prepares us to notice later how they both abuse the trust others place in them—how the King exploits those beneath him in power, and how Horace exploits and feels contempt for those on whom he depends. From different directions but from similar motives, both the king and the poet pervert the ideal of proper patronage relations. Both pretend to respect Terrill more than they really do; both deal with him hypocritically and abuse his trust.

This is why it seems both appropriate and ironic that Horace, in the next scene, is shown laboring over an epithalamion (1.2.1–39). Since marriage songs were quintessentially patronage poems, usually written by poets for their social superiors,[4] Dekker could not have chosen a more appropriate genre with which to mock Jonson's abilities and aspirations as a poet of patronage. Yet the emphasis on the epithalamion also seems clearly ironic, since Horace embodies impulses powerfully opposed to the very creativity, social harmony, and selfless affection a marriage poem exalts. Poetically sterile, lacking in strong attachment to anyone but himself, he hardly seems the perfect writer to celebrate the fecund concord associated with wedded love. His celebration of the marriage, like the King's lecherous presence at the wedding, seems crudely inappropriate. Here as throughout the play, Horace uses poetry not as a means of honoring others or of serving higher ideals but simply as a means of promoting his own self-interest.

If Horace's status as a patronage poet is emphasized implicitly at the opening of this scene, the emphasis becomes much more explicit as the scene proceeds. At one point he openly refers to his patrons as rooks and gulls (1.2.63); at another, he is even more blatantly mercenary. Asinius, the sycophant, asks him about his "fardle":

> *Hor.* Fardle, away, tis my packet; heere lyes intoomb'd the loues of Knights and Earles, heere tis, heere tis, heere tis, Sir *Walter Terils* letter to me, and my answere to him: I no sooner opened his letter, but there appeared to me three glorious Angels, whome I ador'd, as subiects doe their Soueraignes: the honest knight Angles for my acquaintance, with such golden baites . . . (1.2.106–11)

The ironies here are numerous: Horace's hyperbole reminds us of his own idolatry and sacrilege, his own transgression of the deepest religious values of his culture; the reference to "baites," meant to be clever, reminds us of the extent to which he has lowered himself, through his greed, to the level of a rapacious animal; while the self-consciously witty reference to subjects adoring their sovereigns helps prepare us for the later appearance of a sovereign who hardly merits such respect. The passage clearly reveals the pride Horace takes in his relations with powerful people, but it also suggests the extent to which his relations with them are rooted in more than mere vanity. Horace is depicted as incapable of the kind of genuine and ingenuous service that the patronage system ideally called for, but the passage is satirically effective less for what it reveals about Horace's greed than for the warning it imparts to present or potential patrons about his essential selfishness. Yet while the obvious satiric butt of the play is clearly Jonson-Horace, one of the intended results of its satire must have been to suggest to his patrons that, ultimately, they were the ones being made fools of. A little later, for instance, Asinius asks Horace how he has managed to write such a long letter of flattery to a gentleman he had just met only the night before:

> *Hor.* Foh come, your great belly'd wit must long for euery thing too; why you *Rooke*, I haue a set of letters readie starcht to my hands, which to any fresh suited gallant, that but newlie enters his name into my rowle, I send the next morning, ere his ten a clocke dreame has rize from him, onelie with claping my hand to't, that my Nouice shall start, ho and his haire stand on end, when he sees the sodaine flash of my writing; what you prettie Diminitiue roague, we must have false fiers to amaze these spangle babies, these true heires of Master Iustice Shallow.
>
> *Asin.* I wod alwaies haue thee sawce a foole thus. (2.2.27–36)

One need not take this as a literal account of Jonson's dealings with his patrons to recognize that the purpose of such satire was as much to intimidate his supporters as to mock the poet himself. By ostensibly warning his patrons about Jonson's selfishness, the satirists attempt to appeal to his benefactors' own senses of self-interest.

Yet while the play's satire on Jonson is stingingly sharp, Demetrius and Crispinus (the two characters who represent Dekker and Marston) are presented as attractively temperate in their own displeasure with Horace. Their anger with him grows out of a sense of having been betrayed, and indeed their charges that he is an untrustworthy friend are clearly related to the larger theme of betrayal—including the King's betrayal of Terrill—that runs throughout the work. More pained than bitter, Demetrius and Crispinus respond to Horace's falseness with a kind of indignant sorrow that not only implies some genuine concern for the poet, but that also functions much more effectively as satire (and as self-presentation) than if they had simply attacked him (1.2.204–60). Their reasonableness implicitly associates them with the ideal of harmony so strongly suggested by the opening scene, and their comparative mildness stands in powerful contrast with the menacing, abusive threats of Captain Tucca, whose loathing for Horace knows no bounds (1.2.283–86). Tucca's forthright bluster helps highlight the countervailing duplicity of Horace, but while the two seem opposites in most respects, each embodies an essentially combative impulse at odds with the social harmony the play elsewhere celebrates. It is a measure of Dekker's skill that Tucca, for all his wrath, blather, and egocentricity, seems by the end of the play far less disruptive of genuine concord and far more truly sociable than Horace, who superficially seems more affable and urbane. It is Tucca, after all, who wins the widow in the work's final moments, and it is Tucca who steps forth to make common cause with the audience in the Epilogue.

Juxtaposed with the scene that introduces Horace and emphasizes his hypocrisy, the first scene of Act 2 introduces the King and stresses his thinly-disguised designs on the purity of Caelestine. Act 2 opens with mockery of the social pretensions of Mistress Miniver, mockery that looks back to the satire on Horace's own social ambitions in the preceding episode. It seems ironic that the King should enter to the sound of music, since he represents a strong force for disharmony in the world of the play. But the scene also raises other important issues that help connect the play's plot lines while also suggesting the larger theme of patronage. Thus, when Vaughan compliments the King and receives what he falsely takes to be an ambiguous reply, he immediately assumes that Horace has poisoned the King's attitude towards him (although Rufus, in a clever insult, claims not even to know Horace [2.1.101–15]). Vaughan's nervous worries about the King's true feelings underscore the importance of good relations with one's patrons, and in fact Vaughan here voices fears central to the poetomachia itself: the fear that favor might suddenly be lost, the fear that malicious attacks might destroy one's standing with superiors.

Vaughan's fears about the King's possible equivocation may seem simply paranoid and humorous at first, but they take on a retrospective significance when, later in the scene, Rufus does in fact prevaricate while manipulating Terrill. In fact, Vaughan's obsession with ambiguity and his fear that language can be used as a social weapon accentuate an important theme of the play. Horace himself claims at one point that he must carefully weigh each syllable he speaks or writes because his enemies are liable to misinterpret his meaning (1.2.192–203), yet even this claim is consciously hypocritical. In the second scene of Act 2, moreover, Horace brags to Bubo that in writing a letter on Vaughan's behalf, he has "gull'd his Knight-ship heere to his face, yet haue giuen charge to his wincking vnderstanding not to perceiue it" (2.2.50–53). The poet thus behaves exactly as Vaughan had earlier worried the King was behaving, and Horace here does in fact plot against Vaughan, just as Vaughan had earlier suspected. The Welsh knight may indeed be paranoid, but even paranoids have enemies. Like Vaughan, the play itself is obsessively concerned with the use and abuse of language.

Both Horace and Rufus corrupt speech and abuse words to achieve their own limited ends. Language, ideally one of the strongest bonds for holding society together, is perverted through the selfish behavior and pernicious example of this poet and this King, whose social roles give them a special obligation to use words well. No sooner does Vaughan express his worries about linguistic ambiguity than the King begins to address Caelestine in sexually ambiguous terms (2.1.132–48), and it later seems extremely ironic that Rufus—hypocrite that he is—binds Terrill through an oath, a solemn profession of words, to bring his new bride to court (2.1.219–21). The whole confrontation between Terrill and the King, in fact, shows how Rufus exerts his power by imposing control over another's language. Like Horace in the preceding scene, he takes pleasure in his ability to manipulate another person through the clever and disingenuous use of words.

Indeed, here as in the opening scene, the adjacent references to Horace and the King invite us to ponder the thematic parallels between them. In addition to their common abuse of language, both men are essentially egotists and materialists. Horace's professed love of poetry only highlights his greater love of gold, while the King's praise of Caelestine emphasizes her physical attractions rather than her beautiful character. Ironically, some of the imagery he uses to praise her reminds us inadvertently of the same kingly ideals he himself transgresses (2.1.16–64). Dekker could claim, in fact, to have presented a much more complex and searching portrait of kingship in this play than Jonson had presented in *Poetaster*, where the emperor Augustus is idealized in terms that seem relatively unambiguous.[5] Although Dekker's play in some ways seems less "realistic" than Jonson's, in its treatment of the impact of personality on the exercise of public power it seems frankly more stimulating and provocative.

Rufus is hardly the only victim of Dekker's subtle sarcasm. Other patrons within the play also fall short of the ideal behavior associated with their roles. Vaughan himself, for instance, later employs Horace to write poems implicitly attacking Sir Adam (3.1.84–94)—a fact that makes his own earlier fear of slander and ambiguous language seem all the more ironic. Hypocritical in his relations with Vaughan, Horace also serves as the instrument of Vaughan's own hypocrisy. The client-patron relation between Horace and the knight is in several senses perverse, and the parallels between Horace and his patron, like the parallels between the poet and his King, help strengthen the thematic ties between the play's various plot lines. The poet abuses his patron much as the King abuses Terrill, but while Terrill remains innocent, Vaughan falls victim to the very tactics he uses against others. His maneuvers against Prickshaft resemble those of Horace against Tucca. In the world of *Satiromastix*, proper social relations have been poisoned; combativeness and deceit are rampant; the farcically trivial dispute over Mistress Miniver helps emphasize the similar foolishness of other disputes the play presents. The silly pursuit of the old widow by the fatuous old men highlights the equally silly but far more dangerous pursuit of

Caelestine by the King. The play's characters, events, themes, and plot lines are interconnected in ways more intricate and interesting than has usually been assumed.

Whether serving himself or whether apparently serving another, Horace trivializes and degrades his art—much as the King debases the dignity of his office by pursuing private lust. Horace stands in much the same relation to Vaughan as the sycophantic Asinius stands in relation to Horace—a fact that further diminishes the poet's importance. The differences between them, however, damn Horace even more, for whereas Asinius possesses a kind of stupid goodness or naive innocence, Horace not only seems, but thinks of himself as being, shrewd, calculating, and cunning. Like the King, he takes great pride in his own cleverness. However, his poem attacking baldness (4.1.64–101) shows how misplaced is his enormous self-regard; the poem suggests in an especially memorable way just how much Horace has debased his talents. Crispinus's speech defending baldness (4.3.28–68) may seem just as silly, and indeed on strictly poetic grounds the one poem is not much better than the other. If Dekker meant Crispinus's words to illustrate his own superiority over Jonson as a writer, he seems to have badly miscalculated. But Crispinus's speech seems far more important for the thematic issues it implicitly raises than for its quality as rhetoric. Some of its imagery, by alluding to God's kingship and by describing heaven as His court and His court as His masterpiece, indirectly reminds us of the corruption of the earthly king and of the earthly court the play presents. Demetrius's words inadvertently remind us of the ideal standard Rufus transgresses.

The action and phrasing of the play's final scenes dramatically underscore the thematic parallels that have steadily been developing. At the conclusion of Act 4, Tucca, enraged that Horace has betrayed an earlier promise to slander him no more, rushes at the terrified Horace with his sword and seems at first to stab him (4.3.129). Although the poet emerges physically unscathed from this scuffle, the near-stabbing seems an appropriate public humiliation for someone who has spent so much of the play boasting about his valor and metaphorically stabbing others. The irony is increased when Horace charges that Tucca has been "hyr'd" to attack him (4.3.130), since we have earlier seen Horace himself truly attack others for hire. However, Horace's humiliation does not stop here. Charged with all-consuming ambition and with wide-ranging and indiscriminate slander and hypocrisy, he is borne off in a blanket by a crowd, to be publicly mocked at court, the center of power and the magnet of ambition (4.3.245–58). The stage action here is crucially significant: it prepares for a powerful visual parallel later in the play, when the seemingly dead body of the innocent Caelestine is also borne off towards court at the head of a similar procession. And in fact the parallel is explicitly anticipated through Tucca's mocking reference here to the hapless poet as a reluctant "quiuering Bride" who must be forced to go to court (4.3.262).

The jovial, almost festive mood that concludes the fourth act contrasts effectively with the solemn opening scene of Act 5, in which Terrill and Caelestine lament their mutual predicament and her impending danger. Terrill's anguished sense of obligation to the King, his strong commitment to fulfilling his word, his powerful conviction that an oath is "the trafficke of the soule, / [the] law within a man; the seale of faith, / The bond of euery conscience" (5.1.40–42)—all contrast strikingly with the recently emphasized hypocrisy of Horace and with the lawlessness, faithlessness, and lack of conscience thus far displayed by the King. Yet Terrill continues to respect (or at least to obey) a superior who seems to merit no respect—unlike Horace, who betrays his superiors (including Terrill) without hesitation or regret.

Just as Terrill's loyalty highlights the duplicity of both King and poet, so does Caelestine's genuine anguish accentuate the facile dishonesty of both Horace and Rufus, neither of whom worries (as she does) about betraying impersonal ideals or personal trust. Caelestine's determination to preserve her innocence and purity makes the self-prostitution of Horace and the corruption of his own heavenly gifts seem all the more obviously blameworthy. When Caelestine swallows the apparent poison her father has given her (5.1.145 s.d.), the play veers even more sharply towards tragedy. The issues of falsehood, hypocrisy, abuse of trust, and loss of innocence that had earlier been given primarily comic or satiric treatment suddenly seem to take on a darker, more serious significance. Caelestine's role as a symbolic character who personifies and symbolizes heavenly virtues could hardly be clearer than here, where those virtues seem literally to die before our eyes. In a play that deals with the destruction of virtue—both in oneself and in others—this is a richly emblematic moment. The language at the conclusion of this scene, with its emphasis on revels and on leading the bride to court (5.1.169–80), inevitably reminds us of the language that concluded the preceding scene, and helps make the ironic parallels between Horace (carried off in a blanket) and Caelestine (borne off in a chair) even more strikingly obvious. In both cases, dead virtue makes its way toward the court.

The play's final scene, with its opening emphasis on the complacent self-regard and self-indulgence of the King, contrasts strongly with the tragic tone of the preceding episode. Rufus's opening words associating kings with the gods drip with unintended irony (5.2.1–8), but they serve to remind us that Horace also smugly assumes, at various points throughout the play, some higher sanction for his behavior. However, both the King and the poet prostitute the ideals they talk so much about. Both take themselves too seriously, and both dress their motives up in a lofty language that seems grossly inappropriate. Although both men share a kind of duplicitous cunning, both lack true wisdom. Rufus's condescending comments about Terrill in this scene (5.2.27–33), which specifically recall similar remarks made earlier by Horace [1.2.106–24]), illustrate the kinds of ironies Dekker weaves into the King's speeches: "poore soul thou thinkst, / The heart and tongue is cut out of one peece, / But th'art deceau'd, the world hath a false light, / Fooles thinke tis day, when wise men know tis night." It is the King's soul, however, that is truly poor; it is Rufus who is, or is about to be, deceived and caught in another's trap; it is he, in short, who is the true fool.

When the apparently dead Caelestine is brought on stage, the King is devastated. Confronted with a stunning image of death that prefigures his own inevitable demise, he wonders aloud who could dare "blaspheme her beauties, or / Prophane the cleare religion of her eyes" (5.2.59–60). The questions boomerang: Caelestine has chosen physical poisoning over the spiritual poisoning he himself had intended for her. The paradox of poisoning is now picked up by Terrill, who begins a long denunciation of the King with the words, "My tongue is tipt with poison" (5.2.62). But in fact Terrill's words, though harsh, are regenerative; they help convict and convince the King of his own sinfulness and crime. The knight uses language here as a true satirist should, but as Horace never has. Indeed, when Terrill accuses the King of earlier speaking "Vnder the couert of a flattering smile" (5.2.77), we can't help but notice how accurately this also describes Horace's behavior.

However, the King's profound sense of shame and sorrow here contrasts strongly with the way Horace has responded throughout the play to similar accusations. Terrill's indictment of the King, in fact, not only reminds us of similar earlier indictments of Horace by Crispinus and Demetrius (e.g., 1.2.204ff.; 4.3.211ff.), but also looks forward to the climactic "trial" of Horace with which the play concludes. Both the King and the poet face charges in the closing scene, but each responds differently. The King's frank admission of guilt, his sincere regret, and his strong public self-condemnation all have the effect, paradoxically, of making him seem far more worthy and deserving of respect than he had ever seemed before; he embraces his guilt so forthrightly that he suddenly seems somehow innocent. It is no accident that precisely at this moment, Caelestine begins to revive (5.2.90). Viewed as a "realistic" event, her sudden resuscitation seems implausibly miraculous; viewed symbolically, however, it is pregnant with meaning. Her recovery represents physically the spiritual regeneration now taking place within the King; indeed, just as Caelestine never really died, so Rufus's virtues, apparent briefly at the beginning of the play, were never completely extinguished. The King's reformation makes the obstinate pride of his counterpart, Horace, in the second half of this scene seem all the more reprehensible.

When the poet is finally paraded into the court, he and Bubo are *"pul'd in by th'hornes bound,"* and both are dressed *"like Satyres"* (5.2.158 s.d.). The costuming is significant in several ways. It symbolizes Horace's beastly behavior and his corruption of the true office of satirist, but it also reflects obliquely on the earlier goatish lust of the King. The parallels between King and poet are emphasized once more when Horace is symbolically crowned with a *"wreath of nettles"* (5.2.158 s.d.), an act that reminds us both of Christ's crown of thorns and of Horace's unchristian conduct. However, all the parallels between Rufus and Horace help stress the differences that now exist between them. Whereas Rufus had willingly embraced his guilt and accepted his public humiliation, Horace denies the charges levelled against him and continues to protest his innocence. Only when the crown of thorns becomes too painful does he reluctantly confess his misdeeds and vow not to repeat them. Neither his confession nor his oath, however, seems fully convincing.

Unlike the King, whose reformation seemed genuinely inward, Horace's is imposed from without. His previous similar oaths were quickly broken, and Dekker effectively leaves unclear the sincerity of the poet's conduct here. *Satiromastix* does, however, end on a note of other harmonies achieved—not only because the most boisterous and in some ways the most unruly character, Captain Tucca, announces his intentions to marry, but also because in its final moments the play dissolves into a dance. It was at an earlier dance that the King had first attempted to seduce Caelestine, but when he dances with her here, he seems both literally and figuratively in touch with virtue. Horace's reformation may be questionable, but the play's chief patron now seems genuinely changed. In fact, the King's transformation makes the genuineness of Horace's change seem ultimately less important. His rejection of Horace effectively ends the poet's social power. Horace will no longer pose a threat, because his humiliation before the King and his rejection by his other patrons effect a kind of social castration, destroying whatever potency he once possessed. His loss of social power will be rooted less in pious morality than in political pragmatism: to patronize Horace now will clearly mean risking one's own reputation.

The thematic connections between the different plot lines of *Satiromastix* are both numerous and significant, and they help to refute the most common charges leveled against the play—that its tone is incoherent and its structure poorly conceived.[6] Through pairings of scenes, echoes of phrasing, and parallel actions, Dekker stresses the similar shortcomings of the King and the poet in order to stress the similar obligations of each. Behind the play's satiric bite is an implicit idealism about the proper behavior of writers and their patrons; Dekker undoubtedly agreed with Jonson that the true poet and true king shared a similar social importance. Perhaps that is why he took the trouble to emphasize the parallel corruptions of Horace and Rufus and make them central to the play's design and meaning. Perhaps that is also why he chose to stress so strongly Horace's perverse relationships with two other patrons, Terrill and Vaughan. Doing so not only accentuates the theme of patronage but also strengthens the links between the play's various plots.[7]

Of course, Dekker's immediate purpose was to ridicule Jonson, and the mockery of him as a patronage poet in this play seems significant for several reasons. It suggests how important a factor patronage was in the general literary culture of this time. More specifically, it suggests that the competition for patronage may have been a more important factor in the poetomachia than has been previously recognized. Moreover, it implies how important to Jonson (and how widely known) his hopes for patronage must have been during this early period—important enough that his antagonists saw them as effective targets for satire. Their mockery seems designed not only to embarrass and humiliate the poet but also, less obviously, to intimidate and provoke second thoughts among any of his potential patrons. Finally, their attacks suggest one of the ways in which patronage pressures exerted themselves even in the theatre, a sphere in which they might be assumed to have been comparatively less intense.

If the assaults on Jonson in *Satiromastix* emphasize the importance of patronage early in his career, his later epigrams addressed to William Cavendish, the Earl of Newcastle, illustrate the continuing importance of patrons near the close of his life. Poems such as these are easily undervalued. They can be seen as hackneyed rehearsals of tired conventions or as the embarrassing detritus of an aging, declining poet's hunger for social security, written when both his inspiration and his health were beginning to flag. In fact, however, the poems to Newcastle—a patron whose significance for Jonson has not been fully emphasized—illustrate the wit, vitality, and measured autonomy the old poet could assert even during a time when his social and physical power seemed increasingly compromised.[8] The two epigrams to Newcastle reveal both the apparent plainness and the clever sophistication typical of Jonson's poems to superiors; they express clear admiration while simultaneously implying a more subtly critical stance. Rhetorically inventive and full of intriguing nuance, the poems discharge the traditional obligation to teach while pleasing, yet the meanings they impart have a highly personal applicability. Both poems constitute an adroit defense and display of poetic art. Both compare poetry with competing skills, rescuing the latter from overzealous champions in ways that ultimately assert the greater dignity of writing.

Jonson's connections with patrons like Cavendish became, if anything, even more important during the Caroline period than they had been under James. The poet's declining health meant his greater absence from court, so the significance of courtier intermediaries increased. Despite his pension, Jonson's position under Charles seems to have been less psychologically secure than before. Jonson and James had shared much the same temperament, but the new king was more reserved and serious than his father. Moreover, the old poet sensed that his powers—at least in drama—were decaying along with his health, and he knew that the influence of his arch-rival, Inigo Jones, had begun to eclipse his own. Thus while he still obviously sought and frequently won the support of the King, support from the King's subordinates must have seemed all the more crucial. Not only could they provide alternative sources of encouragement and reward, particularly valuable if his standing at court seemed threatened; they could also help shore up that standing through their own mediation, protection, and aid.[9] *Under-wood* 78—an epigram to Venetia Digby addressed through her to her husband, through him to the Lord Treasurer, Richard Weston, and perhaps through Weston even higher—illustrates succinctly the kind of transmission Jonson must have hoped for whenever he addressed a poem to a patron.[10]

Weston's importance as a nonroyal patron of Jonson during the Caroline period seems to have been rivaled only by Cavendish, since 1628 the Earl of Newcastle. Jonson's relations with the Cavendish family provide a pleasant backdrop to the larger but often less cheerful story of his general attempt to win reputation and maintain status during the latter phase of his career. Surviving documents paint an attractive picture of his link with the Earl, whose support he appreciated and whose quest for status provided Jonson with opportunities to promote his own. Yet his poems to Newcastle are hardly simple, straightforward, or uncomplicated. His seemingly relaxed relationship with the Earl may even have contributed to Jonson's willingness to praise him in ways that are subtly and intriguingly qualified. The relative freedom he seems to enjoy in these works seems to have been a freedom he literally took for *granted*—a liberty he could assume partly because the Earl was willing to allow it. In this as in many ways the poems, far from merely expressing the poet's interests or reflecting the patron's, are complex adjustments of the two.

Although Jonson's relations with Newcastle and his family seem to have been most intense during the early 1630s, they apparently began much earlier, during James's reign. He was commissioned to write various works to commemorate important family events, including an epitaph for Sir Charles Cavendish, the future Earl's father, and an entertainment to celebrate the birth of the future Earl's son. To Jonson, William Cavendish himself must have appeared to possess all the qualities one could hope for in a patron. Sir Henry Wotton wrote glowingly of his character and breeding, while Cavendish's connections at court, his vast personal wealth, and his love of verse must have made him seem quite attractive to the aging poet. Clarendon describes Newcastle as having been "amorous in Poetry, and Musick, to which he indulged the larger part of his time. . . ." During the latter part of Jonson's life, he wrote a number of poems and entertainments for the Earl or his family, including two of the more intriguing of his later epigrams.[11]

The two poems Jonson addressed to Newcastle are among the clearest instances in his canon of the poet appealing to a patron's avocations. Cavendish was famous for his devotion to horsemanship and fencing (among other "Qualities . . . which accompany a good breeding," in Clarendon's phrase),[12] and in fact he eventually wrote several treatises on both subjects. Clearly it pleased him to be thought proficient in these skills, so that Jonson's poems not only reflect the Earl's interests but publicize them, too. The first poem, probably written sometime between 1625 and 1628, while Cavendish was still Viscount Mansfield but after he had had an elaborate stable built for his horses, exhibits an attractive playfulness, yet there is also an edge to Jonson's humor:

> When first, my Lord, I saw you backe your horse,
> Provoke his mettall, and command his force
> To all the uses of the field, and race,
> Me thought I read the ancient Art of *Thrace*,
> And saw a Centaure, past those tales of *Greece;*
> So seem'd your horse and you, both of a peece!
> You shew'd like *Perseus* upon *Pegasus;*
> Or *Castor* mounted on his *Cyllarus:*
> Or what we heare our home-borne Legend tell,
> Of bold Sir *Bevis*, and his *Arundell:*
> Nay, so your Seate his beauties did endorse,
> As I began to wish my selfe a horse.
> And surely had I but your Stable seene
> Before, I thinke my wish absolv'd had beene.
> For never saw I yet the Muses dwell,
> Nor any of their household, halfe so well.
> So well! as when I saw the floore, and Roome,
> I look'd for *Hercules* to be the Groome:
> And cri'd, Away with the *Caesarian* bread,
> At these Immortall Mangers *Virgil* fed.

The parallel phrasing in the second line helps emphasize its verbs—appropriate in a poem so much concerned with illustrating and defining proper action. Cavendish can both "provoke" and "command"; he can stir energy but can also discipline and control it, channeling it (as the poem does) to profitable uses. Similarly, the momentarily surprising use of "read" in line 4 makes observation seem more than a passive act, highlighting the epigram's function by forcing us to share Jonson's active scrutiny of the Earl. Seeing as reading involves an act of interpretation informed by an awareness of historical context—an awareness that allows Jonson to appreciate horsemanship without overvaluing its significance. He displays his familiarity with a competing art even while restricting and confining its importance.

The reference to the centaur is witty and playful, but it also introduces a central theme—the conflict between reason and passion. This is a poem partly about the need to discipline oneself as one disciplines a horse, about the need to keep a proper perspective, not to overvalue unimportant things. It is about the need to give greater priority to mind and spirit than to mere bodily activity. Although Jonson praises Cavendish for seeming united with the animal beneath him, the whole poem subtly argues for the need to make and keep distinctions. The reference to Pegasus is significant because Pegasus is a transitional figure—a beast, to be sure, but one already associated with poetry and the muses, with the mental and spiritual qualities that help define human beings and set them *apart* from beasts. Jonson shifts from an image of man literally united with a horse to one of man using and disciplining a particular animal already associated with rationality and mental creativity. The poem draws on traditional imagery associating the rider on a horse with reason controlling passion,[13] yet the work's fundamental seriousness is both balanced and underscored by its sense of humor. The poem's tones are as well poised as the rider it extols.

Ironically, nowhere is this poise clearer than in the apparently awkward lines in which Jonson's enthusiasm pushes him to confess that he almost "began to wish [himself] a horse" (l. 12). The ludicrousness of this acknowledgment is part of its satiric point; it suggests the ridiculous extremes—and the social ridicule—to which the overzealous pursuit of a mere sport can lead. The joke both balances and deflates the apparent hyperbole of the preceding lines, yet the fact that it also cleverly alludes to a famous joke from Sir Philip Sidney's *Apology for Poetry* gives it an even more complicated resonance. The *Apology* opens by implicitly contrasting Sidney's gentlemanly love of verse with the boorish, boastful horsemanship of an Italian named Pugliano. So emphatic was Pugliano's commendation of his own skills, Sidney writes, "that if I had not been a piece of a logician before I came to him, I think he would have persuaded me to have wished myself a horse."[14] Jonson's allusion invokes not only Sidney's text but Sidney's compelling example as an English aristocrat who gave poetry its rightful esteem. One of the poem's most seemingly awkward moments is thus one of its most subtly allusive, one that tests the reader's knowledge even as it superficially seems to display the poet's blunder. Fully to appreciate the joke requires being familiar with a text that gives poetry its proper value. The joke tests the reader even as it entertains him, exemplifying Sidney's dictum of teaching by pleasing. Jonson's skillful insinuation exhibits a polish precisely odds with his apparent clumsiness and with Pugliano's tactless self-promotion. By reminding Cavendish of an earlier horseman who took his sport too seriously, the poem provides a clear but understated warning. Moreover, by placing Jonson in the tradition of Sidney, it gives his warning an intellectual weight and impersonal objectivity it might otherwise have lacked. Sidney's attitude helps sanction Jonson's, making it more persuasive while also rendering it less vulnerable to criticism. The tone of self-assurance and self-respect that characterizes this poem, as in so many poems by Jonson, does not and cannot reflect the writer's essential autonomy.

The reference to Hercules is again a nice joke, helping to emphasize the sheer immensity of the Cavendish stables. But here, as before, the humor serves a serious purpose, reminding readers of the filth of the famous Augean barn Hercules cleaned, and thus of aspects of horsemanship quite different from the stirring images earlier stressed. All the previous emphasis on magnificent physical power, on the strong, supple flesh of horse and rider combined, here gives way to a deflating allusion to horse dung. The joke underscores by contrast the spirtuality, the qualities of *mind*, the work has implicitly ascribed to poetry, but it does so in a way that shows just how encompassing—and how finely nuanced—Jonson's style can be. The closing reference to "immortal mangers" has an intriguing ring in Christian ears and may, just may, have been meant to remind Cavendish one last time of the spiritual values best expressed through poetry. Whether or not this is so, the final lines do clearly allude to a legend that "the young Virgil worked in the imperial stables, displaying such skill that he was rewarded with a double ration of bread."[15] Jonson may have intended the allusion, and his poem's emphasis on the generous provision Cavendish allotted his horses, as a means of jogging the aristocrat's sense of *noblesse oblige*. Surely a poet, Jonson seems finally to imply, deserves to be treated at least as well as a horse. But the poem's method of conveying this message is far more tactful—and far more effective—than any such bald statement could possibly suggest. The indirection is both aesthetically and socially skillful.

Jonson's second poem to the Earl, although even more obviously flamboyant than the one just considered, seems at least as seriously thoughtful. While the first poem played on Cavendish's fascination with horses, this one uses his enthusiasm for swordsmanship to promote an ethical ideal that subsumes valiant action while also transcending it. Jonson conveys the impression that he shares the Earl's devotion to the sport and appreciation of the skill it involves, while also placing them in a larger perspective that gives them meaning partly by denying them any importance in and of themselves:

They talke of Fencing, and the use of Armes,
  The art of urging, and avoyding harmes,
The noble Science, and the maistring skill
  Of making just approaches, how to kill,
To hit in angles, and to clash with time:
  As all defence, or offence, were a chime!
I hate such measur'd, give me mettall'd fire
  That trembles in the blaze, but (then) mounts higher!
A quick, and dazeling motion! when a paire
  Of bodies, meet like rarified ayre!
Their weapons shot out, with that flame, and force,
  As they out-did the lightning in the[ir] course;
This were a spectacle! A sight to draw
  Wonder to Valour! No, it is the Law
Of daring not to doe a wrong, is true
  Valour! to sleight it, being done to you!
To know the heads of danger! where 'tis fit
  To bend, to breake, provoke, or suffer it!
All this (my Lord) is Valour! This is yours!
  And was your Fathers! All your Ancestours!
Who durst live great, 'mongst all the colds, and heates,
  Of humane life! as all the frosts, and sweates
Of fortune! when, or death appear'd, or bands!
  And valiant were, with, or without their hands.

As with many of Jonson's poems, half the skill of this work

consists in the way it evolves. Jonson's reputation as a poet of plain statement has perhaps obscured his talent for manipulating the reader's experience of the unfolding work, his ability to create meaning through accretion.[16] By recognizing how a given passage modifies the significance of one that went before, or prepares expectations that are subsequently either transformed or confirmed, one comes to appreciate how the sheer craft of Jonson's art helped make it a supple instrument for presenting a precise image of the poet to patrons and for shaping their reactions to him and to his work.

The epigram to Newcastle unfolds in four movements. In the first (ll. 1–6), Jonson sneers scornfully at unnamed professors of swordsmanship who, in attempting to regularize the art, to prescribe rules for it and make it a science, in fact trivialize it and rob it of its proper passion. Jonson's sardonic rhyme of "skill" and "kill" reinforces the larger irony of the whole section; the brutal reality of the second word seems out of place in a passage that parodies the overemphasis on technique and moderation that Jonson derides. The precise and mannered movements recommended by such technicians of the sword suggest how unrealistic their detailed advice is in fact, how remote it is from the actualities of combat. It is as if the unnamed "They" *merely* "talke of Fencing," as if they are more concerned with self-conscious display as an end in itself than with the practical realities or ethical implications of swordsmanship.

The style of combat Jonson himself recommends in the poem's second section (ll. 7–14) amounts to a kind of *sprezzatura* of the sword, an artlessness, an effect of unstudied and impassioned immediacy, that achieves a higher kind of art. The kind of fighting he describes and endorses seems at once more realistic *and* more visually stunning than the sort he has just attacked. Display is not its purpose but *is* its practical result, but the display here, Jonson claims, is not an end in itself. Jonson uses a number of phrases to emphasize the overpowering visual impact of the swordsmanship he champions—including one line which, for a moment, seems paradoxically to liken the flash of a blade to the blast of a gun (l. 11). But the "spectacle" here serves the larger ethical purpose, the poet insists, of "draw[ing] / Wonder to Valour!" (ll. 13–14). It advertises the courage of the individual swordsman while more widely promoting the virtue of courage in society. The kind of fighting Jonson recommends is thus doubly commendable: as a display of talent it is far more impressive than the mechanical swordplay discussed in the poem's first section; and it more clearly springs from (and is more clearly subordinate to) larger social values. If the purpose of the first kind of fighting is to promote an attractive image of particular individuals, the second kind does this more effectively while also promoting virtue as well. Here as in so many of his poems for patrons, Jonson seeks to accommodate the individual's drive toward self-assertion to society's interest in promoting cohesive values. And, as usual, in the process he succeeds in implying an attractive image of himself.

No sooner does Jonson suggest this link between moral right and the right kind of swordsmanship, however, than he pulls back from the equation to qualify and limit it. The poem's third movement (ll. 14–18) begins by championing a more passive kind of valor, one that need not be expressed through action, indeed one that is sometimes best expressed by the *refusal* to act. Such valor is "passive" only in the grossest physical sense; Jonson underlines the moral action it entails by his paradoxical reference to "daring not to doe a wrong" (l. 15). The conscious, deliberate refusal to act immorally is itself a daring act, and the section concludes with an emphatic endorsement of suffering as the proper response to some kinds of provocation or danger. Jonson's support for this peaceful, essentially Christian ethic would not be nearly so convincing had he not just previously demonstrated his appreciation of active courage and physical strength. Indeed, his rejection of effete, pedantic rules in favor of a passionate kind of fighting makes his commendation of this superior ethic in the third part seem all the more genuine and persuasive.[17] In place of the moderate physical techniques and tactics lampooned in the first section, part three celebrates an ideal of moral moderation and inner balance. It is these qualities, Jonson implies, that should define and control physical courage. Neither the mechanical rules he derides nor the passionate swordsmanship he commends are sufficient as ends in themselves. Both the stiff, stilted action of the first part and the fiery enthusiasm of the second can only be understood in relation to the internal, seemingly more static but actually more potent ideal celebrated in the third.[18]

If true valor is a function of character, not of action, it follows that only an art capable of delineating the complexities of character will be capable of truly displaying and publicly interpreting it. The present poem demonstrates Jonson's ability as a writer not only to distinguish meaningfully between different kinds of action and to evaluate one kind more highly than another, but to distinguish between mere action and the morals that give it significance. Swordsmanship must have been attractive to men of Cavendish's class largely because of the opportunities it provided for conspicuous self-display and public reputation. Jonson's poem enhances Cavendish's reputation as a swordsman, but another of its effects is to suggest that physical action—even of the highest type—can exhibit only a very limited range of human virtue. The movement of mind and exertion of will that constitute true valor cannot be displayed very easily or fully through bodily movement.

They *can* be displayed or advertised, however, through a poem. Jonson's epigram champions an impersonal ideal of moral achievement while also demonstrating how such individual achievement can be publicly set forth. The poem's stance toward swordsmanship is multivalent and subtle. On the one hand, the second section reveals Jonson's passionate feel for the sport as well as his ability to recreate some of its excitement and kinetic energy in the very texture and movement of his verse. On the other hand, the third section reveals the insufficiency of swordsmanship alone to express publicly anything like the full complexity of human virtue—including the virtue of sometimes *seeming* to do nothing. If the second section ennobles the sport by making it seem an expression of valor rather than of a mere obsession with show, the third section partly undercuts its adequacy to express "All" the virtue the poet claims his patron embodies. The epigram demonstrates poetry's ability both to make and to celebrate the kinds of ethical discriminations the poem discusses. Jonson endorses Cavendish's hobby while tacitly criticizing it. Only a part of the virtue he ascribes to the Earl and his ancestors could be expressed "with . . . their hands" (l. 24). Jonson suggests that through his poetry he can articulate not only those martial virtues but others as well.[19]

Both poems to Newcastle display an intriguing mixture of tones. Explicit praise is combined with implicit warning; playful wit is juxtaposed with serious teaching. Energetic but earnest, the poems exhibit Jonson's gravity, his cleverness, and the depth of his ethical commitment, but they also speak well of Newcastle in ways that transcend the obvious. They imply Jonson's confidence in the fundamental goodness of his patron; they suggest his trust in the Earl, his willingness—but also his permitted ability—to speak frankly to a man whose power far exceeded his own. The confidence the poems embody must have been born of Jonson's prior, deeper confidence in himself, the Earl, and the integrity of their relations. Yet that confidence is also bordered by an ever-present sense of the poet's (and poetry's) danger of being marginalized or devalued through competition with activities more superficially appealing.

The epigrams to Newcastle are all the more remarkable when one recalls the probable circumstances of their composition. There is something both poignant and compelling about the idea of poems so energetic, so vital, so full of an almost palpable, physical *force* being written by a man whose own bloated body was beginning to betray him.[20] The epigrams constitute meditations on both the rewards and the limits of physical action—meditations by a writer whose own activity, especially after his stroke, would become increasingly curtailed. Jonson's declining health must have allowed him to appreciate physical strength in both senses of that verb: to value it, but also to evaluate, not exaggerate, its ultimate importance. The poems embody Jonson's mental agility, vitality, and grace. They display much of the same intellectual toughness and moral vigor they praise.

Like his involvement in the poetomachia early in his career, Jonson's poems to Cavendish—written as that career was drawing to a close—suggest how his life as a writer could never be a solitary enterprise. His status as a social poet—one acutely aware of and involved with his audience, especially with patrons and rivals—is evident throughout his life. The potential threats posed by rivals, as well as the possible protections offered by patrons, inevitably affected his conception and presentation of his works and persona from start to finish. His was a life, like all lives, conditioned by persons, powers, and circumstances he could not entirely control, however much his writings might attempt to assert his own authority. The attacks against him in *Satiromastix* came at a moment when that authority was still quite uncertain; the poems to Cavendish reflect a time when such authority had begun to wane. However, as the next four chapters attempt to show, even in the middle of his career, when he had achieved unparalleled prominence and status, his writing was inexorably tangled in complicated social contexts in which issues of power—and especially of micropolitics—loomed large.

3

Thomas Sutton: Jonson's Volpone?

Jonson's involvement in the poetomachia, and the savage assault on him in *Satiromastix*, both indicate how easily the theater could serve as an arena for personal combat and micropolitical maneuvers. In the case of plays like *Poetaster* or *Satiromastix*, such motives are blatantly obvious, but new evidence suggests that personal satire may also have helped shape the play that remains Jonson's masterwork—*Volpone*. This evidence supports the notion that Thomas Sutton, the founder of London's Charterhouse hospital and the richest commoner in Jacobean England, may have been the model for the play's title character. In the years and decades following the work's first production, this possibility was widely discussed and widely accepted, but more modern commentators have generally dismissed the idea, and most recent editions fail even to mention it.[1] However, several previously unnoted documents throw new light on this old issue, and while they hardly establish that Sutton was Jonson's intended target, they do provide fascinating and valuable evidence about the contemporary context in which his play was written and received and about the whole issue of personal satire on the English Renaissance stage. The documents help illuminate the importance of personal politics for Jonson and his milieu, and they also help to explain why many of the playwright's contemporaries and their immediate descendants believed that Sutton was the object of his satire; why Jonson himself might reasonably have assumed his audience could draw such a conclusion; and how this knowledge may have affected the defensive tone of his play's printed dedication.

It is easy to see why so many commentators have so strongly resisted the notion that Jonson satirized Sutton. During the decades and centuries since his death in 1611, Sutton has been remembered and revered primarily as the pious founder of Charterhouse, one of England's greatest charitable institutions, a residential "hospital" designed to provide lodging, sustenance, and education to needy men and boys. English Protestants hailed Sutton and his hospital as sterling examples of the good men and good works produced by the reformed religion; Sutton was cited repeatedly as a model of Protestant benefaction, useful as ammunition in propaganda wars with Catholics. Until recently, much of the biographical commentary on Sutton had an almost hagiographic tone, and indeed some of the earliest legends verged on the miraculous—such as the amusing claim that his enormous wealth derived from "faery gold" found as he strolled along a beach. Appropriately enough, the first published account of his life (and a source for many subsequent writers) was a commemorative sermon.[2]

A more balanced tone emerges in an important but relatively obscure 1948 article by the historian Hugh Trevor-Roper, himself a product of the Charterhouse school. Although obviously grateful to Sutton, Trevor-Roper provides significant correctives to earlier treatments of "the founder's" life, dismissing most previous accounts as "mythological" and "fabulous."[3] Unfortunately, his own article, while based on archival research, is not specifically documented, which makes it difficult for interested readers to pin down the sources of many of his confident assertions. Nonetheless, his piece is the starting point for any serious investigation of Sutton's life; in fact, Neal R. Shipley, another historian, cautions that "Accounts of Sutton written before the 1940s are, as a rule, wildly inaccurate."[4] For this reason it may be worth quoting extensively from Trevor-Roper's article to establish the basic shape of Sutton's career. Once this has been done, we can better appreciate the significance of the new evidence already mentioned and its relevance to Jonson's play.

Trevor-Roper begins by remarking that "even in his own lifetime Sutton's origins, owing to his own silence, were something of a mystery, which his executors had no sure means of solving. . . . The plain fact is that there is no evidence of any value at all about Sutton before 1569," when he was pensioned by Ambrose Dudley, the Earl of Warwick. Sutton was a dependent of the earl's family: "The Dudleys made his career and fortune, or at least the beginning of it; they provided him with jobs and influence and a wife; and the only family connexions which he seems ever to have had were with them and their circle." Through them he obtained a position by which he acquired the lease of two estates "which he kept till his death [and which] were the solid basis of his fortune." Apparently it was "Ambrose Dudley who had arranged the deal." Dudley also nominated Sutton to the important position of "Master of the Ordnance in the North Parts." During his "period in the North (from 1569 to 1582), . . . he made the first half of his fortune by speculating in coal"; later, while living in the South from 1582 until 1611, "he multiplied it to gigantic proportions by marriage and money-lending."[5]

Trevor-Roper provides a fascinating account of Sutton's struggle for control of the northern coalfields, but it is on the latter part of his life—when, his fortune established, he moved to London and became a notorious money-lender—that we must focus here. He married the rich widow of John Dudley and bought himself

> a house at Broken Wharf in London, and another at Hackney. His illegitimate son, Roger Sutton (now in the army), came frequently to live with him, and so with his wife's daughter, Anne Dudley, and her husband (the son of an immensely rich judge, Chief Justice Popham) he experienced a certain family life; but after his wife's death in 1602 he became more and more a recluse, chiefly concerned with the ultimate fate of his now colossal fortune.[6]

Sutton had boosted that fortune "in the simplest way, by lending it on mortgage." His days as a money-lender coincided with a time of great inflation, when wealthy families were scrambling for the cash they needed for conspicuous consumption or merely to keep themselves afloat. Sutton numbered among his debtors many of the kingdom's most powerful men, including the Earl of Essex; Lord Darcy; Lord Mounteagle; the Earl of Sussex; the Earl of Oxford; the Earl of Suffolk, and many, many others. Some of these people were his friends, and many felt grateful to him; but his enormous wealth (and concomitant power) earned him envy and resentment as well. His scrupulous financial records, many of which survive, provide exceptionally detailed evidence of his activities. Trevor-Roper estimates that "In one form of lending alone, of which we have the records, he lent, in the last sixteen years of his life, £ 220,000 . . . , sometimes lending as much as £ 37,000 in a single year; and at his death, £ 44,891 was still owing to him." Debtors who could not repay their loans often sacrificed their property; land acquired in this way brought Sutton still further sources of wealth. "It seemed that he had only to sit still and let his money multiply. He was known everywhere as 'rich Sutton,' 'Dives Sutton,' 'the English Crassus,' 'the richest gentleman in England.'" Jealousy prompted unfair talk that he was a miserly usurer, but Trevor-Roper comments, somewhat reassuringly, that "his contemporaries never taxed him with extortion; and the inventories of his personal effects—his plate and rich clothes and fine services and damask hangings—prove that he was not a miser in the traditional sense." He was kind to his servants and considerate of the poor. Nonetheless, "in his old age, Sutton became increasingly unsocial, increasingly solitary."[7] One researcher remarks that John Lawe, his chief financial assistant, "was the closest that Sutton ever came to having an intimate friend. . . . Sutton was reclusive and needed the sort of information that Lawe, a born gossip, had in great store."[8]

Strained relations with his son (whom he eventually disinherited) and with other relatives spurred speculation about the eventual fate of his gigantic wealth, and in the decade before his death—when Jonson's play was written—rumors were rife, and schemes and proposals abounded. Everyone wondered what would become of the old man's incredible fortune. Sutton seems to have been attracted at an early stage to the idea of endowing a charity of some sort, but "In the last sixteen years of his life he drafted a new will every six months. Throughout he showed an extreme suspicion. He did not trust his relatives; he feared that his foundation would be dissolved by powerful interests at his death"; in general, "he kept very quiet about his intentions." But if Sutton was not entirely sure how he should dispose of his money, others had more definite ideas. Sir John Harington, the courtier and poet, took an active interest. Although Trevor-Roper asserts, on the basis of published evidence, that Harington came into contact with Sutton in 1607, documents from the Charterhouse records show that their relationship began much earlier. It was in 1607, however, that Harington proposed a plan by which he hoped to benefit Sutton, the King, Prince Charles, and (not incidentally) himself. "Harington's scheme was simple. Sutton was to be persuaded by him to declare Prince Charles his heir. In return Sutton, through the intercession of Harington, was to be honoured by the King with a peerage. Harington, as the skilful broker, would receive a rake-off from both sides."[9]

Harington had not counted, however, on Sutton's determination to be his own financial planner. The old man took offense at the scheme and addressed indignant letters to the Lord Chancellor and Lord Treasurer disavowing it. Moreover,

> To Harington Sutton wrote characteristically protesting that the rumour of the proposal had damaged his money-lending business, since everyone now thought his land was so encumbered that no one would take up leases or borrow money from him. Relations between Harington and Sutton continued after the unfortunate end of this project (in which other members of the court were involved), for Harington was irrepressible.[10]

Further evidence suggests that Harington's scheme was only one of many self-serving proposals outsiders concocted for disposing of Sutton's fortune; indeed, the old man's admirers later applauded his skills at turning the tables on would-be manipulators. Of course, not everyone was self-interested: Joseph Hall wrote a long letter endorsing Sutton's charitable impulses and urging him to act on them without delay. Yet even in the final years of his life, no one could be quite sure what would happen to his money, despite the fact that Sutton by this time had definitely settled on a plan to endow a charitable hospital. After his death in 1611, relatives (spurred on by courtiers, including Sir Francis Bacon) challenged his will, but the document was upheld and the future of Charterhouse finally seemed assured. In the ensuing decades Sutton's fame as a philanthropist grew; any subtler shadings tended to fade from published accounts of his life. In the words of Shipley, the most careful and thorough recent investigator of Sutton's career,

> Secretive and colorless, he provided none of the more obvious virtues upon which an admiring posterity might fasten, so a fictitious life began to evolve immediately upon his death. Sutton's reputation was, in particular, the province of his trustees at Charterhouse and their successors, amongst whom a critical spirit was hardly to be expected, especially as these men were attempting to counter a popular tradition that viewed him as a scoundrel and a miser. Succeeding generations of writers and preachers from Charterhouse gradually elaborated the theme of his sagacity and benevolence, calling into the service of the legend any stray facts or accomplishments not definitely claimed elsewhere. Significantly, one of the first facts to be jettisoned in this refurbishment of his reputation was that he had been a money-lender. Sutton's heirs appear to have been embarrassed by the fact that the wealth they had inherited had been earned in the money market. . . . The definitive formulation was made by Samuel Herne in 1677. According to that version, Sutton combined a variety of government positions with one of the most successful and versatile mercantile careers of the early modern era. Subsequent writers drew on Herne's account for their basic narrative, slowly discarding his more egregious

inaccuracies, but as late as the 1920's it was still hotly denied that Sutton had ever been induced to accept interest on his loans.[11]

As Shipley indicates, the importance of Samuel Herne's *Domus Carthusiana: or an Account of the Most Noble Foundation of the Charter-House . . .* is difficult to overestimate. Although many later writers have been at pains to correct various errors in Herne's account, his book has been the basis of most subsequent versions of Sutton's life. Herne himself claimed to be correcting earlier authors; he emphasizes his reliance on careful investigation, although admitting that "The helps I found in the composure of *Sutton's life* were many of them scatter'd here and there, laid hold on rather by chance than direction . . ." (sig. a3^{v}). Herne's sources included not only "the *Records* of the House" as well as "some Remarks whereof I had from creditable and worthy men, bred in this Foundation long ago" (sig. a4^{v}), but also the early commemorative sermon, *Sutton's Synagogue*.[12]

Herne's most important source, however, was "an Anonymous and Imperfect MS. left, not long since, in the Booksellers hands, which did me very good service" (sig. a4^{v}). This last remark is a bit disingenuous, since the manuscript in question is actually the basis for most of Herne's account of Sutton's life; much of his phrasing follows the manuscript verbatim, but Herne's alterations and deletions are even more interesting than his inclusions. The manuscript, Lansdowne 1198, has been housed in the British Library for many years, although few writers on Sutton seem to have consulted it. Comparing the manuscript with Herne's redaction shows how Herne chose to highlight certain aspects of Sutton's career (and the legends associated with it) while downplaying or ignoring others. The manuscript deals much more forthrightly and at greater length with various controversial aspects of Sutton's life than does Herne. Perhaps this is partly because Herne, in addition to dealing with the Founder's life, was also greatly concerned with the institutional history of the hospital itself; he may have felt that any in-depth treatment of Sutton the man was uncalled for. For whatever reasons, however, the manuscript gives a much fuller and more complex sense of Sutton's life, personality, and times than Herne presents; a full comparison of the two accounts would show exactly how Herne tailored the available data to fit the image of Sutton he tried to construct.

A few examples must suffice. Herne only briefly mentions, for instance, a charge the manuscript dwells on—the allegation that part of Sutton's fortune had been won through piracy (40). The manuscript gives a much fuller sense of the kinds of rumors that swirled around the Founder's reputation; whatever the facts of this particular case, the manuscript provides a far clearer picture of the suspicions and innuendoes that dogged Sutton's fame. The manuscript confronts the charge of piracy head-on and at length:

> If it be objected as it hath beene by some that then it seemes he bestowed that *well,* which he got *ill,* that he maintained charity with *Pyracy;* and releived his own countrymen with what he had taken from strangers, com[m]uting for Robbery with Liberality—
>
> It is answered—that if master Sutton got some part of that [estate] by the *warre* which he bestowed soe well in time of *peace,* he did noe more than Abraham the father of the faithful did who hath Lazarus [the poor] now in his bosome - XXX for Abraham tooke of the Spoyles of his enemies and offered the *Tenth* of them to god Heb: 7.4 and master Sutton it may be took some XXX and justly too [since all we take in warres XXX is ours by the highest law in the world] and gave all unto god[13]

The manuscript's tactic here—defending Sutton by citing Biblical precedent and scholarly theory—is typical of its larger strategy. Nowhere is this clearer than in its later discussion of the charge that Sutton was not merely a money-lender but also a usurer, an issue Herne touches on more briefly and with far less self-assurance (41; 48–49). As part of its attempt to explain "how master Sutton got his vast estate," the manuscript argues that

> and as many merchants cannot trade, soe more gentlemen cannot live without money upon use for want whereof their estates will be swallowed up by mortgages and underrate sales which have been p[re]served by easy borrowing upon interest—whereupon my Lord Bacon say[th] that he Remembred a cruell=monied man in the countrey that would say—"the Devill take this usury. it keepes us from forfeitures of mortgages and bonds.["] and truely considering that it is as lawfull to take use for money; as to take money for the use of any thing bought for money "all states and governem[en]ts have judged it better to mitigate usury by *declaration,* than to suffer it to rage and *bite* by *connivance*["]—allowing the lender an aequitable consideration 1. for the gain he might have made of his money since he lent it, and 2 the benefit the borrower made of it since he had it and .3. for the losse the lender sustaineth in the want of it either after or before the day of payment—I have heard say that master Sutton would never take use for money that was for victualls or other necessaries

> spent by the borrower in the use .1. because it was not only uncharitable but unreasonable to design gain in lending that whereby the borrower relieved onely his necessity and intended noe gain in borrowing; therefore in that case he Lent [as our Saviour commanded and all good men advised] looking for nothing again—this being that usury which the statute Eliz: 13°. c8. Hen: 8.37.c.9. James 2jth. c.17 looke upon as detestable, and forbidden by the law of god; while a more moderate and regulated interest are by both lawes allowed—math: 25.14. to 28. Luc:19.1: to 23. Gen: 41.39 42.18. 47.23–24.[14]

Not all of Sutton's contemporaries regarded Sutton's wealth or his activities as a money-lender so benignly as the author of the manuscript. He was the target of envy and resentment, and the manuscript is extremely interesting in its account of how he attempted to "divert" such feelings. He was a powerful man who sought to maintain his power by not excessively displaying it:

> I say these advantages might honestly make any man rich; as they [~~did~~] made Master Sutton *great*, soe *great* that when it was told him ~~that~~ as a rare thing that such a man died worth 20000^{li} he replyed oh! a *beggar*, a *beggar*—he himselfe being worth betweene 3. and 400000^{li}. a litle before he died - an estate that was the matter of few mens; and therefore was the object of most mens envy—which importune and ~~wicke~~ dangerous passion (for who can stand before envy[)] he avoided as much as he could by his privacy and his meekenesse by not being seene in his grandeur to dazle mens eyes nor carrying things on with insolence and height to provoke their malice nay he would allmost melt men to pitty, when to divert their envy at his plentifull fortune; he would sensibly complain of the unavoidable trouble of it; and suffer himselfe to be crossed and overborne of purpose in the concernes of it; for as nothing increaseth envy more than a violent pursuit of designes soe nothing abateth it more than an unconcernednesse in it—;
>
> Yet because mens minds are naturally inclined to feed either upon their own good; or upon others evill; they who wanted the one in themselves did endeavour to find the other in him; and soe being out of hope to attaine to his condition seeke to come at even hand by depressing him to their own.[15]

Although the manuscript makes clear that many of those who envied Sutton were other (if poorer) commoners, it is not difficult to believe that he must also have been resented by many of his social "superiors," especially those who found themselves in his debt. Sutton had to walk a careful line; he could easily arouse both the jealousy of his inferiors and the indignation of men who had more rank than cash. Given his circumstances—his extreme but somewhat mysterious wealth, his isolation, his dependence on a garrulous factotum, the resentment his position bred—it hardly seems surprising that many spectators of *Volpone* assumed that Sutton was Jonson's target. Other similarities between Volpone's and Sutton's circumstances could only have reinforced this assumption, and many members of the play's audience must have relished the thought of Sutton as an object of satire. The manuscript's discussion of this issue—in a long passage that should be of great interest to Jonson scholars and other students of Renaissance literature—is curiously ambivalent. On the one hand the passage dismisses the possibility that Jonson targeted Sutton; on the other hand it condemns and mocks him for attacking so worthy a figure:

> a particular pique ~~against him~~ was thought to be maintained against him by five sorts of persons whom he used to forebode to misery and poverty viz: concelers, promoters, chemists, monopolists; and poets the last of whom being commonly poore themselves addresse themselves to the rich first by Panegyrickes, and flatteries, and that not working upon them (who deal too much in things to be taken with words) they fall upon them with scoffes and jeares to litle purpose when the wealthy laugh at them at home as heartily as they can laugh at them abroad—
>
> I must confesse I never heard that any poet had soe litle wit as openly to abuse ~~him~~ *Master Sutton* who had soe much wit as to get an estate onely there were severall poems of that time that to some app[re]hensions (and fancy hath made actions XX XX and persons of a 1000 years standing to poynt at those of our own time imagining that the Actions of an old play represented some of their new spectators[)] seemed to touch upon those peccadilloes of his which ~~thay~~ in their opinion he was *thought*, rather than in himselfe *was really* guilty of—and rather expressed their malice towards him, than the poets design *upon him*—and among the rest Ben: Johnsons *Vulponi* is generally reported to be master Suttons humor—concerning this I have thus much to offer 1: that though nothing can be soe excellent nay nothing so sacred but hath beene ~~represented~~ exposed as ridiculous (by the power of that faculty that was given us to conceave things aright that we might judge of them; not to represent them foolishly that we might laugh at them) and soe truely we should take as litle notice of these fancifull affronts as he would have done himselfe (who knew that injuries of this nature got advantage by being taken notice of[)] since good men cannot be concerned at those entertai[n]ments in the world wherein they see god himselfe the maker [&] benefactor of it exposed by men that will hazzard the

being damned that they may be thought witty—yet *Ben: Johnson* himselfe was so farre from owning that design upon master Sutton that XX often frequenting the Schoole [&] the hall since the foundation of the Charterhouse he expressed his great admiration of him who [he sayd] had erected soe noble a foundation that he wished himselfe (as his friend Broome was) a member of it. Ben understood well enough that his mushrome playes could never disparage or outlast mr Suttons ~~lasting~~ good workes where the oddes is as great as between paper and stone; between pleasure and piety; betweene what at present *Ticklish*, and what is for ever *usefull.*

2. If he had designed the portraicture of Master Sutton in that play [as religious Sir John oldcastle is acted on our Stage as a sot: and the Renowned Sir Jo: Falstaffe as a Buffoone] yet Ben: Johnson lived to correct his mistake of him out of a passage in Cicero twice translated by him [in studio rei amplificandae apparebat, non avaritiae praedam, sed instrumentum bonitati quaeri] in ~~his~~ master Suttons great care for the enlarging of his estate it appeared that [he] sought not soe much a prey for his covetousness to enjoy, as instrument for his goodnesse to bestow; who knew that of great riches there is noe reall use but distribution, the rest is conceit—the personall enjoyment of the wealthiest man living can never reach to feel great riches beyond the imaginary way of the custody or fame of them unlesse it be by the phantasticke pleasure of Lavishing them upon vain followers or the real one of dispensing them among needy and poore men.[16]

Herne also denies that Jonson attacked Sutton, but, like the author of the manuscript, he covers all bases, asserting that if the poet *did* have Sutton in mind, then "he was first of all an ungrateful Wretch, to abuse those hands which afforded him Bread, for he allowed him a constant Pension: And secondly, he disowned his very Handwriting, which he sent to our Founder, in Vindication of himself in this matter" (43). It would be interesting to know Herne's sources for his charges about Jonson's pension and his "Vindication"; since, in these respects, he goes beyond the authority of the manuscript, perhaps his information came from the personal testimony he alludes to in his preface. Yet despite Herne's and the manuscript's best efforts at denigrating the possibility that Sutton was Jonson's target, in the very process of doing so they offer evidence which makes it easier to understand why so many in the play's contemporary audiences jumped to this conclusion. Particularly fascinating are their discussions of how Sutton tricked persons who tried to manipulate him into making them his heirs. Neither the manuscript nor Herne denies that Sutton took advantage of such people; instead, both applaud his cleverness and imply that any such operators got what they deserved. The manuscript, in another context, praises Sutton as a shrewd tactician, admiring his

> great abilities in negotiations and dealing being extraordinnarily well seen in the art of working upon men knowing either their nature and temper, and soe ~~working upon them~~ leading them; or their ends and soe persuading them; or their weaknesse and disadvantages and soe awing them; or those that have interest in them and soe governing them.[17]

All these skills were useful, apparently, when it came to dealing with his self-presuming "heirs." Herne asserts that in this case, "The Wisdom of the Serpent [was] as well required, as the Innocency of the Dove. He that strives to outreach his Friend, is justly caught in his own snares" (43). The manuscript's treatment of the same issue is, as usual, much lengthier and more interesting, partly because of its attention to the complex motives engendered by micropolitical maneuvering:

> 3. but that wherein he seemeth to some to be most touched for in that play, and wherein he is by others most reflected on in common discourse is that he served himselfe so much of the hopes so many entertained of being his heires; receaving *hooked* gifts of some who looked to have them returned with advantage, and buying easy purchases of others that expected their land that they passed away by ~~deed~~ their own deed should come again to them by XX his *will*—
>
> here it may be considered that he could not helpe the unreasonable presumptions of men who would needes promise themselves his estate who had so many heires (as appeared afterward) to claim it of his own relations; nor [not knowing their design] hinder their projects in refusing their civilities which they layd as baites; nay if he did know it in respect of some it was not safe for the p[re]sent to neglect their overture, XXXX [for they were great men] in respect of others it was not convenient, they were his friends that he made use of, or his relations; either of which he thought it stood not with his interest to make desperate or Injealous for the present resolving (as he did) to return them their *hookes* for legacies afterwards though if his tendernesse and integrity had not thought fit to have done soe; We suppose the plea of such as complain of him amounts to this that he had soe much of the *subtlety of the serpent, the wisedom of the men of this world in their generation* (which we are allowed) that he would not be overreached by

them, that deceaved themselfes but caught them in their own *crafty wiliness that they had imagined ag[ainst] him*

that he should use so mean an artifice to gain the inheritance of some land where of he had long before had a mortgage, as that we have heard some charge him withall (viz) that they might let him have the land now for his money; XX he had noe heires, and they might hereafter have it for nothing and more with it (upon which terms it is alledged that the parties complied with him, but were not at all considered by him) seemes to us unlikely because it is not so easy to imagine that he should use soe poore and grosse a peice of sordidnesse to *get*, who had no other design in getting than freely to *give*; besides that though it be soe hard a matter to get a small estate that one may be tempted to a litle art of this nature, yet it is soe easy to get a great one (as it is well observed) XXX a stock once able to expect the prime of the XXXXXXXX markets, overcome those bargaines which for their greatnesse are few mens money, and make a man partner in the industries of younger men growing upon its selfe; that a man hath noe occasion for it.[18]

What seems clear both from Herne's account and from the manuscript is that however much the genesis of Jonson's play may have been rooted in his reading or his own imagination, and however innocent his own intentions may have been, the resemblances between Sutton's circumstances and Volpone's were striking enough—and well enough known—to spark the kind of suspicions the play immediately provoked. It is not at all difficult to believe that Jonson, perhaps encouraged by a friend or patron who had reason to resent Sutton, had the old man at least partly in mind when he wrote his play. And it certainly is not difficult to imagine that some spectators or readers may have assumed a satirical purpose even if none had been intended. Indeed, a fragment of evidence in a letter to Sutton from Sir John Harington raises intriguing possibilities (although these must remain highly hypothetical in the absence of further data). Written on February 5, 1609/10, Harington's letter informs Sutton of the death of Sir John Skinner (or Skynner), with whom both Harington and Sutton had had extremely complicated and acrimonious financial dealings in the middle years of the decade just ending. Harington's letter begins by asserting that

Yt is not one of the least signes of God's favour unto you, that he hath taken out of this world the man that above all others, without cause or desert, did seke your disturbance and defamation. But that he should dye in such miserie as ys reported, and under the arrest of the sherrifs balyfes; *and that in his life tyme hee should bee playd uppon the stage soe extreme scornfully;* which, I suppose, of all the rest did most breake his heart; this ys to my thoughts a fearfull example of God's judgments, *that even in this world sometimes punisheth men in the same kynd and measure they offend; one particular of which concerninge yourselfe I will reserve till I meete you.*[19]

This is a tantalizing letter: the italicized passages strongly suggest that Skinner, who had definite reasons to dislike Sutton, may have encouraged theatrical satire against him, only to be subjected later to the same kind of ridicule himself. Surviving documents suggest that the height of the Sutton-Skinner feud was reached in the first half of 1607—which is to say, at least a year after *Volpone* was first staged, but at around the very time when the printed version of the play was first being circulated and read (H&S 5: 4). It would be fascinating to know whether Jonson had any links with Skinner or with Skinner's sympathizers, but no hard evidence of such a connection presents itself. However, even if Harington's letter has no reference at all to Jonson or to *Volpone*, the document still contributes valuably to our understanding of the context in which Jonson's play was first staged and read. The letter provides further evidence of the use of the stage for personal satire in Jacobean London,[20] but it also shows that being satirized on the stage could be a particularly painful experience; that playwrights could be influenced by private parties to engage in such satire; and that personal attacks were easily recognized by many members of the audience. All of these facts are relevant to the circumstances surrounding *Volpone* and its reception, even if the play had no intended connection at all to Sutton.

Certainly Jonson could not have been surprised to learn that others spotted a connection. There is no way to know, of course, whether he deliberately intended any personal satire, and there is even less evidence about his more precise motives even if such satire *was* intended. However, the standard assumption of earlier scholars—that Jonson could not possibly have aimed at Sutton—seems less convincing than it once did. After all, their picture of Sutton—a picture stressing his piety and exemplary character—has been drawn largely from the very sources that sought to whitewash his contemporary reputation. Yet even those sources (especially the unnoted manuscript) offer evidence that many people of Sutton's time viewed him far less benignly than subsequent generations have done.

The fact that the resemblances between Sutton and Volpone are not even more striking does not necessarily prove that no satire was intended. Indeed, if the playwright *had* wanted to mock Sutton, he would have had to guard against mocking him too obviously, lest he be charged with personal libel. Moreover, in deciding about charges of personal satire on the English Renaissance stage, textual evidence alone can never be entirely conclusive; much would have depended on how the actor playing Volpone chose to move or to speak his lines.[21] However, Jonson's intentions or even those of the actors are less important than the interpretations his audience could reasonably have made of his play. What seems clear from a fuller investigation of Sutton's life is that, given the old man's circumstances, Jonson would have had few grounds to complain if Sutton, his friends, or his enemies detected some personal application in the work. The play's subplot, with its English characters and its many references to contemporary English events, would have given comfort to any spectator who wanted to view the main plot in similar terms. The Venetian setting distances the work only partially from relevance to life in London. Whether by accident or design, *Volpone* treats a subject that was highly topical at the time the work was written. The extraordinary speed with which Jonson penned his masterpiece—he claimed to have composed it in five weeks—can reasonably cause one to wonder if something other than his reading alone may have jogged his imagination. In any case, and for whatever reasons, he hit upon a subject that must have struck many auditors as especially timely and pertinent.

Certainly the play's dedicatory epistle seems preoccupied with the issue of personal satire. Although often read as an epitome of Jonson's most enduring assumptions about the nature and purposes of art, the epistle also seems to reflect quite specific and contemporary concerns. Never before in this way had Jonson felt so elaborate a need to explain and justify his intentions; he even jokes about the dedication's extraordinary length. The epistle goes out of its way to deny—repeatedly—that *Volpone* is aimed at anyone in particular; the extent and intensity of its denials are striking, and raise the possibility that Jonson may have been rebutting specific charges. Of course, as Annabel Patterson has pointed out, vigorous denial of topical applications could in fact invite readers to search for them, so the very words that seem to rule out personal satire could have been read, at least by some, as covert encouragement to seek it out.[22] In a sense, Jonson's very vehemence undermines any certainty about his sure intentions or about how his words may have been received. The dedication raises more questions than it settles.

Whether or not Jonson intended any personal satire, his epistle seems concerned to answer such charges. At times it seems to preempt, point-by-point, the kinds of attacks leveled against him in the British Library manuscript. Even—or perhaps especially—if such allegations were untrue, Jonson would still have felt a strong need to confront them. Almost at once the epistle indicates his awareness that his reputation and status were in others' hands, that his power to affect others' renown could be turned against him. He distances himself from licentious "*Poetasters*" (H&S 5:17)[23]—a word, ironically, that would have reminded his audience of his own involvement in the bitter "War of the Theaters" a few years back, with its stinging personal satire. His very claim of lofty superiority over the hacks who debase art oddly recalls one of the least savory episodes of his career; the very words that seem to distance him from theatrical abuses could be read as belated theatrical abuse. The petulancy he attributes to others might seem his own, while his claim that only a good man can be a good poet is as much a tactical maneuver as an expression of serene self-confidence (H&S 5:17).

Rhetorically brilliant, the epistle turns all the standard charges against poets back upon their accusers while endorsing measured criticism—thus making the attackers seem the true extremists. If poets were alleged to be unmannerly and undignified, the epistle makes their critics seem even more guilty of these faults. If poets were attacked as licentious, Jonson makes their critics seem libelous and slanderous, since they tax all writers with the crimes of some. Jonson bitterly rejects his persistent reputation for "sharpnesse," for being "bitter"; what "publique person," he asks, has he provoked? Has he not always in fact "preserv'd their dignitie, as mine own person, safe?" (H&S 5:18) The inserted clause is telling: avoiding the appearance of personal satire was not only right but sensible. Indeed, his entire self-defense is intriguingly ambivalent. He denies personal abuse so vehemently and at such length that one cannot help but wonder why such denials seemed so important. Jonson, however, seems to have been less confident than subsequent commentators that no personal satire could be discerned in his play. His claims to self-assurance suggest a more fundamental insecurity:

> I know that nothing can be so innocently writ, or carryed, but may be made obnoxious to construction; mary, whil'st I beare mine innocence about mee, I feare it not. Application, is now, growne a trade with many; and there are, that professe to have a key for the decyphering of every thing: but let wise and noble persons take heed how they be too credulous, or give leave to these invading interpreters, to bee over-familiar with their fames, who cunningly, and often, utter their owne virulent malice, under other mens simplest meanings. (H&S 5: 18–19)

A subsequent sentence attacks those who "care not whose living faces they intrench, with their petulant stiles"; Jonson would almost rather see antiquated plays revived than "behold the wounds of private men, of princes, and nations" on the contemporary stage. He quotes a passage from Horace he had already translated in *Poetaster*: "In satyres, each man (though untoucht) complaines / As he were hurt; and hates such biting straines" (H&S 5:19).[24] This buried echo from one of his own most bitterly personal plays seems unintentionally ironic; in any case, it could hardly innoculate *Volpone* against suspicions of personal satire. No number of denials could do the trick, and for readers predisposed to view the play this way, even the denials themselves must have seemed suspicious.

The epistle, in short, sheds no certain light on the issue of whether Jonson satirized Sutton, although that issue itself casts back an interesting and provocative glow on the epistle. It provides an intriguing contemporary context for what might otherwise seem a timeless statement of general poetic principles. Even if Jonson did have Sutton partly in mind when he wrote his play, or even if he knew that many in his audience could not help but think of Sutton when they saw it, this hardly means that the dedication is an exercise in hypocrisy, that Jonson used it to deny a libel he secretly intended. Any resemblance between Volpone and Sutton would surely have seemed, to Jonson, not libelous but actually (if paradoxically) well-intentioned. As the epistle makes clear, Jonson saw it as part of the poet's duty to educate his society, to uphold the highest moral standards, to impart and instill virtue by reminding men of their obligations to themselves, to each other, and to God. The true poet, he writes, "is said to be able to informe yong-men to all good disciplines, inflame growne-men to all great vertues, keepe old-men in their best and supreme state, or as they decline to child-hood, recouer them to their first strength . . ." (H&S 5:17). Any satire on Sutton intended or perceived in Jonson's play could have been interpreted as being in Sutton's (and society's) best long-term interests. Any implied criticism could have been read as having been designed, like Bishop Hall's letter, to spur the old man to use his wealth well, to finalize and implement the charitable designs he had long ago set down. Any implied attack on Sutton in the play could have been read by Jonson, his audience, and even by Sutton himself as a well-intentioned (if pointed) reminder about what really mattered in life, and about the proper uses of prosperity.

Whatever Jonson's private intentions may have been, it seems clear that many of the play's first auditors and readers saw a connection to Sutton. The Beinecke Library at Yale owns Lord Charles Stanhope's baroquely-annotated copy of Jonson's 1640 Folio. The margins are filled with curious notes and observations, including one passage next to the first few lines of the famous "Argument" to *Volpone*:

> VOLPONE, childlesse, rich, faines sicke, despaires,
> Offers his state to hopes of severall heires,
> Lies languishing; His Parasite receaves
> Presents of all, assures, deludes. . . .

Beside this, Stanhope has simply written: "This was [just] / ritch ould / Suttons case."[25]

Like many other members of Jonson's earliest audiences, Stanhope seems to have had no difficulty imagining that the playwright's works for the public theatre were often tinged by micropolitical motives. Our latter-day preoccupation with the "larger" political ideologies of earlier writers and with the involvement of their writings in "great" historical movements or events can often lead us to neglect such motives and meanings, but as the next few chapters will suggest, micropolitics of some sort seems frequently to have been a matter of some concern to Jonson and his contemporaries.

4
Political Contexts of *The Devil is an Ass*

Unlike *Volpone, The Devil is an Ass* is not one of Jonson's best-known plays, but in many respects it is one of his most interesting. Written in 1616, the same year in which he received a royal pension and witnessed the publication of his massive first folio, the play was produced at a time when its author must have seemed near the height of his public career. Although the work has rarely been judged a complete artistic success, it has hardly been considered a total failure. Instead, critical assessments have usually been mixed, with many readers acknowledging the play's genuine strengths. Anne Barton, in fact, has recently called it "an immensely courageous play, far better and more interesting than most of its critics have made out"; she sees it as both a summation and a new departure in Jonson's development as a dramatist.[1] Her discussion invites new attention to the play's aesthetic success, but our understanding of the work can also profit from a renewed examination of its place in history, of the ways it is at once embedded in, and emerges from, specific historical contexts. Leah Marcus has recently gone far towards helping us understand those contexts,[2] yet a wealth of further evidence links the work to contemporary personalities, issues, events, and texts that have yet to be fully explored. Examining this evidence will reveal how tightly the play can be tied to its own time and place, and thus how many resonances it may have had for its original audience. Reading the play with a fuller awareness of its historical dimensions can heighten rather than reduce our sense of its artistry and complexity. Moreover, the test case the play provides may suggest the need to reexamine many of Jonson's other works with renewed attention to their historical contexts.

Jonson's comedy was first staged in the fall of 1616, probably in October or November; it seems to have been written sometime during the preceding several months.[3] This dating is crucial and crucially helpful, for 1616 was an especially momentous year in Jacobean history. The political situation was unusually fluid at this time: King James's old favorite, the Scotsman Robert Carr (Earl of Somerset), had recently been convicted for his role in the murder of Sir Thomas Overbury—the greatest scandal of the reign. Meanwhile the new favorite, the Englishman George Villiers, had yet to establish firmly his independent power. The opportunities for factional competition and intrigue, especially those tinged by ethnic prejudices, were thus particularly abundant. The Earl of Pembroke, one of Jonson's most important patrons, had only recently succeeded the disgraced Carr as Lord Chamberlain, and Pembroke was known for his antagonism toward the Scots. However, domestic British politics was not the only focus of contention. Rumors abounded of a planned Spanish match for the young Prince Charles—a marriage and a policy strongly opposed by many powerful people (such as Pembroke) but strongly supported by others, including many courtiers who were on the Spanish payroll. King James's own intentions regarding the possible match were, as usual, somewhat mysterious—a fact that could only exacerbate uncertainty and tensions. This very fluidity meant that a play seeking to influence current events, or to contribute to contemporary dialogue, could hardly have been written at a more propitious moment.

As if all this were not enough, 1616 was also a time of great conflict between competing legal philosophies and between competing courts and jurists, the latter most notably including Sir Edward Coke (the Lord Chief Justice) and Sir Thomas Egerton (the Lord Chancellor). The King's sympathies were clearly with Egerton, and the monarch's 1616 speech in the Star Chamber, in which he enunciated quite clearly his own thinking about the law, was one of the most important pronouncements of his reign. Yet while Coke's power could seem to be waning, so, clearly, was Egerton's health. Once again, uncertainty and instability were the results. This was true, too, in another important matter — "Alderman Cockayne's Project," perhaps the most volatile topic in contemporary political debate. Jonson's preoccupation in *The Devil is an Ass* with the heated issue of monopolies is inescapable; by satirizing "projectors," the play targeted a problem of exceptionally current relevance. Several commentators have previously noted the play's possible allusions to the Cockayne project, but this connection has never been explored in much detail. In particular, Cockayne's own role as Jonson's patron earlier in 1616 has not been mentioned in recent discussions of the play. The fact that the fierce satirist of monopolies had lately been employed by the era's most infamous monopolist adds another layer of complexity to the work's already tangled contexts.

Finally, another complicating factor seems to have gone almost completely unnoticed—the evidence that Jonson, in writing his play, seems to have had in mind another recent comedy by another author. This work was *Ignoramus*, a university drama in Latin by the Cambridge scholar George Ruggle. Ruggle's work was one of the most notorious plays produced during James's reign. It had touched off fiery controversies, not only between partisans of Oxford and Cambridge, but more importantly between representatives of competing legal traditions. It was thus linked, in important ways, to the issues animating the conflict between Coke and Egerton, but this is merely one aspect of its relevance to Jonson's play. The connections between the two dramas are numerous, and much evidence suggests that Jonson may have been deliberately and consciously alluding to *Ignoramus*. In this respect as well as in the others already touched on, Jonson's work seems very much to have been a product of a particular time and place.

I

Addressing his friend Dudley Carleton, the Jacobean letter-writer John Chamberlain reported in June 1616 that on the eighth day of that month, King James had dined "at alderman Coquins, where he was presented with a bason of gold, and as many peeces in yt as together made up the summe of 1000^{li}, the Prince after the same manner with 500^{li}: so that the whole charge of that feast stoode the new companie in more then 3100^{li} the thanckes remaining wholy with the Alderman who at parting was knighted with the Citie-sword."[4] Evidently this dinner attracted a good deal of attention; Chamberlain had already mentioned it in an earlier letter (2: 8), and it was also touched on in another note to Carleton, this time written by George Gerrard. Gerrard reported that the King had been "feasted by Alderman Cockayne and the new Company of Merchant Adventurers, who gave him 1,000*l*. in a basin and ewer of gold. Dyers, cloth dressers, with their shuttles, and Hamburgians, were presented to the King, and 'spake such language as Ben Jonson putt in theyre mouthes.'"[5]

Jonson's involvement in this project has not received much attention, and in fact Cockayne's name is not even listed in the index to the standard edition of the poet's works. Although Jonson preserved and published many of the poems, masques, plays, and entertainments he wrote during the latter part of his career, a text of his "speeches" for Cockayne has not survived. Whether it was simply lost, burned in the famous fire of 1623, or was deliberately suppressed is unclear. What seems likely, however, is that Jonson may later have felt some misgivings about his involvement with Cockayne, as he had earlier felt misgivings about his works celebrating the marriage of Somerset, which had precipitated Overbury's murder. Just as Jonson afterwards attempted, like many others, to distance himself from the disgraced favorite, so he may also have felt some need to undo the public perception of his connection with Cockayne. To understand why, we need to review the history of Cockayne and his "new Company of Merchant Adventurers." Doing so will also shed light on some other figures and issues relevant to a fuller understanding of *The Devil is an Ass*.

Astrid Friis long ago wrote what remains the fullest account of Cockayne's "project."[6] Cockayne, an important figure in the City, seems to have long been behind efforts to undermine the monopoly the government had granted to the old Merchant Adventurers, who possessed the right to export undressed cloths. Cockayne and his associates (the "new company") argued that domestic profits would increase, and more people would be put to work, if the cloths were dressed *before* exportation, rather than leaving such essential processing to foreigners. The "Dyers, cloth dressers, with their shuttles, and Hamburgians" mentioned in Gerrard's letter suggest how closely Jonson's speeches must have reflected Cockayne's ideas. In any case, by 1613 Cockayne had succeeded in interesting the government in his proposals, which seemed to promise not only increased employment and prosperity but additional revenues for the financially troubled bureaucracy. Almost from the beginning, however, there was skepticism; Friis notes that many of the King's Privy Councillors

> expressed their absolute sympathy with the principle of the proposal, for it would serve to give work to the poor handicraftsmen, but they added that it was even more important to keep up the free and ample sale of cloth in foreign parts, and it was exceedingly doubtful whether this was possible when all cloths were dyed and dressed before the exportation. (240)

The old system, whatever its faults, was well established; and besides, foreigners might retaliate against the new scheme, either by barring English imports or by seeking supplies of undressed cloths from other sources. If successful, Cockayne's proposal would enhance the nation's prosperity. If it failed, however, it could severely damage the country's chief industry at a time when the economy was already suffering. And, of course, Cockayne's ideas threatened the self-interests of the "old" Merchant Adventurers. In fact, B. E. Supple, another historian, has described the plan of Cockayne and his cohorts as merely a devious scheme to muscle in on the exportation of undressed cloths; it was, he says, an attempt "by seventeenth-century racketeers, to gain, by conspiracy and misrepresentation, a share in a profitable monopolistic trade."[7]

Hindsight, of course, is always clear, and if Cockayne had succeeded he would have been hailed as a hero. Success, however, seemed unlikely to many at court, and the fact that the scheme was being pushed by Somerset, the favorite, and by the Earl of Northampton and other members of the Howard family (who were all alleged to have been bribed),[8] made it almost inevitable that the debate would soon become tangled in factional intrigue. The Earl of Pembroke was suspicious of Somerset and a rival of Northampton, and Northampton himself had long been unfriendly toward Jonson.[9] Northampton died in 1614, but Cockayne had other powerful backers, particularly Sir Edward Coke (who in other respects was a member of Pembroke's faction [Prestwich 170]). Even Coke's old rival, Sir Francis Bacon (whom Jonson greatly admired), claimed to have initially supported the plan,[10] so that the diverse motives and personalities swirling around the proposal make easy assessments difficult.

Most important of all, however, the King had begun to take a definite interest in the project. It might seem easy to regard James's growing support as an indication either of his greed or of his economic naïveté, but if he was naive he was no more so than some of his most accomplished Councillors, and the charge of greed seems even less easy to support. In fact, James had been offered "a considerable profit" by the old company for permission to maintain their monopoly (Spedding 12: 169–70), and by 1615 Bacon, in a letter to the monarch, was alluding to the "great annual benefit" the King could reap if he abandoned Cockayne (Spedding 12: 171). Yet even after the project's financial failure had become widely apparent, James was reluctant to cut his losses, arguing (in Friis's paraphrase) that he "had not aimed at any personal advantage, on the contrary, his annual loss was £ 30,000. Only the good of the country had been in his thoughts" (Friis 288). Samuel Gardiner, still one of the most reliable historians of the period (and certainly no apologist for James), concludes that the King did indeed act disinterestedly in this matter.[11] But he also acted, as most students of the subject have concluded, with his typical stubborness and with a willful sense of his own correctness. By 1616 James seems to have been far less worried about losing money than about losing face; he was determined, if possible, to make the project work, especially since he had sanctioned it with (as he thought) the best of intentions, and especially since (as he felt) the prosperity of his subjects was at stake. James, it must have seemed, could not win: if he abandoned Cockayne, his initial judgment would be questioned; if he stuck with Cockayne, people would question his judgment. Only success could free the King from his dilemma, and success (he hoped) might still be grasped. When he sat down to dine with Cockayne and to hear Jonson's "speeches," he was still clinging to the fading chance that things might turn out for the best.

In the interim, events had made this unlikely. When the members of the "old company" at first refused to give up their charter, Coke suggested that it be undermined by legal means (Friis 270). However, the efforts of the "new company" began to fail almost immediately. Exports fell and production dropped, and in addition it was found that Cockayne and his group "were not fulfilling their obligations with regard to the fully-manufactured textiles which they *did* export" (Supple 42). By 1615 opposition to the project had begun to mushroom, especially among the Privy Councillors. But Somerset and his allies continued to support the project, and so did the King, who was reluctant to seem inconstant (Friis 274–76). By 1616, however, Somerset had fallen, and a new favorite—Villiers, who had been promoted by Pembroke and his allies—was clearly on the rise. In addition, Pembroke himself had recently been appointed Lord Chamberlain. And finally, by 1616 even James had begun to have doubts about the project. Evidence of fraud had been uncovered, and further investigation began (Friis 287). A letter from the King, read at the Privy Council meeting of 14 January, provides clear proof that James had begun "to feel ill at ease at the thought of the responsibility devolving on him in this matter. His perplexity and irresolution are plainly evident" (Friis 288). The King stressed that the Privy Council had approved the plan and that Coke had strongly advised it, but he seemed unwilling simply to let Somerset take the blame, and equally unwilling to abandon the project without giving it further chance to work. He did, however, order further investigation, and directed that "if the present state of affairs could be traced to bad practices or private gains of the members of the new company, Cockayne was to be questioned" (Friis 288). This was a directive that most of the Privy Councillors were quite ready to pursue.

Within a few days, the investigation had turned up a number of disturbing facts, and at a meeting on 18 January, sentiment in the Council had turned even more sharply against Cockayne. According to Friis,

> The Lord Chief Justice, Sir Edward Coke, formerly one of the promoters of the new company, no doubt seized this opportunity to turn against it with the greatest eagerness, the new company having developed into something quite different from what he had imagined and no less objectionable to him than the old company. It was not for this that he had employed his brilliant legal knowledge. It did not improve his mood that he was often reminded that he had been one of the agents in the formation of the new company. That his great antagonist, Sir Francis Bacon, had drawn up the charter was only another reason for attacking it. (292)

Coke's switch was significant; it deprived Cockayne of one of his most forceful advocates. And, as I shall suggest later, this switch may be glanced at in Jonson's satirical depiction of Justice Paul (or "Povle") Either-side in *The Devil is an Ass*. Either-side can be linked with Coke for a number of different reasons, but certainly the Chief Justice's dramatic about-face in the matter of the Cockayne project (and in the face of the King's growing dissatisfaction) may have struck many contemporary cynics as itself a cynical maneuver. However sincere Coke's new thinking may have been, it was bound to lend itself to other interpretations.

During much of the rest of 1616, the fate of the "new company" hung in the balance. Opposition among the Privy Councillors continued to grow, and even the King's stance seemed to shift from time to time (Friis 295–301). Clearly he was growing impatient, although just as clearly he seemed determined to salvage the project if he could. The dinner in June that Cockayne hosted for the monarch, complete with Jonson's "speeches" (which Friis even calls a "masque" [303]), was obviously designed in part to shore up faltering support. However, in spite of James's decision to knight Cockayne and in spite of the King's willful efforts to make the business work, by late summer and early fall (the period when Jonson was probably at work on his play)the situation had considerably soured. By 6 August, James had issued detailed instructions

> as to how the Councillors were to deal with Alderman Cockayne. They were to summon him before them privately and seriously represent to him that his Majesty's honour was at stake, and point out the incalculable damage that would ensue to the commonwealth from the universal decay of cloth manufacturing. . . . They were further to remind Cockayne of what had passed between his Majesty and himself in private, and how his Majesty had often warned him to be wary and circumspect and "not to embrace more, then well hee was assured, his forces were able well to weeld." Moreover, his Majesty had commanded him to advise him from day to day of the progress of the work, so that, in case the project should threaten to fail, his Majesty's wisdom might prevent it in time, in order that "no preiudice might befall to his honor or detrement to his subiectes." (Friis 308)

Punishment was threatened for those members of Cockayne's company who had committed "'a playne Cosonage, not sufferable in a well-gouerned Commonwealth'" (Friis 308). By the beginning of autumn the Councillors could feel some confidence that Cockayne's influence was waning and that they had the King's support (Friis 309).

However, James still resisted the dissolution of the new company. "It hurt his pride too much to admit that he had been wrong. On the other hand, his feelings toward Alderman Cockayne had definitely changed. He no longer trusted him." At one meeting in September the King angrily cut the Alderman short (Friis 317). Determined to preserve not only the cloth trade but also his own reputation, he alternately threatened and accommodated Cockayne and his crew (Friis 318). He even promised to commit £ 40,000 from his own funds to help sustain the project (Friis 327). By mid-October, Bacon was advising Villiers, the new favorite, that "his majesty must either lay the fault upon the matter itself, or upon the persons that have managed it; wherein the king shall best acquit his honor, to lay it where it is indeed; that is, upon the carriage and proceedings of the New Company, which have been full of uncertainty and abuse." He further noted that the "subjects of this kingdom generally have an ill taste and conceit of the new company, and therefore the putting of them down will discharge the state of a great deal of envy" (Friis 84). By November, during or shortly after the period when Jonson's play may actually have been staged, the King (according to Archbishop Abbot) told Cockayne "'in could bloud before ye Council Table yet if he had abused him by wrong information his 4 quarters should pay for it,'" at which, continues Abbot, "'ye poore Alderman stood infinitely amazed'" (Friis 352). Earlier that month he had warned the new company that he would take any delays "as a double contempt" (Friis 348).

By the beginning of the new year, the old company had been restored. Cockayne's project had collapsed, and *The Devil is an Ass*, Jonson's very timely satire on projects and projectors, had been written and performed. Jonson's motives in writing the play were undoubtedly complicated, but surely one of them must have been to distance himself from his earlier involvement with Cockayne. This is not to impute hypocrisy or insincerity to the poet; his commission to write his earlier "speeches" may have been a task he could not have refused, whatever his personal feelings. By the same token, we do not know the precise tone of his speeches; they may have been more admonitory than simply celebratory. In writing them he may have felt that he was serving not so much Cockayne's interests as those of the commonwealth and the King. The fact that the speeches have not survived makes speculation somewhat fruitless, but there seems little doubt that Jonson would have wanted to allay any misunderstandings that his involvement with Cockayne may have aroused. By the time he wrote *The Devil is an Ass*, Jonson was in part expressing widely held sentiments about projectors—sentiments the King currently had good reason to share, and sentiments that were, in any case, already part of official royal doctrine. Attacking corruption may have seemed particularly worthwhile at this time, when court policies and personnel were being altered and when the opportunities for genuine reform may have seemed more promising than they had been in years.

Whether James himself was embarrassed by Jonson's satire on monopolies is impossible to say. Several ironic references to aldermen might have reminded contemporary auditors of the most famous alderman of the day (2.1.42; 3.2.32) and of his involvement with the King, but by the time Jonson wrote, even the King had become suspicious of Cockayne. At another point, it is true, the play's chief monopolist, Meere-craft, mentions to the chief object of its satire, Fitz-dottrell, a project for the recovery of flooded land, "Whereof the *Crowne's* to haue his moiety, / If it be owner" (2.1.46–47). James could conceivably have interpreted this as satire on his own greed, but if he did, he did not order the lines suppressed, and in any case it was pride more than greed that seems to have dictated his behavior in the Cockayne affair. If Jonson intended this comment as a slap at James, he seems to have felt free to deliver it. More likely, however, Jonson's phrase alludes to the royal bureaucracy or to the state rather than to the King himself. In that case, Meere-craft's comment reflects more on him than on James, and in any case it would not have been unreasonable for the crown to receive some share in profits from the drainage of royal lands.

James could not have been surprised to hear a projector talk as Meere-craft does, nor could it have startled him to learn, by way of Jonson's comedy, that courtiers could be bribed to promote projects. If James was at all a target of the play's satire, he seems not to have noticed or to have been bothered. The fact that Jonson felt free to write a play so explicitly and obviously topical, at a time when it might embarrass the King, says much about his trust in the monarch's tolerance. Moreover, the fact that the play was not suppressed suggests that James found little in it to trouble his own conscience or to threaten his keen sense of his reputation. It was Jonson, as much as James, who needed to worry about gossip concerning his involvement with Cockayne. Perhaps the ferocity of the poet's satire on projectors reflects the need he felt to distance himself from the alderman, and to undo any damage done to his own reputation by the public's knowledge of his earlier "speeches."

II

Although King James seems to have tolerated or even to have enjoyed Jonson's general satire against monopolists, evidence survives that he did request at least one change in the play. Jonson would later tell his friend William Drummond, in connection with Meere-craft's previously mentioned scheme to make Fitz-dottrell the Duke of Drowned Land, that "the King desyred him to conceal it" (H&S 1: 144). Jonson called *The Devil is an Ass* "a play of his upon which he was accused" (H&S 1: 144)—suggesting, as Ian Donaldson has noted, that in the Drowned Land satire "a particular target must have been seen."[12] Who could this have been, and why would James have intervened? This has always been one of the most fascinating puzzles connected with the play.

Leah Marcus has recently made a strong case that the target of Jonson's satire may have been Sir Robert Carr (or Ker)—not the royal favorite of the same name (who became Earl of Somerset and then fell as a result of Overbury's murder), but rather a kinsman to Somerset, also named Sir Robert Carr, who was a Gentleman of the Prince's Bedchamber. Marcus notes the report of "a grant to Sir Robert Carr and Thomas Reade recorded in the Docquet 11 August 1614 for sole drainage of the king's drowned lands." She observes that there had been several attempts in the early seventeenth century to reclaim fens, and she contends that the grant to Carr and Reade was the most recent of those recorded (Marcus 100). Although I shall later suggest that another powerful figure may just as well have been the target of Jonson's satire, Marcus's suggestion remains a very real possibility. Before exploring alternatives, it seems worth seeing what else can be said in favor of her suggestion.

Why Carr? Why would Jonson choose to focus (if he did) on this particular courtier and on this particular aspect of that courtier's life? If his point was to mock a man whom Marcus calls "a royal favorite" (104), why did he choose *this* favorite at *this* time? Several answers suggest themselves. In the first place, the Carr whom Jonson may have mocked had been a close ally of the Carr (Somerset) who had recently been disgraced and replaced. Carr, therefore, was vulnerable in 1616 in ways that he had not been even two years earlier. His connection with the fallen Somerset would have made him an obvious and somewhat easy target. It was Somerset, after all, who had helped "plant" him in the Prince's Bedchamber in 1613,[13] and a courtier such as John Donne soon recognized Carr's value as an intermediary with the Earl.[14] Jonson would have known Carr from his participation in the poet's masque for 1615, *The Golden Age Restor'd*, and Carr would later take part in the masque for 1618, *For the Honour of Wales* (H&S 10: 430). Even King James recognized—and used—Carr's connection and influence with Somerset.[15] Taken together, these facts suggest that because of his link to Somerset, Carr would have been as vulnerable in 1616 as he had been strengthened by it earlier. In fact, in April of that year Carr had even been investigated and briefly imprisoned on suspicion of assisting his fallen patron. John Chamberlain reported that

> Sir Robert Carre (neere about the Prince) and Gibbe of the bed-chamber were examined the last week about conveying away and burning of papers, and letters, and were restrained to Sir James Fullerton . . . but I heare Sir Robert Car hath found meanes to be inlarged, whatsoever becomes of Gibbe. (1: 625–26)

This arrest, it should be noted, shortly preceded Somerset's trial, and both events must have made Carr seem relatively defenseless. Evidence survives that as early as 1611, before his ascendance, Carr had worried about his vulnerability to detraction,[16] and surely such thoughts must have entered his mind again. If it was Carr who complained to the King about being mocked as the Duke of Drowned Land, it is not hard to see not only why he complained but also why Jonson may have felt able to mock him. And as it turns out, several other factors could have made Carr a tempting target. One was simply his nationality: like his patron he was a Scot, and the effort to replace Somerset with Villiers had been motivated, in part, by the desire of certain powerful Englishmen to reduce Scottish influence at court. Another factor was, of course, Carr's continuing proximity to, and influence with, the Prince. If Somerset's fall was to be made final, and if the influence of Somerset's faction was to be counteracted, then men like Carr could not be allowed to retain their former power. The same figures who helped engineer Somerset's eclipse may have put Jonson up to his possible satire of Carr. Who might these have been? One likely candidate is the Earl of Pembroke, well known for his suspicion of the Scots and a prime mover in the effort to undermine Somerset. And, in fact, evidence survives that there was bad blood between Carr and Pembroke. Thus, Carr's brief imprisonment in April 1616 was due in part to the suspicion that he had written a tract attacking Pembroke, among others. Although his innocence was "at once established" and another Scotsman was implicated instead,[17] this datum nonetheless reveals that there was tension (as one might have assumed) between Carr and Pembroke. When satire of Pembroke was uncovered, Carr was immediately suspected.

Jonson's link with Pembroke is well known; in some ways he can be seen as the poet's most important patron during this period. His recent advancement to the post of Lord Chamberlain, his role in advancing Villiers, and the generally auspicious outlook for his faction at court all made him an especially powerful figure in 1616. Jonson's folio *Workes*, published that year, had abundantly acknowledged the poet's respect for the Earl, and a few years later he would report to Drummond that Pembroke had been giving him £ 20 each new year's to buy books (H&S 1: 141). Jonson would have had many reasons, then, for mocking Carr, especially if it was suspected that Carr was capable of mocking Pembroke. As a leader of the faction opposed to Carr's and as a lightning rod for anti-Scottish sentiment at court, Pembroke would have had many reasons to encourage Jonson to take a swipe at Carr. And James, with his usual interest in making peace among his courtiers, could have been expected to "desire" Jonson to conceal any satire that was too blatantly personal. What we seem to glimpse, then, in Jonson's possible attack on Carr is not so much a reflection *on* the state of the court as a reflection *of* it—specifically, of its factional intrigues and tensions. What such satire may reveal is not the poet's indictment of "the court" as such but rather his involvement, on one level, in the personal politics that his play otherwise so effectively mocks.

There seem good reasons, then, to accept Marcus's suggestion that Carr was the prototype of Jonson's "Duke of Drowned Land." At the same time, however, another possible candidate seems worth mentioning. Many of the same factors that might have prompted Jonson to satirize Carr could also have encouraged him to mock another Scotsman—Archibald Campbell, the seventh Earl of Argyll. In the first place, records survive of a grant, dated 3 July 1615,

> to Chas. Glemmond and John Walcott, of London, nominees of the Earl of Argyle, of certain marsh grounds left by the sea in Wigtoft, Moulton, Holbeach, and Tydd-St.-Mary, co. Lincoln, to be drained at the expense of the Earl, with reservation of a fifth portion, and a rent of £ 50, to the King, and of certain common lands to the neighbouring townships, &c.[18]

This grant was thus more recent by more than a year than the one given to Carr, and, as it happens, events in the county of Lincoln in 1616 would have given any drainage projects in that area a certain degree of notoreity at precisely the time when Jonson was probably at work on his play. H. C. Darby reports, for instance, that in "January 1616 a commission of sewers at Wisbech was attended by 'soe great an assembly of commissioners and inhabitants' of the fen countries as had 'seldome been seen together att any one tyme before.'"[19] Controversy about drainage schemes continued throughout the rest of 1616 and indeed for the next several years.[20] In his reference to the drowned lands as in his more general comments on monopolies, Jonson once again had touched on a very timely topic.

Why might Argyll have been targeted, if he was in fact targeted at all? Several possibilities suggest themselves. The fact that he was a Scot should not be forgotten, particularly in light of other events occurring in 1616. Argyll had been among the original contingent of Scottish lords to follow James south in 1603, and, as I shall indicate shortly, his relations with English aristocrats were from the start somewhat strained.[21] Moreover, the fact that Argyll was also a Scot who hoped to profit from the recovery of English land may also have annoyed some Englishmen in 1616. Argyll, as it turns out, had good reason to be interested in earning profits during this period; despite (or because of) his lofty rank, he was burdened with debts and "hounded by creditors."[22] His financial problems would, in fact, soon be one of the causes that would prompt him to leave Britain to live abroad for a number of years. In the year in which Jonson wrote his play, however, Argyll had reasons to be hopeful.

Although James himself had at one time joked at Argyll's discomfiture after a lost battle,[23] in 1616 the King had good reason to be pleased with the Earl's military prowess. In the preceding year he had been in charge of subduing the rebellious Macdonald clan and had done his job effectively (Paul 348). James could not help being grateful, and Argyll's English rivals may have felt good reason to fear that the Earl's influence would grow. He seems, by 1617, "to have been in high favour at court,"[24] and he was also back in England throughout 1616.[25] In other words, he was well positioned to exercise his influence with the King that year, and at the very end of 1615 the Queen and Prince had stood as sponsors at the christening of the Earl's recently born twin sons.[26] The fact that Argyll's wife was a Catholic would not have given any peace of mind to the Protestant faction at court (a faction headed by Pembroke), nor would the Earl's presumptive sympathy for Spain have comforted the anti-Spanish faction (also headed by Pembroke), especially during a year swirling with rumors about a Spanish marriage for the Prince. In fact, Argyll's pro-Spanish views (combined with his financial problems) would cause him, before long, to desert Britain, travel to the continent, and spend the next several years fighting on behalf of the Spanish king.[27] In 1616, however, that move was still two years in the offing.

Pembroke and his followers, then, may have felt a number of general misgivings about Argyll's growing influence. Even other

Scotsmen feared it.[28] As it happens, however, Pembroke had very personal reasons to dislike his Scottish rival. A letter by William Trumbell, written around the time of the performance, on 6 January 1610, of Jonson's *Speeches at Prince Henries Barriers*, reports

> the marriage between the Scotch Earl of Argile and Mrs. Anne Cornwallis. Who being bidden last week to a feast at my Lady Hatton's for that occasion, where many other lords and ladies were invited, among whom were the Earls of Pembroke and Montgomery, there was like to fall out a quarrel between Pembroke and Argile for the places of sitting, which the last had taken amongst the ladies above the other, who rose from the table at the second course and so disordered all the feast and the company, who muttered much with him at the Scotch Earl's presumption, Pembroke saying that if he offered him any more such an affront he would run him through with his rapier. The other withdrew into another room, and for the time there grew no further inconvenience of it. They departed without any satisfaction one of the other. It is thought that the prosecuting of that matter hath been hitherto only hindered by the occupation which the parties had about the Prince's combat.[29]

Surely Jonson, the author of the speeches for that mock "combat," would have heard of this nearly real one, and surely his sympathies would have been with Pembroke. By 1616, in any case, his allegiance to Pembroke was clear and obvious, and one can imagine that Argyll would have known it. After his marriage Argyll spent most of his time in England (Paul 347), so opportunities for further tension between the two earls would have been numerous. Evidence survives, in fact, that in 1614 Pembroke's brother, the Earl of Montgomery, "was lasht with a riding rod by one Mr. Ramsey a Scotchman, but . . . twas well taken up by the King, and the Erle well rewarded by the King for his patience."[30] The same source also alludes to the duel, in August 1613, in which another of Jonson's patrons, Sir Edward Sackville, killed the Scottish aristocrat Edward Bruce.[31] Sackville's political leanings would seem to have made him a natural ally of Pembroke, and, interestingly enough, he himself would much later become involved in efforts to drain the fens.[32]

Such efforts themselves probably did not bother Jonson; indeed, the policy seems to have made good sense, as Jonson's friend Sir Clement Edmondes would soon testify at length.[33] Instead, it was probably some of the men and some of their methods for winning grants that most probably annoyed Jonson and the faction with which he seems to have been allied. Whether the playwright, in mocking the "Duke of Drowned Land," was aiming at Sir Robert Carr, at the Earl of Argyll, or at someone else, there is good reason to think that he was motivated not simply by a detestation of monopolies but also, paradoxically, by the same kind of courtly infighting that his play also attacks. This would help to explain both the accusation the play provoked and the King's method of handling it. He did not, after all, order Jonson to eliminate the satire on monopolies; he simply "desyred him to conceal" an apparently personal attack on a man with connections at court (H&S 1: 144). General satire was fine; satire that might too clearly antagonize a powerful figure—as Argyll was, and as Carr still was to some degree—was undesirable. It would stir up the kind of factional tensions that James seems genuinely to have dreaded. After all, the King's only earlier known intervention with one of Jonson's plays (*Eastward Ho*) had resulted from the complaints of an offended Scotsman (H&S 1: 140). That Jonson seems to have been willing to risk once more the King's displeasure by mocking a Scot may suggest the depth of his own feelings, the confidence he now felt, and his trust in the power of his allies. In any case, this time he did not go to prison; he went to the King, who simply advised him to tone down any personal satire. Domestically as well as in foreign relations, James took his motto seriously: Blessed are the Peacemakers.[34]

III

James's interest in making peace, in fact, was a source of special concern in 1616, at least to those courtiers and politicians who worried about the prospects of a marriage between Prince Charles and the Spanish infanta. In fact, William Savage Johnson has even seen an allusion to the infanta—or at least to her title—in Act 4 of *The Devil is an Ass*,[35] and indeed that act is much concerned with satirizing Spanish fashions and conduct and the current enthusiasm for both among some members of the English court. Like so much else in the play, Jonson's stinging satire of pro-Spanish attitudes was particularly timely during the year in which his play was written and first staged. Rumors had been circulating for many months that negotiations for a Spanish match were seriously under way, and this was of course a policy that Pembroke and his faction vigorously opposed. Jonson's satire of things Spanish would not have displeased the Earl, who was described by one contemporary writer as distrustful of foreign modes and manners.[36] As early as 1614, Lord Chancellor Egerton and Sir Henry Neville, also patrons of Jonson, already opposed a Spanish alliance (Gardiner 2: 149), while the poet's enemy, the Earl of Northampton, not only supported such a link but was receiving a secret pension from the Spanish (Gardiner 2: 167). By 1615 Somerset, the then favorite, realized that the anti-Spanish faction comprised his chief antagonists, and he urged the King to allow him to supervise the secret marriage negotiations that were then under way (Gardiner 2: 321). As was often the case, James's own intentions were somewhat mysterious. Although he pursued the talks, he may have been influenced by Bacon's advice (in September 1615) that worry about such an alliance would make a future parliament more pliable and more forthcoming with financial support (Gardiner 2: 367). By the end of 1615, James was telling the Spanish king that the marriage still interested him, but in the same month he promoted the anti-Spanish Pembroke to the post of Lord Chamberlain (Gardiner 2: 368–69). The next month, however, saw the appointment to high positions of several Spanish sympathizers (Gardiner 2: 369), only to be followed, in March, by the favor James showed to the English ambassador to Spain, who had advised him against a Spanish match (Gardiner 2: 390). Meanwhile, both the Queen and Villiers, the new favorite, had become allied with Pembroke's faction (Gardiner 2: 381–82).

During the year in which Jonson's play was written, the prospects for a Spanish alliance seemed continually in flux. Some measure of the uncertainty can be glimpsed in the reports dispatched by the Venetian representatives to the English court. In January 1616, for instance, it was reported that the pro-Spanish faction had been dealt a serious blow (*CSPV* 105), but a dispatch written two months later claimed that although the negotiations were progressing, those who opposed them were optimistic (*CSPV* 147). By May it was reported that rumors about the Spanish match were widespread, but that some were speculating that the King was using fear of the alliance to generate support at home (*CSPV* 192). Later in May the match seemed imminent, and many English courtiers were reported to have a stake in promoting it (*CSPV* 208–09). By June it seemed almost a *fait accompli*, although still not yet assured (*CSPV* 220), and a week later it was reported once again that many courtiers had financial interests in advancing the negotiations (*CSPV* 226). A week later still, the

King was thought to be moving forward, and even Archbishop Abbot, Pembroke's ally, was rumored to have come around (*CSPV* 234). Within another week, however, prospects for the match seemed more distant, and a French alliance was being rumored instead. Negotiations for the Spanish marriage now seemed likely to drag on (*CSPV* 245). Later in July, the likelihood of a French match seemed to be dimming (*CSPV* 264–65), and in August talk of the Spanish alliance had revived, winning support even among some Puritans (*CSPV* 276–77). By the early fall the negotiations with the French had reportedly encountered difficulties, and sentiments among the powerful seemed to be leaning toward a link with Spain (*CSPV* 292). In October, Lord Roos, a Scotsman, was dispatched to Madrid to negotiate, but his precise instructions were unknown (*CSPV* 322). By December, however, it was reported that the negotiations had bogged down and that no imminent match was in sight (*CSPV* 381).

Whatever their precise accuracy, the Venetian reports suggest how fluid were the perceptions and status of the Spanish match throughout the period when Jonson's play was being conceived, written, and performed. Once again the evidence suggests that Jonson's comedy was exceptionally timely, and once again, too, the data imply the poet's sympathy with Pembroke's basic positions. It might seem easy to view Jonson's satire of things Spanish as satire of the King's policy, but the King's real policy and ultimate intentions were far from immediately obvious, and powerful figures at court—including the new favorite—were doing their utmost to discourage a Spanish alliance. Nothing, however, had been certainly decided. It seems sensible, then, to see Jonson's anti-Spanish satire as a part of a campaign to influence the opinion of the King, his courtiers, and the public at large. In this as in so much else, Jonson's play does not stand back from contemporary political and factional disputes and simply comment on them. Instead, it is deeply implicated in the factional politicking that on one level it derides.

IV

Another link between Jonson's comedy and the politics of its day concerns a famous speech that King James delivered in the Star Chamber in June 1616. Leah Marcus has already suggested how several of the speech's themes affected *The Vision of Delight*, the masque that Jonson would compose for the following Christmas season (Marcus 68–78). She has also touched briefly on a possible link between James's speech and one theme of *The Devil is an Ass*—a link I wish to explore much more fully. Marcus suggests that Jonson's depiction of Sir Paul Either-side in the final act of his play resembles two disgraced judges who were associated with "Lord Chief Justice Coke, whom James I had suspended for insubordination after his Speech in the Star Chamber" (Marcus 91). However, I wish to reinforce my earlier suggestion that Coke himself may have been touched on in Jonson's depiction of Either-side, whose very name, as I have noted, was suited to his notoriously ambiguous role in pushing and then abandoning the Cockayne project. The notion that Coke was the model for Jonson's Either-side is not a new one; William Savage Johnson suggested it years ago, arguing that "In obstinacy, bigotry, and vanity this character represents the class of judges with which Coke identified himself in the Overbury trial. Nor are these merely class traits. They are distinctly the faults which marred Coke's career from the beginning. It is certain that Coke is partially responsible for this portrait" (Johnson lxxii). Although certainty is difficult to come by when trying to document personal satire, Johnson's suggestion can be buttressed with evidence not cited by Johnson himself.[37]

Much of that evidence is freely available in James's Star Chamber speech, one of the most significant pronouncements of his reign. In it the King sought to clarify his own thinking about judicial matters—a decision prompted in part by recent jurisdictional disputes between the common law courts, headed by Coke, and the Court of Chancery, headed by Egerton. In the words of S. R. Gardiner,

> A custom had gradually arisen of seeking redress in Chancery, in cases where the Common Law courts had failed to do justice on account of the strictness of the rules which they had laid down for their guidance. Such a practice was, naturally enough, regarded with dissatisfaction by the Common Law judges, and by none more than by the Chief Justice of the King's Bench [Coke], who had long looked upon the Chancellor [Egerton] in the light of a personal opponent, as well as in that of a thoroughgoing supporter of an obnoxious system. (Gardiner 3: 10)

Two cases in 1616 helped prompt James's decision to make his own feelings clear. The first involved Coke's attempts to protect the priority of his court by appealing to the statute of *praemunire.* Unfortunately, this involved him in an effort to protect a judgment rendered in favor of two swindlers, whose victims had appealed for help to the Chancery court. It would have been easy for contemporary observers to feel that Coke's effort to observe legal technicalities meant subverting true justice, and in fact a grand jury resisted his efforts to "bull[y] them into submission. They returned once more into court, and, to Coke's disgust, returned an *ignoramus*" (Gardiner 2: 12). Coke, angered, promised to turn the cases over to a better jury in the next term. The fact that one of the swindlers had over-priced a jewel, and that a similar incident occurs in Jonson's play, may simply be a coincidence, or it may be one more indication that the poet was alluding to contemporary events (Gardiner 3: 11; *DA.* 3.1.11–14). In any case, at around the same time, another dispute arose, this time more obviously involving the royal prerogative. In a case concerning the king's power to grant commendams, James had requested that Coke and his fellow judges not rule until they had consulted with him. When Coke and his colleagues proceeded nonetheless,

> James had now the advantage on his side. In his reply, he told the judges that he had no wish whatever to interfere in any question which merely concerned the interests of parties; but in the present case he himself was, to all intents and purposes, a party to the suit. Was it fitting, therefore, that his rights should be adjudicated upon without his being allowed to say a word in his own defence? (Gardiner 3: 16)

By the late spring of 1616, then, James had at least two reasons to feel impatient with Coke. Egerton, the ailing Lord Chancellor, saw the case of premunire as a challenge to his own power and to the power of his court (Spedding 12: 249), and Bacon concurred in this assessment (Spedding 12: 350). In the case involving commendams, the King had written to Coke, ironically applauding him for his concern with rapid justice but arguing that delaying the case until James had had his say would hardly delay justice.[38] James's position was unanimously supported by Egerton and by the Privy Council,[39] and the King decided to spell out his legal philosophy in an important and widely noted speech, delivered in the Star Chamber on 20 June 1616. Not long after its delivery, the speech was printed, so that both Jonson and his audience would not have had to depend on being present or on word of mouth to know what the King had said.

Jonson's friend Camden called it a "fine speech" and noted that it had given the judges "a gentle touch,"[40] while another writer has noted that one purpose of the speech was to support the Court of Chancery, where mercy could moderate harsh justice (Spedding 12: 395). The speech—which Arthur Wilson called long and well-tempered[41]—apparently reflected Bacon's legal thinking (Spedding 12: 381), and it was widely seen not only as a gesture of support for Egerton, the ailing Lord Chancellor, but also as an attempt to encourage harmony among the different courts and judges (Wilson 706–07). What is striking about the speech, when it is read in conjunction with *The Devil is an Ass*, is how neatly it jibes with Jonson's satirical presentation in the concluding act of Justice Either-side. Jonson may or may not have intended Either-side as a reflection on Coke, but the parallels between Either-side's conduct and the conduct against which James warned his judges are often striking. Coke may not have been Jonson's only target, but the playwright's depiction of Either-side strongly suggests that Jonson may have sympathized with James's recent statement of judicial principles.

In the final scene of Jonson's play, when Fitz-dottrell, the chief fool, pretends to be possessed by the devil, Justice Either-side is called in to assess the case. As G. L. Kittredge has argued, Either-side's behavior in this scene reflects poorly on his judicial wisdom and may have been intended to mock the behavior of two of Coke's fellow judges (and close associates) in a recent case involving the hasty trial and precipitous execution of a number of women falsely accused of being witches.[42] It was James himself who had eventually exposed the fraud, and the case's notoriety helped strengthen James's stance in relation to such judges as Coke. The fact that Jonson chose to allude to this incident already suggests where his sympathies lay, but the possibility that his depiction of Either-side may also allude to Coke's recent conduct is also worth exploring. In his hastiness, passion, prejudice, intolerance, close-mindedness, self-interestedness, and proud sense of personal correctness, Either-side seems to exemplify many traits that critics also found troubling in Coke.

Jonson's first references to Either-side come in Act 4, where the judge's wife reveals that he is closely involved with projectors and with money-making schemes (4.2.8ff.). Whether Jonson intended this to allude to Coke's involvement with Cockayne is impossible to say, but the possibility is nonetheless intriguing. In any case, Either-side's relations with Meere-craft and with Lady

Taile-bush hardly make him a disinterested judge when they and their cohorts (including Either-side's wife) attempt to persuade him in Act 5 that Fitz-dottrell has been possessed. James had recently declared that he had refrained from involving himself in cases in which he "might seeme, as it were obliquely, to be in favour of one partie, and for that cause this Counsellor, or that Courtier might be thought to mooue me to come hither."[43] Either-side, on the other hand, involves himself in a case in which his wife and her friend and his own associate (Lady Taile-bush) have a direct and obvious interest.

At the same time, Either-side's very first words show that he has already made up his mind; he has come to "punish the impostors" (5.8.7), although of course he does not stop to consider that it may be Fitz-dottrell who is guilty. He quickly, and credulously, accepts that Fitz-dottrell is possessed, showing none of the skepticism that James had so wisely demonstrated in the recent case involving the accused witches. Like Coke in the case concerning commendams, Either-side seems ready to rush to judgment, without considering all the relevant evidence or hearing all the appropriate testimony. He does, it is true, request the presence of a constable, "the King's *Officer* . . . and some Cittizens, / Of credit," but only in order that they may witness him "discharge [his] conscience clearly" (5.8.11–12). Either-side's repeated references to the word "conscience" may allude to Coke's alleged attempts to usurp the prerogatives of Egerton's Chancery court, where conscience rather than strict legality was expected to be considered. And, as I shall later suggest, there may have been still another reason that Jonson chose to have Either-side harp on this word. In any case, Either-side's whole performance seems to fly in the face of James's recent declaration that it was the business of judges "not to take vpon them to make Law, but ioyned together after a deliberate consultation, to declare what the Law is" (James 327). Either-side, with his excited sense of personal inspiration, of being prompted by his "conscience," seems to neglect the law and proper legal procedures and to operate almost as an autonomous agent. Ironically, his irrational responses make the Justice himself seem somewhat lawless.

In the Star Chamber speech, James had urged his judges to "doe Iustice boldly, yet I bid you doe it fearefully; fearefully in this, to vtter your owne conceites, and not the trew meaning of the Law. And remember you are no makers of Law, but Interpretours of Law" (James 332). He further reminded them that "your interpretations must be alwayes subiect to common sense and reason"—a point he chose to reiterate repeatedly. They were to remember that "what you doe, that you should doe with aduice and deliberation, not hastily and rashly, before you well study the case, and conferre together; debating it duely, not giuing single opinions" (James 332). Either-side, of course, violates all these prescriptions. He shows no fearfulness about following his own "conscience," and he demonstrates little concern with common sense or reason. When Fitz-dottrell's own wife chides her husband for "counterfait[ing]," Fitz-dottrel accuses her of pricking him with needles. Either-side's immediate response is to command, "Woman, forbeare," and to pronounce her alleged pricking "A practice foule, / For one so faire" (5.8.48–53). When the hero, Wittipol, expresses amazement at the judge's reaction ("Hath this, then, credit with you?" [5.8.54]), Either-side at once replies, "Gentlemen, I'll discharge / My conscience. 'Tis a cleare conspiracy! / A darke, and diuellish practice! I detest it!" (5.8.55–57). Furthermore, he warns Wittipol and Manly, the two sensible males, "not to confront / Authority with impudence" (5.8.59–60). He thus not only violates James's injunctions against deciding "hastily and rashly," but he also demonstrates the kind of high-handedness in the face of common sense that Coke had demonstrated in dealing with the jury who had refused to rule in favor of the jewel swindlers. As if to underline this possible connection, Jonson makes Either-side in the final scene address his "good friend, Master *Guilt-head*" (5.8.63). In *The Devil is an Ass*, it is Guilt-head who is involved (along with Either-side's other friend, Meere-craft) in a swindle involving a jewel (3.2.1–7).

However, the most striking instance of Either-side's possible resemblance to Coke occurs when Manly, speaking as well for his friend Wittipol, asks the judge,

> Are you phrenticke, Sir,
> Or what graue dotage moues you, to take part
> With so much villany? wee are not afraid
> Either of law, or triall; let vs be
> Examin'd what our ends were, what the meanes
> To worke by; and possibility of those meanes:
> Doe not conclude against vs, ere you heare vs.
> *Pov.* I will not heare you, yet I will conclude
> Out of the circumstances. *Man.* Will you so, sir?
> *Pov.* Yes, they are palpable: *Man.* Not as your folly.
> *Pov.* I will discharge my conscience, and doe all,
> To the *Meridian* of Iustice. (5.8.91–102)

For anyone prone to see an analogy between Coke's alleged rush to judgment in the commendams case and Either-side's equal unwillingness to consider relevant evidence, this is a memorable moment. Either-side's behavior in the final scene graphically illustrates James's warning in the Star Chamber that "euen as a King, (let him be neuer so godly, wise, righteous, and iust) yet if the subalterne Magistrates doe not their parts vnder him, the Kingdome must needes suffer" (James 339). If Jonson had set out to illustrate this warning, he could not have done a better job than in his depiction of Justice Either-side. And if he had set out to mock the aging Coke covertly, he did little to disguise his intent. The fact that the elderly Either-side, in the passage just quoted, invokes his "conscience" for the fifth time in this scene seems more than coincidental. Jonson seems to have intended a deliberate pattern. Why? A possible answer may be found in a report to the King from Bacon dated 2 October 1616 (that is, around the time when Jonson seems to have been finishing his play). Bacon reported that he and Egerton had discussed with Coke (who had been suspended as a judge that summer) the possibilities of errors in his legal reports. Coke admitted to finding only five such errors, but he also claimed "that it was a sin for a man to go against his conscience, though erroneous, except his conscience be first informed and satisfied" (Spedding 13: 77). Whether Jonson was aware of Coke's insistence on his "conscience" is unclear, although it seems reasonable to assume that James was not the only one whom Bacon and Egerton informed, and indeed Coke himself may have made the same point in conversations with his own adherents.

The number of Coke's friends had been shrinking, and at the time when Jonson's play was written and performed, his power seemed seriously in jeopardy. Coke, like Cockayne, was a vulnerable target in the late summer and autumn of 1616. In June he had been called before the Privy Councillor on account of financial irregularities; a few days later his suspension was announced (Gardiner 3: 23). Although Coke asked the Queen and Prince to help him, his wife's attacks on the mother of Villiers, the new favorite, did him no good, and there was even talk of his treason (*CSPD* 380). In July he was alleged to have done damage to the King's interests by his dealings with the admiralty (*CSPD* 380), and by early fall rumors circulated that he would be not only suspended but replaced (*CSPD* 397). The Venetian representative reported that James was angry with Coke and that the judge was hated by all the nobility (*CSPV* 245). Throughout the fall Coke's fortunes seemed uncertain. October brought rumors that the King would eventually show him clemency, despite the power of Coke's enemies.[44] Coke himself reportedly hoped to win back his influence by marrying his wife's daughter to Villiers' brother (*CSPD* 402), but by December even his wife had abandoned him, claiming to have been damaged by his fall (*CSPD* 411). At the same time, however, the King was beginning to show him signs of renewed favor, and Coke seems to have benefited from some support from the Queen and Prince (*CSPD* 413). For Coke as for the country in general, 1616 seems to have been a year of unusual instability. The very flux of events that gave Jonson so many topics for his play also created real anxiety for figures such as Coke.

V

The Devil is an Ass shows how clearly Jonson could respond to contemporary events, but the play also shows how his work may have responded to other texts. James's Star Chamber speech may provide one example of such influence, and Leah Marcus has called attention to others. No one, however, seems to have stressed the many resemblances between Jonson's work and an even more famous comedy that shortly preceded it—George Ruggle's *Ignoramus*. Ruggle's Latin comedy is little known today, but it seems to have been one of the most memorable and sensational works staged during James's reign, and the controversy it touched off reverberated for years. First acted during a royal visit to Cambridge University in March 1615, the play has been called "the most notorious play ever performed at Cambridge,"[45] and one historian has argued that the impact of its staging was "undeniable" and was "discernible almost to the end of James's reign."[46] Certainly James himself was delighted by his visit; John Chamberlain reported that "the King was excedingly pleased many times both at the playes and disputations, for I had the hap to be for the most time within hearing, and often at his [m]eales he wold expresse as much" (Chamberlain 1: 588; Nelson 540).

Nor was Chamberlain the only courtier present to witness the King's reaction; *Ignoramus* was acted in a hall at Trinity College "so well ordered for roome that above 2000 persons were conveniently placed" (Chamberlain 1: 287). For a number of reasons the King's visit "was a political event of some magnitude," and

Ignoramus was conceived as "not merely a college play but a production representing the whole university."[47] The comedy itself, Chamberlain noted, "was full of mirth and varietie, with many excellent actors . . . but more than halfe marred with extreme length" (Chamberlain 1: 587). James, however, seems not to have been bothered by the fact that the play took five hours to perform (Mullinger 2: 540); one contemporary witness reported that "his ma*ies*tie was much delighted w*i*th ye Playe and laughed exceedingly and offentymes w*i*th his handes and by word*es* applauded it" (Nelson 542). Much later, another writer noted that "Never did any thing so hit the Kings Humour, as this Play did, so that he would have it Acted and Acted again, which was increased with several Additions, which yet more pleased the King" (Nelson 864). So pleased was he with the initial performance, in fact, that within a few weeks Chamberlain reported that "The King hath a meaning and speakes much of yt to go again privatly to Cambrige to see two of the playes, . . . but yt is not likely he will continue in that mind, for of late he hath made a motion to have the actors come hither . . ." (Chamberlain 1: 591). In the end, however, it was James who did the travelling; Chamberlain wrote that in mid-May

> the King went again to Cambrige to see the play *Ignoramus* which hath so netled the Lawiers that they are almost out of all patience, and the Lord Chiefe Justice [Coke] both openly at the Kings Bench and divers other places hath galled and glaunced at schollers with much bitternes, and there be divers ynne of court men have made rimes and ballades against them, which they have aunswered sharply enough. . . . (Chamberlain 1: 597–98)

Barnabe Googe, the Master of Magdalene College, also noted that the play had "woonderfully discontented the Lawyers," including some powerful patrons, and he urged the university's Vice Chancellor "to take som cours*e* for the staye of thes*e* bitter inuectiues: certenly yf they goe one, in this kind: we shall growe odious amongst [the lawyers]" (Nelson 552). Nor were the common lawyers the only ones bothered by *Ignoramus*; jealous Oxonians resented the work's success and unloosed a barrage of satirical ballads, which their rivals at Cambridge were only too ready to answer. Ruggle's comedy thus touched off a mighty war of words whose spent ammunition survives in many texts and anecdotes, while the play's popularity is attested by the existence of numerous manuscript copies and several printed editions and translations.[48] Jonson, then, could hardly have been ignorant of Ruggle's comedy or of its enormous contemporary impact.

Why was the play so controversial? Why did James enjoy it so much? The answers are multifaceted and concern both the manner and matter of the work. Ruggle wrote what has been called "vivacious and racy Latin,"[49] while another writer has referred to the play's double meanings, coarseness, and "broad obscenities" (Mullinger 2: 542). James would have appreciated all these qualities, and most contemporary comments suggest that the King was delighted by the play; certainly its genuine humor must have been the chief reason for its appeal. Yet humor was not the only reason for the comedy's popularity; as with *The Devil is an Ass*, Ruggle's satire was bitingly topical and personal, and this helps account for much of the outrage it provoked. The play "at once appealed to . . . royal predilections, to professional jealousies, to political rivalries, and to local animosities" (Mullinger 2: 528), and Ruggle "made the best of his opportunity in catering to the King's interests, as demonstrated in the anti-Jesuit satire, the scenes involving the exorcism of evil spirits, the assault upon the worst aspects of legal jargon, and the lampooning of Schioppius," a foreigner who had attacked the King in writing.[50] Most important of all, however, was the playwright's mockery of his title character, Ignoramus, who was modeled on a Cambridge town official but who could be seen as representing the worst aspects of the common lawyers, such as Coke, with whom the King's relations were often tense. As E. F. J. Tucker has shown, Ruggle was drawing on and thus sustaining a satirical tradition that had long associated lawyers with the devil—a tradition Jonson himself had already exploited in *Volpone*.[51] Coke and his associates recognized only too clearly what Ruggle had done and why the King found it so funny.

Jonson, it seems, also took notice. He could hardly have helped knowing about Ruggle's play; it had literally been a scandalous success. Thousands had witnessed it and numerous others had heard about it; it was the talk of the circles in which the poet moved, and the fact that it had so obviously pleased the King would surely have caught Jonson's attention.[52] *Ignoramus*, it is true, was staged more than a year before *The Devil is an Ass*, but at the time Jonson was writing his comedy, Coke and his associates were even more vulnerable than than they had seemed a year before, and any resemblances between Jonson's work and Ruggle's would have added to the sting of Jonson's play. James's continuing interest in Ruggle's comedy, and the play's continuing notoriety, is suggested by a little-known incident that occurred in the spring of 1616—that is, in the months just prior to the composition and staging of Jonson's drama. J. L. Van Gundy has reported a French account of a play staged before James in May of 1616 that featured not only satire on Schioppius but also the character of "un certain docteur Ignoramus."[53] According to Van Gundy,

> How far this play was an imitation of Ignoramus [sic] we cannot say; but it is certain that the character Docteur Ignoramus as well as his speech, . . . which caused the king to laugh so heartily, were borrowed directly from Ruggle's drama. (70)

Van Gundy even suggests that James may have commissioned Ruggle to write this new version of his earlier satire (70), although this possibility is pure speculation. What seems plain, however, is that in the spring of 1616, Jonson had good reason to be reminded of *Ignoramus*, as well as good reason to think that James had not forgotten it. One can only imagine what Coke's reaction may have been to this new resuscitation of a character he personally resented so strongly.

As it happens, the resemblances between Jonson's play and Ruggle's are numerous. Whether this was deliberate or merely coincidental, it is hard to see how members of Jonson's audience could have missed the many similarities. One of the central characters of Jonson's play—Manly—shares the name of an unseen but frequently mentioned character in Ruggle's (Manlius). This fact alone might seem insignificant, but the standard source reports no play other than Ruggle's that is earlier than Jonson's and that uses such a similar name.[54] Jonson, then, may have been inspired to choose this name with Ruggle's play in mind, and many people who witnessed the performances of both works may have caught the allusion. In any case, other general connections between the two works are worth noting. Both, for instance, draw explicitly on the tradition of English morality plays. E. F. J. Tucker has emphasized that "the outstanding characteristic of Ruggle's lawyer is the manner in which the author transforms the [classical] *advocatus* type into the typically English Vice figure."[55] The debt Jonson's comedy owes to the morality tradition, including the focus on the Vice, has always been considered one of the most intriguing aspects of his play. Tucker notes that

> Ignoramus' first name of Ambidexter provides a sufficient clue to his real identity by aligning him with undoubtedly the most famous of the Vice characters: Ambidexter in Thomas Preston's *Cambyses*. His very first entrance confirms our suspicions, for his opening speeches abound with expressions like "phy, phy," "ho, ho," and "hi, ho," reminding us of the typical first appearances of the Vice figures in the old interludes.[56]

The very first words of Jonson's play, of course, are "Hoh, hoh, hoh, hoh, hoh, hoh, hoh, hoh, &c." (1.1.1.)—Satan's jocular response to the request by Pug, a minor devil, that he be allowed to go to earth. In addition, Jonson's opening scene very prominently features a traditional vice ("old *Iniquity*" [1.1.43]), and perhaps even the name "Ambidexter" that Ruggle gave to his chief legal character may have inspired Jonson's choice of "Eitherside" for the name of his play's judge. In any event, the fact that both plays so heavily satirize abuses committed by members of the legal profession is another link between them, as is their common emphasis on what Tucker has called "witchcraft and demon lore," to which he finds "scores of allusions" in Ruggle's play.[57] In addition, Tucker himself has noted the similarity between the scene in Ruggle's play in which Ignoramus, because of his reliance on legal jargon, is thought to be possessed by the devil, and the similar scene in Jonson's play in which "Pug the demon from the underworld encourages Fitz-Dottrel in his pretense of being possessed by evil spirits."[58] Certainly this is one of the most striking resemblances between the two works, but it is simply one of many that can be noted.

Before discussing such resemblances, it may be useful to summarize both works briefly. Thus, *Ignoramus* focuses on the love between Antonius and Rosabella, whose custodian is the pander Torcol. Antonius's father, Theodorus, decides to send his son from Bordeaux (their residence) to London; Antonius is then to bring back Theodorus's wife (Dorothea), his other son (Antoninus—Antonius's twin), and his step-daughter (Catharina), all of whom Theodorus has not seen in almost twenty years. Theodorus had married Dorothea after the death of her first husband, Alderman Manlius, with whom she had produced two daughters—Catherina and another girl lost during childhood. Now, after their long separation, Theodorus proposes to reestablish his links with his wife, his twin sons, and his remaining step-daughter. Antonius, however, with the help of his father's servant, Trico, manages to escape from the London-bound ship so that he can prevent Torcol's intention to arrange a mercenary marriage between Rosabella and Ignoramus, a ridiculous English lawyer who lives in Bordeaux and speaks (and woos) in fantastical legal jargon. Through a series of complicated maneuvers, Antonius and Trico, with the help of Cupes and a friar named Cola, trick Torcol and Ignoramus. They manage, for instance, to convince other characters that Ignoramus is possessed and that he must be exorcised. Although their deceptive schemes are threatened when Dorothea, Antoninus, and Catherina suddenly do arrive from London, all (of course) turns out well in the end. We discover (as we might have expected) that Rosabella is really Isabella, the long-lost daughter of Dorothea and Alderman Manlius, and that she had been promised in marriage to Antonius when both were children. Ignoramus is defeated, the clever servant is rewarded, and the two young lovers anticipate a happy life. Yet Ruggle breathed life into this somewhat predictable plot through his clever phrasing and biting satire.[59]

The basic plot of Jonson's play can also be recounted quickly. After some hesitation, Satan permits Pug, an inexperienced devil, to try his skills in London. Soon after his arrival there, Pug meets Fitz-dottrell, the play's chief gull, who, as it happens, has been curious to meet a real devil. Although Fitz-dottrell is not convinced that Pug is the genuine article, he nonetheless hires him as a servant. In that capacity, Pug witnesses the efforts made by the gallant Wittipol (aided by his friend Manly) to woo Fitz-dottrell's abused and beautiful wife. Fitz-dottrell, meanwhile, is himself being courted by a conniving projector named Meere-craft; among other proposed money-making projects, Meere-craft proposes to help Fitz-dottrell become the Duke of Drowned Land through a scheme for draining the fens. He also offers to introduce Fitz-dottrell to a great Spanish lady who can teach Mrs. Fitz-dottrell better manners, although he indicates that Fitz-dottrell will need to present this lady with a gold ring to win her help. This ring—inflated in price—is procured from the goldsmith Thomas Guilt-head.[60] Wittipol, posing as the Spanish lady, eventually reveals himself to Mrs. Fitz-dottrell, but instead of continuing to court her, he vows true friendship and pledges his assistance. Still posing as the Spanish lady, Wittipol talks Fitz-dottrell (who anticipates a duel with his rival) into temporarily signing his estate over to Manly. When this is done, Wittipol reveals himself to the outraged Fitz-dottrell. Although Manly intends to use his power for Mrs. Fitz-dottrell's benefit, her husband is infuriated. Prompted by Meere-craft and Meere-craft's cousin, Everill, Fitz-dottrell pretends to have been bewitched, possessed, and cheated; through this ruse he hopes to win the sympathy of the credulous Justice Either-side. In the end, though, all is revealed, and Mrs. Fitz-dottrell emerges not only with some measure of economic independence but also with the virtuous friendship of Wittipol and Manly.

Although a few resemblances between Ruggle's play and Jonson's are obvious even from such cursory summaries, many other parallels emerge when the two works are examined more closely. Both plays center around the conflict between a mercenary fool and a good man for the affection of a virtuous but exploited woman. Wittipol is to Antonius as Fitz-dottrell is to Ignoramus. In both plays the attractive woman is dominated by a man who should genuinely care for her but whose motives are purely selfish and monetary. In both plays the woman is brighter and more independent than the fools assume, and in both plays the fools (Ignoramus and Fitz-dottrell) exhibit an interest in trivial amusements (*Ig*. 1.5; *DA*. 1.6). In both works unsavory characters mock the value of formal learning and emphasize the importance of purely financial gain (*Ig*. 1.3; *DA*. 3.1). In both plays the heroes must court the virtuous ladies surreptitiously, and in both cases the heroes must eventually use tricks to gain access to the women they love. In both plays conversations between the heroes and the good ladies are interrupted by malignant characters, and in both works the servants appointed to guard the women fail to do their jobs effectively and are physically beaten by their frustrated masters (*Ig*. 1.7; *DA*. 1.7). In both plays the sympathetic characters must resort to using disguises (*Ig*. 2.3; *DA*. 4.1),[61] and both works contain numerous allusions to the devil and to diabolical behavior (*Ig*. 2.3; *DA*. throughout). Both works satirize lawyers, and Ruggle seems to have shared Jonson's general distrust of Puritans (*Ig*. 2.6; *DA*. 1.1.).

Other similarities are also worth noting. Thus, in both plays arcane knowledge and technical jargon are strongly emphasized, whether this involves Ignoramus's fantastical legalisms or Meere-craft's intricate disquisitions on projects and schemes. Both plays prominently feature disputes about golden rings of inflated value (*Ig*. 2.5; *DA*. 3.1). Moreover, just as Ignoramus feels physically threatened by Antonius in Ruggle's play (*Ig*. 2.7, 8), so Fitz-dottrell anticipates duelling with Wittipol in Jonson's work (*DA*. 3.1). Thus, in both works the prospect of physical violence between the hero and the fool adds suspense. In addition, both plays show fools being tricked in connection with legal documents (Ignoramus's marriage indenture; Fitz-dottrell's deed of estate), and both works also prominently depict the duping of the fools' servants (Dulman in Ruggle's play, Pug in Jonson's [*Ig.* 3.1; *DA.* 3.3]). Both comedies feature scenes in which sympathetic characters not only pretend to be people they are not, but in which they pretend to be foreigners (*Ig.* 4.1; *DA.* 4.1). Both works feature indignant accusations—and brazen defenses—concerning suspect clothing (*Ig.* 4.4.; *DA.* 5.2),[62] and both plays move toward conclusions involving legal accusations and arrests (*Ig.* 4.12; *DA.* 5.3). While many of these resemblances may have been merely coincidental or can be explained by pointing to the typical conventions of Renaissance comedies, the sheer number of similarities, combined with the often striking nature of the parallels and with the fact that *Ignoramus* had had such a recent and memorable impact, suggests that Jonson, consciously or unconsciously, may have had Ruggle's play on his mind when he came to write his own.

The most intriguing similarity, of course, and the one that most strongly suggests that Jonson was deliberately thinking of Ruggle's work, is the climactic scene involving Fitz-dottrell's pretended "possession." This moment of Jonson's play is so strongly reminiscent of the equally funny and equally important moment in Ruggle's, in which Ignoramus is "exorcised," that a contemporary auditor who witnessed both works would have been hard put to overlook the resemblances. In Jonson's play, it is true, the fool deliberately pretends to be possessed, whereas in Ruggle's work the fool is victimized by accusations of possession. In both plays, however, the chief fools are associated with the devil, and in each instance the "devil-possessed" fool is shown to be an ass. In both Jonson's play and Ruggle's, the "bewitched" fools seem to confirm their possession by speaking in fantastical jargon—in Fitz-dottrell's case a strange polyglot of languages, and in Ignoramus's case frustrated legalese. In fact, Ruggle's scene of "exorcism," in which Ignoramus vomits up one strange term after another, may itself have been indebted to the highly memorable moment in Jonson's own play *Poetaster* in which the foolish poet Crispinus is forced to disgorge the worst examples of his perverse vocabulary (5.3.463–530). And, as has already been noted, Ruggle's presentation of a possessed lawyer is strongly reminiscent of Jonson's own depiction of Voltore in

Volpone (5.12.21–35). It is just possible, in other words, that Ruggle himself borrowed from Jonson, which would have given Jonson all the more reason to return the compliment.

VI

The likelihood that Jonson was thinking of Ruggle's comedy when he wrote *The Devil is an Ass*, as well as the likelihood that many members of Jonson's original audience would also have witnessed *Ignoramus* and would have spotted the parallels between the two works, both suggest again how tightly Jonson's play seems to have been tied to its contemporary contexts. In its relevance to the infamous Cockayne project; in its allusions to contemporary drainage schemes; in its reflections on Spanish influences at court; in its concern, like the King's Star Chamber speech, with the proper conduct of judges; and, finally, in its apparent debt to Ruggle, *The Devil is an Ass* is very much a play written in and for a particular historical moment. Understanding that moment can help us better understand—and better appreciate—the nuances of Jonson's play, not only as an historical document but especially as a work of art. Paradoxically, the more fully we appreciate how Jonson's play was rooted in its own time, the more fully we may appreciate its artistry and thus its continuing interest and relevance.

Contextual study suggests that *The Devil* is a much more complicated and interesting play than it might initially appear. Far from being the first of Jonson's "dotages," the work seems much more vital and responsive when we understand more fully the circumstances from which it arose. This seems true of all of Jonson's works, including one he wrote not long after *The Devil*—his famous masque entitled *Pleasure Reconciled to Virtue*, one of the best but also one of the most curious works in a genre that Jonson helped transform.

5

"Other Men's Provision": Jonson's Parody of Robert White in *Pleasure Reconciled to Virtue*

Pleasure Reconciled to Virtue is now regarded as one of Jonson's most sophisticated and accomplished masques, which is why the reception that greeted its original performance has always seemed somewhat puzzling. Various evidence suggests that its first audience—including King James—found the masque dull and disappointing, and although Jonson himself claimed that the work was well received, he quickly dropped the whole first section, improvising a new antimasque for a revised version of the work entitled *For the Honour of Wales*.[1] Different explanations have been offered for the poor reception accorded the original masque, including the audience's inability to appreciate the innovative nature of its design, as well as their possible offense at the masque's satirical implications, particularly its satire of courtly self-indulgence.[2] However, contemporary evidence that has received insufficient attention throws an entirely new light on the masque, not only helping to explain its genesis but perhaps also providing new insight into the reasons for its poor reception.

That evidence is embodied in a masque by Robert White entitled *Cupid's Banishment*, which was performed only months before the first staging of *Pleasure Reconciled to Virtue*. Peter Walls long ago noted briefly the resemblances between the antimasques of the two works, but in fact the similarities between White's masque and Jonson's are far more striking and pervasive than Walls's short note could indicate.[3] In fact, it seems undeniable that Jonson's work was intended as a conscious and deliberate response to *Cupid's Banishment*, and that the motives behind Jonson's invention may have had as much to do with micropolitical rivalry as with the larger political issues that have recently been stressed in commentary on *Pleasure Reconciled*. A strong circumstantial case can be built to suggest that Jonson may have felt significantly threatened by (or at the very least significant disdain for) White's masque-writing, and that *Pleasure Reconciled to Virtue* was conceived partly as an attempt to beat White, and beat him publicly, at his own game. The similarities between the two masques—in their characters, their themes, their stagings, their structures, and their overall designs—are remarkable, and would have been readily apparent to the many courtiers and other prominent people who must have witnessed both performances. As I shall suggest, Jonson's masque may have been badly received partly because the resemblances between the two works were too obvious, so that he may have seemed to be usurping an important court occasion to score personal points against a private competitor. Evidence from other periods of Jonson's career suggests his willingness to use masques to attack his rivals, and other evidence indicates that Jonson's attacks on other artists were not particularly appreciated by the Stuart kings and their courts.

Cupid's Banishment was performed on May 4, 1617 at Ladies Hall in Deptford, a girls' school not far from the royal palace at Greenwich, where Queen Anne spent much of her time.[4] The Queen was building a new residence there, and another of Jonson's rivals—Inigo Jones—had been commissioned to design it and to supervise its construction.[5] Thus Jonson may have had more than one reason to feel some discomfort with the Queen's recent patronage of other artists. For Anne was present at the performance of *Cupid's Banishment*, and indeed White paid her special honor near the work's conclusion, in which two of her goddaughters (performers in the masque and apparently students at Ladies Hall) presented her with needlework gifts emblazoned with her initials. Anne, of course, had always been one of the prime patrons of masques at court and had taken an active interest in commissioning, staging, and dancing in them. It was she who had witnessed, more than a decade earlier, Jonson's first entertainment of the new king's reign (H&S 2: 260), and it was she who seems to have commissioned his first such work for the Jacobean court, *The Masque of Blacknesse*, taking a detailed interest in overseeing its features and design (H&S 2: 265).

There is no evidence that Anne was similarly involved in dictating the details of *Cupid's Banishment*, but White must have realized that the staging of his masque before the Queen gave him the opportunity to display his literary abilities before one of the kingdom's most powerful and influential patrons, one with a particular interest in the masque as an artform. Certainly Jonson must have realized this, too, and if he felt threatened at all by the opportunity the occasion provided White, it is not difficult to understand why. Perhaps White hoped—and perhaps Jonson feared—that success before the Queen at Deptford might lead to future commissions for masques at Whitehall, where Jonson enjoyed a near-monopoly as chief masque-writer of the Jacobean court.[6] King James, on a progress to Scotland, was not present for the staging of White's work, so the importance of the Queen's reaction was magnified all the more. Jonson himself had benefited early in the reign by making a good impression on the Queen while the King was absent, and it would not have been too difficult for him to imagine (or fear) White's work having a similar effect. If such thoughts entered his mind at all, it is not hard to understand why he may have felt an impulse to rival White's work.

Several commentators have noted the unusual ambitiousness of *Cupid's Banishment*, which went far beyond the simple revels typical of scholastic entertainments. Such revels (according to C. E. McGee) had themselves proven "popular enough to be the butt of one of Jonson's jokes" in *Christmas His Masque*, produced a few months earlier, but White had taken the unusual step of "blending the customary revels of the school with the lavish display of the court masque" (McGee 231). Similarly, G. E. Bentley also notes that White's masque "seems rather elaborate for the school," and points out that a total of thirty-one performers were named.[7] These included at least two members of the King's Music and may have included other "professionals" as well (McGee 228). In other words, *Cupid's Banishment* may have been performed in part by the sort of men, and perhaps even by some of the very same men, who performed in Jonson's masques at court. The mere presence of the Queen was enough to ensure that this would be no normal school revels, but White seems to have gone out of his way to design a masque that aspired to be worthy of its occasion and its audience. White seems to have been the headmaster or some other official at the school, but the masque he designed for the Queen's visit to Ladies Hall suggests that he thought of himself and his work in loftier terms. Like Jonson, he seems to have taken the task of writing a masque quite seriously indeed.[8]

Besides the Queen, the original audience for *Cupid's Banishment* also probably included many other influential figures.

McGee notes that Ladies Hall may have been "a school attended by the daughters of learned officers of the court," and he suggests that a number of the young women who participated in the masque may have been the daughters of particular members of the Jacobean elite (McGee 259). Indeed, one purpose of the masque may have been to display eligible young women as potential marriage partners (McGee 231–32), so that the event may have had a social significance that went beyond mere entertainment. These reasons, combined with Anne's presence, suggest that *Cupid's Banishment* was probably witnessed by many of the same 600 or so very important persons who later crowded into Whitehall to view Jonson's *Pleasure Reconciled to Virtue*.[9] If Jonson's masque was in fact intended as a comment on White's, many members of his audience could not have failed to appreciate that fact, for White had been attempting to appeal to many of the very same people whose approval Jonson needed to maintain his own status at court.

One of those people had not only been a highly significant figure in Jonson's career, but seems also to have been the chief patron behind *Cupid's Banishment*. This was Lucy, Countess of Bedford, one of the most influential ladies at court and one of the most significant of Jonson's own patronesses.[10] Lucy, in fact, had played an important role in the staging of *Lovers Made Men*, a masque by Jonson that preceded *Cupid's Banishment* by only a few months (H&S 10: 566). Indeed, the resemblances between these two masques are themselves noteworthy, and if Jonson was in fact commenting on White's work in *Pleasure Reconciled to Virtue*, perhaps it was partly because he felt that White himself had used *Cupid's Banishment* to respond to *Lovers Made Men*. Both of the latter masques feature Mercury and Cupid, and in both masques Cupid is a particularly prominent and somewhat disruptive character. But whereas *Lovers Made Men* closes with the explicit reconciliation of love and wisdom (thus anticipating the theme of *Pleasure Reconciled to Virtue*), in White's masque, as its name implies, Cupid is banished for being too unruly. *Pleasure Reconciled* may have been intended by Jonson not only as a riposte to White's masque but as an explicit defense and reassertion of the theme broached less than a year earlier in *Lovers Made Men*. Although White may not have intended consciously to compete with Jonson, it is not difficult to imagine why Jonson could have viewed *Cupid's Banishment*—with its elaborate design and production and its focus on the very themes that Jonson himself had most recently explored—as a kind of challenge to his preeminence as a masque-writer.

Jonson's annoyance—if he was annoyed—may only have been increased by Lucy's patronage of White. What seems to have bothered Jonson as much as (if not more than) his rivals themselves was the support his own patrons sometimes gave them. As Jonson recognized, the power his rivals enjoyed—like his own power—depended as much on the patronage his competitors received as on their own talents and accomplishments.[11] More than once Jonson voiced frustration with his patrons' support of rival artists, and one of the most memorable of these complaints had focused on Lucy herself. In the famous epistle to the Countess of Rutland (which had just recently been printed for the first time in the 1616 folio), Jonson, with muted sarcasm, had called attention to Lucy's neglect of him in favor a "better verser . . . / (Or *Poet*, in the court account)" (H&S 8: 115).[12] There was precedent, then (or at least there must have seemed precedent to Jonson), for Lucy's patronage of an unworthy "verser," and certainly White himself goes out of his way to thank Lucy for her support. The unique surviving manuscript of his masque is dedicated to her, and the dedication opens with an expression of gratitude for "the honorable furtherance and noble encouragement your La: gaue vs in presentinge our maske to hir Magesty," thanking her particularly for her "worthy protection" (29–33). To Jonson, it may have seemed one thing for White to pen a masque on a theme with which Jonson himself had only recently dealt, but it may have seemed another thing altogether for White to pen his work at the encouragement of one of Jonson's own patrons, who was also one of the Queen's favorite ladies. The Countess's close involvement with the work is suggested by White's reference to the masque as "the fruits which your honor first sowed" (43). White, by himself, posed little threat; White with Lucy as his patron could prove a threat indeed. Whatever Jonson's attitude toward Lucy's involvement with White, there is evidence to suggest that Jonson's subsequent attitude toward Lucy soured considerably. In the margin of an edition of Martial that Jonson could not have read any earlier than 1619, he apparently penned her initials next to an unflattering epigram that describes a vain and insubstantial woman.[13]

The protection that White solicits from Lucy may have been especially welcome if, as I wish to suggest, Jonson had taken some offense at *Cupid's Banishment*. Much of the phrasing in

White's dedication and in the text of the masque itself strongly implies that *someone* had been bothered, and the specific objections to which White responds sound thoroughly Jonsonian. Moreover, the kinds of attacks that White levels against his unnamed antagonist could easily have applied to Jonson. Admittedly, some of White's comments on the envious reaction to his masque sound thoroughly conventional; thus he asks for Lucy's continued support "in despight of enuies raginge winter," and claims that thanks to her encouragement, it matters not if "the enuious spitt theire veneme, and tipp theire toungues with gall" (46–48). Even claims like this, however, raise curious questions. Why would a schoolmaster need to defend the annual entertainment against envious attacks unless that entertainment had in fact provoked someone's ire?

It is when White turns from defending his work in general terms to responding to specific criticisms that the possibility that Jonson was the critic he had in mind becomes most provocative. Someone, apparently, had objected to the indecorous nature of the masque's characters and action. "I heare," White tells Lucy,

> some curious Criticke allready, whose hungry eares feedes still on other mens prouision, and perchance his teeth on other mens tables, hath spyed an error and as his perspectiue informes him, a grosse one too! He abruptly demaunds what should Hymen haue to do, where Diana is? or why there should bee a marriage solemnised by the Queene of Chastity; yf his refined witt would bee confind with reason, I can awnsweare him; but I thinke hardly satisfie him; . . . it was no marriage, but a forme of vnitinge chast harts, to shew a defiance to Cupid, and his contracts, and that there could bee a chast combination without his powers. yf this will not satisfie; I referre him to the speeches; and thus Madame, holding you no longer with preambles, and superfluous apologies, especialy to them that rightly vnderstand mee: I rest. (50–65)

It is impossible, of course, to say with certainty that Jonson was the critic at whom White was aiming, although the description here fits Jonson perfectly—or at least it matches, point for point, the surprisingly consistent negative image of Jonson left by many of the playwright's own antagonists. The unnamed critic was apparently someone who was eager to find fault with other men's work; someone who was open to the charge of being imitative, of "feed[ing] on other mens prouision" (a charge White expands upon in the masque itself); someone who frequently depended on others to supply his meals; someone who was likely to criticize another artist less for lacking aesthetic talent than for making "an error"; and someone who was fastidiously concerned with the proper, almost scholarly use of mythological characters and sources.

It would be very easy to list numerous similar charges leveled, again and again, against Jonson himself over the course of his career.[14] If Jonson was in fact the object of White's sarcasm, then other details of the Dedication's phrasing take on a richer significance. Thus, the closing appeal to "them that rightly vnderstand mee" may have been intended as a deliberate echo of one of Jonson's own favorite words and tactics. Similarly, the reference to the critic's "perspectiue" may have been a subtle allusion to one of the sophisticated devices of staging associated with Jonson's own masques for the court. Finally, White's claim not to have written "from affected singularity, or from any conceite of worth in my labors" (36–38) can easily be seen as a muted indictment of Jonson's well known self-regard and claims to superior artistic merit. Certainly Lucy would have been as familiar as anyone with Jonson's characteristic rhetoric and self-image, and part of the sting of White's attack—if Jonson was indeed its target—would have been that the indictment was intended to be read by a woman whose importance for Jonson clearly involved (but also went beyond) their personal relationship. It would have been annoying enough to be attacked by White, but to be attacked by him in front of Lucy, particularly since Jonson's indebtedness to Lucy was well known, may have seemed an offense more deserving of retaliation.

White's defense of himself and his work against envious criticism is not confined to the dedication. Like several of Jonson's own masques, *Cupid's Banishment* itself develops a number of themes enunciated in the prefatory matter that accompanies the work.[15] (Or rather, since the masque presumably preceded the writing of the dedication, that section elaborates upon themes first broached in the masque proper.) By drawing connections between the masque's fiction and the real problems dealt with in the dedication, White makes more obvious the relevance of the masque's themes to the concerns of everyday life. Certainly that relevance is suggested by the masque's opening speech, which was spoken by the character Occasion. This part was played by White himself—a fact that would have given his words particular prominence and point. Addressing Anne, Occasion celebrates "female worth" (80), thereby not only complimenting the Queen and calling attention to the special circumstances of a masque performed at a girls' school, but also anticipating Cupid's later attacks on women and Occasion's apologies for those attacks during the masque's conclusion. Yet the speech soon turns from simple praise to an expression of thanks, as Occasion declares that if "free acceptance of noble fauor" had not armed that character's breast

> with that stronge temper of resisting proofe
> against Enuies hissinge adders
> Tymes handmayd had bene dumbe
> despayre and feare had ouercome our weake designes
> (80–85)

The Queen's presence

> . . . frees each thinge that liues in doubt
> no harmeles thought now feares the banefull stinge
> of fell detraction nor here no carpinge god
> bereaues tru meaninge of hir worth . . . (90–93)

This might seem an odd way for a work of this sort to begin—unless, of course, White was referring to some real source of envy, some real attacks that had been leveled against his work even before it was staged, while it was still being planned. It would have been extremely unlikely for Jonson to have been totally ignorant of the preparations being made for White's masque, especially since the work was to be performed so near to London, and since it closely concerned so many prominent figures. Moreover, the masque involved a number of "professionals" with whom Jonson probably had regular contact, and it dealt with a theme that Jonson himself had very recently treated. It is not hard to imagine, then, that Jonson heard of the work or of White's plans for it, and that he publicly mocked White's ambitions. In any case, Occasion's speech implies that the envy of a "carpinge god" (perhaps a jibe at Jonson's status and lofty self-regard) had almost inhibited the author from undertaking the work. Ironically, the opening speech is positively Jonsonian in its prickly self-consciousness, in its tone of self-justification and of undeserved injury. Like a number of Jonson's other rivals, White sometimes comes close to resembling Jonson himself.[16] Certainly the unusual prominence White enjoyed in a work of his own devising smacks of Jonson's similar involvement in his own art, and it may partly have been annoyance at White's use of his work for self-advertisement that prompted Jonson's possible rejoinder in *Pleasure Reconciled to Virtue*. Of course, if Occasion's attack on the "carpinge god" in Queen Anne's presence was in fact aimed at Jonson, the embarrassment would have provided the playwright with still another motive to respond.

Occasion's "complaints" about her "wrongs" (118–19) are interrupted by the appearance of Cupid, who snatches the long single lock of her hair and urges her to "inuite fresch youth to some amorous sceane" (121). Cupid had also been a prominent figure in two masques by Jonson performed within the past year. White's Cupid bears more resemblance to the figure in the very recent *Lovers Made Men* than to the Cupid in *Christmas His Masque*, yet White's Cupid quickly evolves into a far more threatening and disruptive figure. If White thought he could go Jonson one better in presenting a more complicated Cupid, perhaps Jonson decided to go White one better by revising large segments of the latter's entire masque. In any case, Occasion resists Cupid's blandishments, insisting that "this is no tyme nor place for Cupids wiles / thy plotts and subtle shifts are all delusions / to mocke mortality and idle fict[i]ons / forgd by some Poets fruiteles brayne" (139–42). And so Occasion dismisses Cupid's "wanton subiect and laciuious Muse" (147).

Attention now shifts to Diana, goddess of Chastity, dressed all in white and standing in an arbor on or near a mountain. Surrounded by her nymphs, she shows herself; while the mountain opens, loud music plays and Diana, too, rebukes Cupid. The god of love, unintimidated, argues with the goddess and speaks the first of a number of slurs on women. Diana, becoming increasingly irritated, orders Cupid away, claiming that his "very breath corrupts a Virgins vow" (205). She commands Occasion to remove Cupid from the hall, and Occasion obediently complies. Next Diana summons Mercury—also a figure in *Lovers Made Men* and soon to be a very prominent figure in *Pleasure Reconciled*—and orders him to summon Hymen. No sooner has Mercury departed than two of Diana's nymphs, singing from the mountain, call for Hymen, who soon enters, followed by the King and Queen of the revels. After Diana welcomes Hymen, she points to Fortune, who also welcomes Hymen and Mercury while standing at the bottom of the mountain. Hymen briefly addresses the assembled goddesses, emphasizing his "chastest resolution" (268).

At this point, Bacchus unexpectedly bursts in, and at this point, also, the resemblances between White's masque and *Pleasure Reconciled* become particularly striking. Bacchus rides in a chariot, carrying a "truncheon in one hand and a bole of wine in the other" (274–75). He is accompanied by two boy "Bacchanalians with wreaths of iuy" (276), who also are carrying bowls of wine. Bacchus brings the now-disarmed Cupid with him and attempts "to reconcile the / Goddesse Cinthia and / the God of loue" (281–83). In other words, he attempts to reconcile pleasure and virtue, insisting that "weele make you all freinds . . ." (288). Cupid complains "By Venus apron strings" about having been disarmed (290), the quoted phrase perhaps reminding the audience of the boy Cupid and his humorously overbearing mother as presented during the past year in Jonson's *Christmas His Masque* (H&S 10: 560). This possibility is reinforced by Bacchus's response, which alludes to Venus as "some scoldinge butterwife" (296), a description very much in the spirit of Jonson's recent presentation of the goddess. The emphasis on Cupid's immaturity—also stressed in *Christmas His Masque*—continues when Bacchus refers to him as "this little boy" (308) and "my little rouer" (313). In the spirit of reconciling pleasure and virtue, Bacchus urges the other figures to "conclude with loue" (316), and Diana responds by indicating her willingness to admit Bacchus and Cupid to her court so long as they "conteine with in the bounds of modesty" (319).

Next, Fortune and Hymen help solemnise the coronation and marriage of the revels King and Queen, an event that takes place at the foot of the mountain. In a prose note, White is careful to insist that "there reuells / did wholly tend to Chastity . . . w[th]out / any preiudice to virginity or / scandall to any entire vow" (336–42). This seems to be another explicit response to the kinds of carping objections mentioned in the Dedication, particularly to the charge that Hymen had no place in such a ceremony. Cupid, upset that he has been excluded from the marriage, bursts out angrily and once again attacks the assembled women. Diana responds with equal anger, claiming that Cupid "dost profane our presence" and declaring that "loue can neuer conquer Chastity" (374; 376). Eight wood nymphs now rush out from a grove adjoining the mountain and surround Cupid "in a figure" (391), put horns on his head, and, after dancing "many pret- / ty figures" (394–95), chase him from the masque for good. Perhaps significantly, "figure" is also the term used in *Pleasure Reconciled* to describe the masquers' dances (H&S 7: 488–89), while an ensuing reference to Cupid as "Venus bratt" (409) may perhaps allude again to the kind of Cupid Jonson had so recently presented in *Christmas His Masque*. In any case, Bacchus's attempt to reconcile pleasure and virtue has proven, at least on this level and at least for the time being, a dismal failure.

Despite the recent excitement, Bacchus apparently has dozed off. Occasion now awakens him and warns him not to make the same mistake as Cupid. Although Bacchus protests that he is still very sleepy, he nonetheless introduces another antimasque involving some of his bacchanalian followers, including "a grand Bacchus skippinge in / with a belly as bigg as a kinderkin / all in flesh coulord buckram w^th / a wreath of vine leaues aboute / his head a red swolne face / full of pimples" (430–35). This figure is accompanied by four attendants, two of whom "at theire backs . . . haue barrells / with bellies like a tunn" (453–54). They in turn are accompanied by five drunkards, each of whose entrances is heralded by rowdy verses (including some that must have seemed a bit risqué in a girls' school revels), and who then dance with the four bacchanalians, who are described as having "wreaths of iuy on / their heads and girdles with twists of iuy, barrells at / their backs with red fiery faces longe hayre great bellies / and red pumps" (494–97). A prose note describing this dance concludes that these figures "shew the seuerall humers of drunkards / with many pretty figures befitting that vayne" (514–15). The references to humours (a term associated with Jonsonian comedy, as the recently published folio had reminded everyone) and to "figures" (a term soon to be emphasized in *Pleasure Reconciled*) may be merely accidental, but as I shall suggest, the strong resemblances between the actions and appearance of these characters and those in Jonson's forthcoming masque seem to have been designed by Jonson to remind his audience explicitly of White's preceding work.

Once the dances have ended, Diana introduces twelve nymphs, who "descend from the mount attired all in white / tinsie" (523–24), six wearing blue mantles and six wearing red. These nymphs spell out the names of Anne, James, and Charles through their dances, and then they separate, six to one side and six to the other. Diana then "descends from the / mount with 2 of the Queenes godaughters" and presents them to Anne (542–43), to whom they in turn present needlework gifts bearing the Queen's initials. Then they reascend the mount, singing a final song that celebrates "the true loue, and ioyfull peace" with which "Cynthias triumphs begin to cease" (575–76). In other words, in this way and on this level, and despite or precisely because of Cupid's banishment, White's masque also glorifies the reconciliation of pleasure and virtue. Bringing the masque's design full circle, Occasion ends the work with another speech to the Queen. White uses the address to call attention to his personal contribution by alluding to the "nimble minutes" that "Occasion hath aduentured to bestow" (588–89). He begs pardon for any offense that Cupid's speeches may have caused, but, more significantly, he also uses nearly the very last lines of the masque to allude to the work as "our childish sports" and to claim that "wee professe [our] stage no Helicon / our Muse is homespun our action is our owne" (604–06). After Occasion asks the Queen to grace his efforts with a smile, the masque concludes.

Occasion's final speech, by reminding us of her first one, not only gives the masque a symmetrical structure but also seems to revive some of the themes of the opening address. Perhaps it also continues the submerged satire on Jonson which, I have argued, was part of the purpose of Occasion's opening words. It is not difficult at all to see the description of *Cupid's Banishment* as "our childish sports" not simply as an allusion to the masque's emphasis on the boy god and to the young girls who performed in it, but perhaps also as another swipe at what White may have considered Jonson's pretentious claims for his own works in this genre. Even more relevant is White's claim that his muse is "homespunn," perhaps alluding to Jonson's dependence on classical and foreign models, a possibility reinforced by the immediately succeeding claim that "our action is our owne." If White was indeed attacking Jonson as an imitative writer, he was only following the lead of many of Jonson's other critics, and if Jonson did indeed decide to imitate White's masque when he wrote *Pleasure Reconciled*, he may have viewed this decision as a particularly appropriate and ironic response to White's allegations.

The assumption that Jonson is the target of Occasion's concluding remarks is reinforced by one other bit of evidence, and in fact, accepting this assumption makes sense of the manuscript as it stands and obviates the need for any emendation. Line 605 of the surviving manuscript reads, "wee professe no stage no Helicon," but White's most recent editor has emended this line to read, "wee professe [our] stage no Helicon." Either reading would support the argument that this is an attack on Jonson, with his exalted notions of the poet's role. However, the unrevised manuscript reading seems even more obviously directed at Jonson, not only as a poet with laureate ambitions but also as a professional dramatist. White would thus be mocking Jonson—or defending himself—in two ways rather than one, and the lightly punctuated manuscript could stand free of any need of the single substantive emendation that Professor McGee introduces.

However convincing or unconvincing the argument that White may have had Jonson in mind when he wrote *Cupid's Banishment*, it seems nearly undeniable that Jonson had White's masque in mind when he came to compose *Pleasure Reconciled to Virtue*. The resemblances between the two works are remarkable and are far more extensive than previous commentators have noted. This, at any rate, is how I would justify the extended summary of White's masque that I have just offered. When we turn now from his work to Jonson's, the parallels—and the significant distinctions—become immediately obvious.

The most obvious resemblance would have been apparent to the spectators even before a single word was spoken. The setting of *Pleasure Reconciled*, like that of *Cupid's Banishment*, was dominated by a huge mountain, which Jonson's stage directions identify as Atlas (H&S 7: 479). But the mountain in Jonson's masque seems to have been a far more imposing and technically ingenious contraption than the hill in White's. It extended nearly to the ceiling of the hall and was capped by a "huge head" that "rolled its eyes and moved itself with wonderful cunning."[17] Thus, right from the start it must have seemed clear that Jonson and his collaborator, Inigo Jones, were bent not simply on imitating White's work but on surpassing it. For instance, the fact that the mountain in *Pleasure Reconciled* is clearly identified, whereas the one in White's masque is not, must immediately have given the former structure greater resonance and symbolic value. Surely the spectators at Jonson's masque who were also present at White's could not have helped but notice the striking similarity between the settings of the two works, and the obviousness of this resemblance would have cued them to look for all the others that soon follow.

One of these others, again introduced immediately (as if Jonson could not wait to call attention to the resemblances) is the boisterous entrance of Comus, "ye god of *cheere*, or y^{e} *belly*" (H&S 7: 479), a figure often associated with Bacchus. And, just as Bacchus enters *Cupid's Banishment* drawn in a chariot, so does

Comus enter *Pleasure Reconciled* "riding in tryumph" (H&S 7: 479). In both cases the gods' attendants are crowned with wreaths of ivy—a detail that may have been merely conventional but one which, nonetheless, could not help but remind Jonson's audience of White's masque, staged less than a year earlier. In both masques, wine bowls are prominently featured in association with the gods of revelry, but in Jonson's work the bowl is borne not by Comus himself but by a drunken attendant, who speaks one of the liveliest and most waggish speeches of the whole work. His prosy wit and cleverness seem much more vital than the tamer songs sung about the drunks in White's masque (none of which is in prose). It is almost as if Jonson intended to demonstrate how a poet trained in writing plays for the theater, with their frequent alternations between prose and verse, could achieve more dramatic and daring effects than those conceivable to a schoolmaster. This sort of contrast is underscored in other ways, as well. Thus, whereas White opens his masque with a decorous and highly self-conscious address to the Queen, Jonson, with the assurance of a master, plunges *in medias res;* the opening of his work is much more startling, spontaneous, and dramatic than the opening of White's.

In *Pleasure Reconciled,* the speech by Comus's bowl-bearer is followed immediately by the dancing of the first antimasque, featuring *"Men in the shape of bottles, tuns, &c."* (H&S 7: 482n)—in other words, details precisely reminiscent of the similar dancing of the Bacchanalians in *Cupid's Banishment.* Any member of the audience who had seen or heard about White's masque and who had not by this point noticed the echoes of it in *Pleasure Reconciled* would surely have noticed them now. It hardly seems accidental that the features of *Cupid's Banishment* that Jonson chose to echo most clearly were precisely the features which, because of the vitality and excitement associated with them, would have been most readily memorable. By the close of the first antimasque, the nature of Jonson's design—as a partial parody of White's—would have been clear to many, if not most, of the people present.

Perhaps in part because this aspect of his design was indeed obvious by this point, Jonson now shifts from his close imitation of White's work. He introduces the figure of Hercules, who banishes not Cupid but Comus, and who has no obvious male counterpart in White's composition. Even in this instance, however, there are intriguing similarities between the two works. Thus, a memorable moment in *Cupid's Banishment* was the moment when Bacchus fell asleep and had to be revived by the touch of Occasion's wand (414–17). In *Pleasure Reconciled*, it is Hercules who falls asleep, not because of self-indulgent indolence but because of justifiable fatigue from his exertions. As he sleeps, he is approached by a band of pigmies who intend to slay him. However, when he is roused by the music that accompanies their dancing, they immediately flee. Perhaps Jonson identified with Hercules, who is described as a "*Great frend, and seruant of the good*" (H&S 7: 483), as an "active frend of *Vertue*," who is crowned with a garland of poplar by Mercury (H&S 7: 485), and who in various ways seems to function as the poet's representative in this masque, as Occasion had in White's. (In White's work, for instance, it is Occasion, played by White, who is initially charged with the role of ejecting Cupid, just as in Jonson's masque it is Hercules who banishes the equally disruptive Comus, his crew, and the pigmies.) If this possible resemblance between Hercules and Jonson seems legitimate, then Jonson's decision to show Hercules being pestered by pigmies—unworthy opponents—may have had some relevance to Jonson's opinion of White. So, too, perhaps did Hercules's annoyance that it was *his* wine bowl ("ye crownd reward / of thirstie Heröes after labour hard" [H&S 7: 482]) that had been usurped by Comus's servant. And perhaps there was also some personal point in Jonson's allusion to one of Hercules's less famous labors, when Mercury praises him "for rescuing [Atlas's] faire Daughte[rs]: then ye prey / of a rude *Pirat*, as thou cam'st this way" (H&S 7: 485).[18] This, of course, is pure speculation, but it seems significant that Jonson provides details that make such speculation possible.

Whatever the possible resemblance between Hercules and Jonson, and whatever the possible relevance of this resemblance to Jonson's feud with White, it seems clear that *Pleasure Reconciled* was intended to echo *Cupid's Banishment* not only in its first antimasque but also throughout. Both Jonson and White, for instance, feature Mercury as characters in their works, although Jonson, typically, takes the briefly mentioned character from White's masque and transforms him into a major figure in his own. It is Mercury, a god often associated with wisdom, who thanks Hercules for his services to Virtue and who rewards him in the presence (and on behalf) of Hesperus (King James). However, what must have seemed one of the most vivid similarities between the two works—the introduction of the chief dancers of their respective main masques—is one that is not entirely obvious from the surviving texts. To be sure, some of the similarities are plain. For instance, just as there are twelve nymphs whose dances are central to *Cupid's Banishment*, so are there twelve princes whose dances are the highlights of *Pleasure Reconciled*. Just as the twelve nymphs descend from the mountain in White's work, so do the twelve princes descend from the mountain in Jonson's composition. In White's masque, the twelve dancers are preceded by the goddess Fortune; in Jonson's, the twelve princes are preceded by Daedalus, who introduces and supervises their dancing. Perhaps the dancing at this point in *Pleasure Reconciled* was more sophisticated and subtle than the dancing at the comparable point in White's work, with its almost mechanical spelling out of the names of the King, Queen, and Prince. In any case, Daedalus goes out of his way to interpolate and explain the significance of the dances in Jonson's masque, so that the sense of dance itself as a worthy and legitimate art-form seems much more explicit in his work than in White's.

Some of the similarities between these two moments of the two masques, however, survive not in the extant texts but in an extremely valuable account left by a member of the audience of *Pleasure Reconciled*, a chaplain associated with the Venetian diplomatic delegation. His letter refers to Daedalus and the dancers, but it also mentions "a goddess in a long white costume"—a figure not specified at this point in Jonson's text but one who may have reminded spectators of the similarly dressed Diana in White's work.[19] The Venetian's letter further mentions that six of the princes in Jonson's masque were dressed in one style, while six were dressed in another. The same kind of division was true of the twelve dancing nymphs in *Cupid's Banishment*. Moreover, just as the Venetian was careful to report that Jonson's twelve princes wore "long hair," White was careful to specify that the twelve nymphs wore "their hayre disheueld" (526). In other words, the original spectators of the two works would have been able to notice even more resemblances between them than are apparent from the surviving texts. At the conclusions of both works, the dancers reascend their respective mountains, and the masques draw to their respective ends.

For all the similarities between these works, the distinctions also seem significant. Whereas in *Cupid's Banishment* the chaste nymphs danced alone, in *Pleasure Reconciled* the dancing princes take lady partners, thus emphasizing the masque's titular theme of the reconciliation of opposites. Similarly, whereas in White's work only the peformers themselves dance, at the conclusion of Jonson's work the whole audience joined in, again suggesting the theme of concord and inclusion. Love is presented less crudely and ridiculously in Jonson's masque than in White's, but perhaps for that reason, undisciplined love is also presented as a more potentially tempting distraction. Commentators have remarked on the moral seriousness of Jonson's conclusion, its emphasis on the importance of making virtuous choices.[20] Perhaps this emphasis was designed not only to give Jonson's masque greater significance and wider import than White's, but also to contrast with the self-congratulatory (but also self-defensive) tone of Occasion's final speech in *Cupid's Banishment*.

Although Jonson undoubtedly believed that his masque had far excelled White's, surviving evidence indicates that this opinion may not have been widely shared by his audience. The negative reaction the masque elicited has already been mentioned, but the flavor of that reaction is best communicated by a few quotations. Ironically, one commentator found the most imitative part of the work the most appealing. Sir Edward Harwood reported that the antimasque "of little boyes dressed like bottells and a man in a great tonn w[ch] the bottells drew out & tost too and fro" was "not ill liked: the masqu[e] it selfe in generall not well liked: the Conceite good, the poetry not so" (H&S 10: 576). If this reaction was common, and if it was communicated to Jonson, his decision to jettison the originally effective antimasque and replace it with a new one in *For the Honour of Wales* may seem illogical, unless, perhaps, he was piqued that some observers preferred the part of *Pleasure Reconciled* that was most obviously derivative.

Other reactions were less precise than Harwood's but are still suggestive. Edward Sherburn wrote that the masque "came far short of thexpectac[i]on and M. Inigo Jones has lost in his reputac[i]on in reguard some extraordinary devise was loked for (it being the Prince his first Mask) and a poorer was neuer sene" (H&S 10: 576). This is a particularly intriguing comment, since it suggests that Jones as well as Jonson suffered a loss of reputation from the disappointment the masque provoked. If the main objection to the masque was the politically daring nature of its writing, it is difficult to see why Jones would have been held accountable. Instead, the thread that runs throughout almost all the reactions to the masque emphasizes its dullness, the audience's sense of aesthetic—not political—frustration. We may now regard their judgment as misguided or unsophisticated (although they were the ones who actually witnessed the masque's performance), but it at least seems worth stressing that most of them seem to have condemned the work according to aesthetic criteria, rather than because they found its political implications offensive. Of course, it may seem a bit surprising that Sherburn found the masque lacking in "some extraordinary devise," especially when we remember the Venetian chaplain's fascinated reaction to the huge and mechanically ingenious Mount Atlas. However, Sherburn's response seems more comprehensible when we recall that an earlier masque had so recently featured another such mountain. Jones's attempt to surpass the mountain in *Cupid's Banishment* may have fallen flat, perhaps seeming merely imitative to many of the spectators who had witnessed the earlier work. Today it seems hard to imagine a more "extraordinary devise" than the one Jones concocted, but for the original spectators the design may have seemed not so much to excel White's as merely to mimic it.

This may also have been true of some of the negative reactions to Jonson's writing. John Chamberlain reported of the masque that "there was nothing in yt extraordinarie but rather the inuention proued dull . . ." (H&S 10: 576). Similarly, Nathaniel Brent wrote that "The maske on 12th night is not com[m]mended of any ye poët is growen so dul yt his devise is not worthy ye relating, much lesse ye copiing out. divers thinke fit he should retourne to his ould trade of bricke laying againe" (H&S 10: 576). Once more, what seems to have impressed these contemporary witnesses was not anything in the masque that struck them as politically provocative but rather the supposed dullness of its conception. If Jonson was defiantly indicting the corruption of his courtly audience, few of them seem to have noticed or to have commented on it. What they did notice—or at least discuss—was an evident flagging in the poet's powers of invention, a reaction that seems especially comprehensible if they believed that he was simply parroting White's masque of less than a year before. What Jonson may have intended as a subtle form of one-upsmanship, his audience may have perceived as an indication of artistic sterility. Ironically, his decision to parody White's masque may only have confirmed, for many observers, the frequent charge that Jonson was imitative and uninspired.

Such an assumption would help to explain why Jonson decided to drop the most obvious aspect of his parody from the revised version of his masque. *For the Honour of Wales* deletes the whole episode dealing with Comus and his bacchanalians, even though that section would seem to have had the potential of being the most lively and entertaining part of the masque, and even though Harwood seems to have regarded it as the best part of the piece. However, it is easy to imagine that Jonson may have felt that his parody had backfired, and it is equally easy to imagine that some members of the audience were offended by his use of such an important court occasion to score points against such a minor personal antagonist. We have evidence of a similar reaction when Jonson used a later masque, *Time Vindicated to Himself and to His Honours*, as a means of attacking his rival George Wither in 1623. John Chamberlain reported that "Ben Iohnson they say is like to heare of yt on both sides of the head for personating George withers a poet or poetaster as he termes him, as hunting after fame by beeing a crono-mastix or whipper of the time, w[ch] is become so tender an argument that yt must not be touched either in iest or earnest" (H&S, 10: 648). Similarly, there is evidence that Jonson lost credit at court and with the King for attacking his erstwhile collaborator, Inigo Jones, when Jones seemed to be usurping Jonson's role of "Fabler" in the production of the masques (H&S 11: 151–52). As so often happened in Jonson's career (and as may have happened with *Pleasure Reconciled*), the poet's attempts to defend his interests against antagonists seemed only to undermine his public standing.

Reaction to Jonson's revised masque seems to have been mixed. John Chamberlain reported that the masque "was represented again wth some few alterations and additions, but little bettered" (H&S 10: 576), but another correspondent noted that the new version "was much better liked then twelueth night; by reason of the new Conceites & ante maskes & pleasant merry speeches made to the kinge . . . " The reference to "new Conceietes & ante maskes" is particularly interesting if Jonson was in fact attempting to make *For the Honour of Wales* seem less obviously imitative than its predecessor. Apparently this time his intentions were better achieved.

Ironically, it was the Welsh masque, rather than its predecessor, that seems to have sparked concern about the offensive nature of its writing. Nathaniel Brent wrote that the Welsh speeches in the work were "sufficient to make an English man laugh and a welsh-man cholerique" (H&S 10: 577). Certainly *Pleasure Reconciled* seems hardly more daring, in its satirical verve and political implications, than *Cupid's Banishment* itself, a work encouraged by the Countess of Bedford and apparently enjoyed by the Queen. Thus, at one point in White's work Diana instructs Cupid to leave her presence and "steale to some amorous court and tutor / wanton ladies how to wo" (195–96). This could have been interpreted—by those so inclined—as a critical comment on the immorality of the Jacobean court, but if White intended any such implication, he seems to have felt little compunction about expressing it before the Queen and an assembly of other powerful figures. Again, when Bacchus alleges that the disruptive Cupid must have had "some Lawier" as his father (295), the social satire seems at least as explicit as anything in Jonson's masque. Similarly, if references to kings, courts, and courtiers would have reminded Jacobean audiences of the real king and his real court, what are we to make of the reference, in connection with one of the drunkards in White's masque, to "the crew of drunkards trew / that do belong to Bacchus court"? (483–84). If one of Jonson's main purposes was to satirize the excesses of the Jacobean court (as in fact it may have been), then it seems that he was echoing White in this as in so much else.

It seems, however, that micropolitics may have played at least as great a role in determining the shape and nature of Jonson's masque as his undeniable concern with macropolitical issues. Personal rivalry and worry about the maintenance of personal status seem to have been at least as important as motives for the composition of *Pleasure Reconciled* as a concern with contemporary politics or with arcane aesthetic theory.[21] One of the texts that Jonson seems to have had most clearly in mind when he wrote his masque was the text—or at least the plot summary—of *Cupid's Banishment*. That work, interestingly enough, features as one of its most memorable characters a large, loud, wine-guzzling entertainer, "with a belly as bigg as a kinderkin" and with "a red swolne face / full of pimples" (431; 434–35). Perhaps it is merely coincidence (or perhaps it is something more) that this careful description calls up another one, written not long afterwards by Jonson himself, in which he refers to his own "mountaine belly" and "rockie face" (H&S 8: 150). Was White thinking of Jonson when he described his "grand Bacchus"? The possibility is tantalizing, but uncertain. Was he thinking of Jonson when he attacked the "curious Criticke" mentioned in his dedication to Lucy? That possibility seems more likely. Finally, did Jonson have *Cupid's Banishment* in mind when he came to write *Pleasure Reconciled to Virtue*? That much seems sure.

Jonson's awareness of White's masque, and his response to it in his own, suggest again the importance of rivalry in his career, especially as a writer of aristocratic entertainments. Such concerns seem present again in another important masque written a few years later, *The Gypsies Metamorphos'd*. However, the artist to whom Jonson may have been responding in that work—Thomas Campion—is of altogether greater importance than Robert White.

6

Jonson, Campion, and *The Gypsies Metamorphos'd*

Jonson's detailed response to the work of Robert White suggests the depth of his awareness of other writers. Various recent scholars have emphasized this point. For instance, Richard S. Peterson and Katharine Maus have demonstrated the alert and discriminating intelligence with which Jonson read and imitated the works of important classical authors, while Robert N. Watson and George E. Rowe have argued that Jonson's drama is rooted in a fundamental effort to distinguish his own works from those of other authors.[1] Recent studies of Jonson's reading have tried to show how he responded to various texts,[2] and the preceding chapter has, I hope, shown how one of his most famous masques, *Pleasure Reconciled to Virtue*, was written partly as a detailed reply to White's masque, staged only a few months earlier. The present chapter discusses a relationship that is much less certain and clear-cut, but one that is nonetheless intriguing. This involves the possibility that Jonson's well-known masque of 1621, *The Gypsies Metamorphos'd*, also echoes an earlier masque by another writer: Thomas Campion's *Ayres Sung and Played at Brougham Castle*, initially performed in 1617 and published the next year. Apparently Campion's work was the only recent royal entertainment before Jonson's that had given such prominence to gypsies.

King James, who was present at the performances of both works, would have been hard put to overlook their similarities. Although both works emphasize the activities of gypsies, both also share similar themes, structures, and phrasing. And, of course, such parallels naturally invite attention to differences. Examining the links between the two works will also permit more detailed discussion of the relationship between Jonson and Campion, which has rarely been studied at any length and which seems to have been a bit ambivalent. Evidence survives, in fact, that Jonson had already mocked a masque by Campion in a masque of his own, and this precedent—along with the kinds of similarities already mentioned—adds to the possibility that in writing *The Gypsies Metamorphos'd*, Jonson may have been glancing over his shoulder at Campion's earlier work. In any case, whatever Jonson's precise intentions, it seems likely that many members of his audience would have spotted the resemblances between the two entertainments. Exploring those resemblances may help provide not only a better grasp of Jonson's masque and of his relations with Campion but also a fuller comprehension of the contexts to which he seems to have been responsive.

The lives of Jonson and Campion reveal a number of interesting parallels. Both had lost parents at an early age, and both had had experience with apparently unsympathetic stepparents.[3] Both had apparently served as volunteer soldiers during the early 1590s—Jonson in the Netherlands and Campion in France (Vivian xxxii). Indeed, Jonson seems to have known and alluded to a Latin epigram Campion wrote as a result of his military service, a poem in which he, like Jonson in a number of works, mocks the claims of a bragging soldier (H&S 1: 150). Both Jonson and Campion were apparently linked in the 1590s with Thomas Nashe, who seems to have been a friend of Campion's and with whom Jonson collaborated on the infamous *Isle of Dogs* (Vivian 27). Both men seem to have had strong ties to the Inns of Court (Vivian xxviii), and although Campion actually studied there, he seems to have shared Jonson's suspicions of a career in the law (Vivian xxxi). Both men, during the 1590s, were establishing their reputations as poets (Vivian xxxvi), and by the early years of the next century both were listed by William Camden—Jonson's mentor—as among the best contemporary authors.[4] Nor was this the only time that the two poets were praised by the same man; John Davies of Hereford, for example, seems to have respected them both (Vivian xli). By the same token, both Jonson and Campion wrote poems praising Alphonso Ferrabosco, the court composer with whom both had at various times collaborated and who had set the words of both men to music. Both poets wrote whimsical works celebrating Thomas Coryate's *Crudities* (Vivian xli), and both had links during the early years of James's reign with members of the powerful Cecil family.[5] During this time both wrote masques designed to promote the interests of that family (Lindley 176), and both masques dealt with strikingly similar themes and involved a number of the same aristocratic participants.[6] Jonson and Campion apparently shared a number of the same friends (Vivian xlix), and both seem to have valued friendship (Vivian xlviii). However, no record survives of any particularly friendly relations between them. They seem to have exchanged no commendatory poems, and, as we shall see, Jonson's few definite comments about Campion suggest some traces of conflict.

The literary links between Jonson and Campion are also worth noting. Campion apparently had collaborated on the early *Masque of Proteus*, a crucial work in the development of the genre and one that provided an important precedent for Jonson's own later work.[7] Moreover, in the first decade of the new century Campion helped develop the emphasis on antimasques, and Jonson seems to have been influenced by his example (H&S 2: 275–76). Campion, in turn, seems to have been familiar with Jonson's masques (H&S 2: 281), and similarities between the various royal entertainments the two men provided have been noted by Jonson's editors (H&S 2: 302; 321). Moreover, similarities also existed in their practice of lyric poetry. David Lindley, for instance, has noted that Campion's "ayres" often have a "sententious, epigrammatic style" that anticipates the achievement of Jonson (138), and indeed Campion himself explicitly equated his airs with epigrams (Lindley 73), a genre in which Jonson felt he had composed "*the ripest of* [his] *studies*" (H&S 8: 25). Both men had a sure command of Latin and were proud of that attainment (Vivian xxxviii), and the epigrams of both are satirical in ways reminiscent of Martial.[8] Both Jonson and Campion adapted the very same lyric by Catullus (Lowbury 49), and in fact the striking similarities between the two works strongly suggest that Jonson was responding as much to Campion as to their common Latin source.[9] Typically, though, Jonson's version of the poem is as interesting for its differences from Campion's text as it is for any similarities (Sternfeld 320). What the two poems clearly indicate, though, is the interest both men shared in incorporating the best apsects of classical literature into their English compositions. Both were strongly influenced by classical precedents, and indeed Catherine W. Peltz has suggested that Campion's influence was "of first importance" in paving the way for Jonson's achievement as a lyric poet (6). In their actual practice as well as in their literary theories, the two men seem to have had much in common.[10]

Given all their personal and literary similarities, one might expect Jonson and Campion to have been at least friendly, if not friends. However, the scanty surviving evidence suggests, if anything, that their relations were occasionally strained. In fact, as George Rowe has argued, the very parallels between Jonson and some of his contemporaries may have encouraged him to distinguish himself from them, and perhaps this was true of his relations with Campion. The possibility that there may have been tensions between these two talented men—who moved in many of the same circles, were concerned with many of the same issues, and worked in many of the same genres—should seem no more surprising than the hostility that definitely existed between Jonson and his longtime collaborator, Inigo Jones. Campion, in fact, seems to have had very warm relations with Jones, with whom he also collaborated on at least two masques and to whom he seems to have been much more deferential than was the combative Jonson.[11]

Perhaps the friendship between Jones and Campion seemed reason enough for Jonson to suspect the latter, especially since Campion was himself a distinguished poet and was one of Jonson's few serious rivals in the business of writing masques. This must have seemed especially true in 1613, when Campion published two collections of songs and was commissioned to write no less than three separate aristocratic entertainments, including the main masque for the marriage of Princess Elizabeth as well as an important masque for the wedding involving Robert Carr (the Earl of Somerset and the King's favorite) and Frances Howard. Campion's status as a client of the Howard family may also have troubled Jonson (Lindley 190–91), since the Howards—particularly the Earl of Northampton, whom Jonson considered his "mortall enimie" (H&S 1: 141)—had long been been contemptuous of Robert Cecil (now deceased) and of the Earl of Pembroke, with whom Jonson seems to have been allied. As David Lindley has suggested, Campion's extraordinary productivity at this time was probably due in no small measure to the "confidence and security" he must have felt because of "his adoption by the Howard family" (Lindley 210–11). Given these circumstances, it is not hard to imagine that Jonson, in 1613 at least, saw Campion as a potential threat to his own status as the chief writer of masques for the Jacobean court.[12]

Such an assumption would help explain why Jonson apparently felt compelled to mock Campion's *Somerset Masque* in his own *Irish Masque*, also written to help celebrate the favorite's wedding. David Lindley notes at least four specific resemblances between Jonson's work and Campion's, which had been staged not long before. He speaks of Jonson's "detailed parody" of Campion:

> Specifically, in presenting twelve masquers hindered from arriving at the celebrations, Jonson adopts the same fiction that Campion employed. He then contrasts his "realistically" naked masquers with those in Campion's work who had the benefit of "a deuoish vit a clowd to fesh 'hem out o' te bottom o'te vayter". . . . In the dispute regarding who is to speak first he also pokes fun at Campion's masque, as he does in allusions to the symbolic use of the number four. ("Embarrassing," 357)

Stephen Orgel also notes Jonson's mocking allusions to Campion's masque, as do Herford and the Simpsons.[13] That the allusions were in fact meant to mock, and not merely to allude, seems clear from Jonson's explicit reference to the "deuoish vit a clowd." As it happens, we know from the surviving report of an ambassador who was present at the staging of Campion's work that this "device" had been a source of unintended amusement and ridicule.[14] In the words of the ambassador (translated by John Orrell), the masque's architect or designer had

> disgraced himself, if truth be told, and misspent much of these gentelemen's money . . . what they had thought would be a marvelous thing—the descent of a cloud with the twelve lords, richly clothed and much adorned, who were to perform the masque—turned out to be that he had fixed a lowering device behind the cloud just like one used in dropping a portcullis. . . . when it came down one could see the ropes that supported it and hear the pulleys, or rather wheels, making the same noise as when they raise or lower the mast of a ship . . . the lords came down without any music, with no other sound but the screeching of the wheels. (304n)

Campion himself seems to have been embarrassed by all this; he apologizes for it in the printed preface to the masque (Davis 268). That Jonson chose to allude precisely to those aspects of Campion's masque that had caused the most ridicule suggests that he was having fun at his rival's expense, not paying him tribute. Lindley in fact sees these allusions as "cheap jibes" (Lindley 234) that reflect Jonson's "arrogant sense of his own superiority as a writer of masques" ("Embarrassing," 358). He is quick to challenge Orgel's claim that Campion's masques were less coherent and more flattering than Jonson's (Lindley 175–76), and in fact Lindley's comments on both Jonson and Orgel sometimes seem to reflect the same touchiness that may have existed between the two poets.

In addition to the mocking allusions in *The Irish Masque*, other evidence also suggests that Jonson may have felt some ambivalence toward Campion. For instance, he told William Drummond of Hawthornden "That next himself only Fletcher and Chapman could make a Mask" (H&S 1: 133). Yet neither Fletcher nor Chapman had had the kind of experience as a masque writer that Campion had had, and Jonson's editors suggest that "The point of the remark . . . is that Daniel and Campion could not write masques" (H&S 1: 155). If this interpretation seems plausible (and it does), then this remark was not the only time during his conversations with Drummond that Jonson thought of Daniel (another rival) and Campion together. In what is perhaps his most famous and certainly his most explicit reference to Campion, he told Drummond that "he had written a discourse of Poesie both against Campion and Daniel especially this Last, wher he proves couplets to be the bravest sort of Verses . . ." (H&S 1: 132). Unfortunately, Jonson's "discourse" is now lost, like many of his other writings. It would be foolish to speculate at length about what, precisely, the discourse may have said, especially regarding Campion and his ideas. In 1602 Campion had issued his *Observations in the Art of English Poesie*, in which he had attacked rhyme and argued in favor of quantitative verse. Campion's treatise was immediately answered by Daniel's *Defence of Rhyme* (1603), which is thought to have finally killed the quantitative movement. Several commentators have remarked that most of Campion's own poetry uses rhyme—a concession, it seems, of his defeat. Jonson's own attitude toward the controversy would be worth knowing; presumably he tried to stake out an alternative to both Campion and Daniel—to "distinguish" himself (in Rowe's sense) from both of his competitors. Presumably he expressed some sympathy with Campion's dislike of many forms of rhyme (an attitude also expressed, it would seem, in his famous poetic "Fit of Rime Against Rime" as well as in his *English Grammar*), but presumably he also endorsed some forms of rhyme, as his own practice would suggest. His regard for couplets may have been the point he chose to emphasize; he would later tell Drummond that he "destest[ed] all other Rimes" (H&S 1: 132). Whatever the case, it seems clear that in his prose, his masques, and his attitudes toward poetry, Jonson saw certain clear distinctions between himself and Campion.

And distinctions there clearly were. Campion, a medical doctor, was more clearly in the long tradition of amateur poets, whereas Jonson, with his links to playwriting and with his laureate ambitions, was more obviously a poetic professional (Lindley

136). Campion tended to be less up-to-date in his subject matter and in certain aspects of his style (Lindley 138). In the words of one commentator, "Formal speeches were more congenial to Campion's idiom than the racy dialogue and irony in which Jonson excelled and which were the life of the antimasque" (Lowbury 104). Finally, even Peltz concedes that Campion's "advocacy of approximating classic meters in English lacked the sturdy common sense of Jonson's point of view upon the same subject" (Peltz 5). Jonson, for all his classicism, wrote almost entirely in a vigorous English full of the rhythms of good prose, whereas Campion was proudest of his Latin epigrams, while his English "airs" are distinguished chiefly by their flowing lyricism. If Jonson knew of the *Ayres That Were Sung and Played at Brougham Castle*, and if he knew that they were by Campion, and if he thought of them at all when he came to compose *The Gypsies Metamorphos'd*, he may have noticed the differences as well as the similarities between his own masque and the work composed by Campion.

Ian Spink, in a little-known article published more than twenty years ago, seems to have been the first person to call attention to the basic resemblance between Jonson's masque and Campion's work.[15] However, Spink's comments were very brief and very general; as an historian of music, his chief interest was in Campion the lyricist rather than in Campion the writer of masques. Nonetheless, Spink's article is extremely valuable for a number of reasons. In the first place, it provides even firmer evidence than had previously been offered that the words for the *"Ayres That Were Sung and Played at Brougham Castle"* were indeed composed by Campion. Since Campion's name does not appear on the title page of the collection of songs printed in 1618, the question of attribution is important. Spink offers new historical evidence, in addition to what was already available, to support the generally accepted view that Campion had the chief hand in preparing the words for the entertainment (57–59). Secondly, Spink offers a very plausible argument about the structure and format of the entertainment and about the order in which the songs were presented, and once again he provides new historical data that strongly support his assertion that the entertainment was broken into two basic parts, presented on two separate nights (60–61). Thirdly and most importantly, Spink briefly outlines what he calls the "Jonsonian" aspects of the masque, and he suggests that "consciously or unconsciously, Jonson may have been influenced by reports of the Brougham Castle entertainment in his *Gipsies*

Metamorphosed, performed almost exactly four years later . . ." (61). He points out the similarities between the plots and structures of the two works, and concludes by noting that

> both masques have three stages in common. First, the arrival of the gypsies; second, the rural interlude, or anti-masque; and third . . . the gypsies' praise of the King in terms that are impressive enough, but all the more so because of the gypsies' supposed supernatural powers of divination. Jonson's masque is a work of considerable intricacy, more so than Campion's is likely to have been; but reduced to essentials, the relationship between the two seems quite pronounced and may indicate some sort of influence on Jonson by Campion. (Spink 61–62)

At this point, Spink's comments on the possible Jonson-Campion connection cease, and he now proceeds to the main focus of his article. However, the connection he suggested can be developed in much more detail, and the case for the connection can be greatly strengthened. Spink confines himself to discussing basic structural similarities between the two works, but more detailed parallels—not only of structure, but of theme, characterization, and phrasing—can be sketched. These, combined with a number of historical data, make it quite likely that there was in fact "some sort of influence on Jonson by Campion," and that not only Jonson but also many in his audience were probably conscious of the similarities between his masque and Campion's *Ayres*.

The mere fact that the text of Campion's *Ayres* had been printed, and that the songs were thus available for repeated performances, would have given Campion's work greater currency (and would have made it literally more memorable) than if the songs had simply been presented once. Thus, the fact that Campion's work was presented several years before Jonson's is in itself no reason to question its possible influence as a source, nor does the length of time make it unlikely that Jonson's audience would have forgotten Campion's work. By their very nature, songs would have been easy to remember and easy to perform repeatedly and in small groups, especially since both the words and music were in print. Moreover, another consideration that strengthens the possible connection between the two works is the simple fact that King James and many of his most powerful courtiers were present for the performances of both works. A variety of texts have been mentioned as possible and quite plausible sources for Jonson's masque, but in most cases we cannot be sure whether James and other members of the audience for the *Gypsies Metamorphos'd* were personally familiar with those texts.[16] However, we have abundant evidence to show that James was present for the performance of Campion's work, and if that work was, as Spink so persuasively argues, a masque or entertainment that prominently featured wandering gypsy fortunetellers, then its relevance to Jonson's masque dealing with exactly the same subject seems undeniable.

The other texts suggested as possible sources for Jonson's work include plays and pamphlets, but Campion's seems to have been the only recent masque or entertainment to place so much emphasis on gypsies. The two works were thus similar not only in their subject matters and structures, but also in their genres, in the composition of their audiences, and in the circumstances of their first performances. Both works were commissioned by important aristocrats for presentation in their own homes to commemorate and celebrate a visit by the King. As many scholars have emphasized, the King was the most important member of the audience for any royal entertainment, and it is first and foremost James's presence during the staging of Campion's work that would have made it a likely influence on Jonson's. We have already seen that in the *Irish Masque* Jonson was more than willing to invite his aristocratic auditors to contrast his work with one by Campion. In the *Gypsies Metamorphos'd* he seems, once again, to be looking over his shoulder at a previous composition by Campion. Whether his motive was to pay tribute to Campion (who by this point was dead), or whether it was to demonstrate his own skill in dealing with a subject already handled by a significant predecessor, or whether it was to give a new twist to a popular theme, or whether his motive (as seems likely) was some mixture or combination of these, what does seem clear is that Campion's work was on his mind when he came to write his own. Moreover, the fact that the text of Campion's words was readily available would have made it quite easy for Jonson to borrow if he had so desired.

The resemblances between the two works in words, themes, characters, and structure are all worth noting. In many cases the parallels are undoubtedly coincidental and unavoidable—the result of two talented poets working in the same basic genre and dealing with very similar subject matter. However, as I have already suggested, Jonson's decision to present the same subject in a similar genre may not have been either a coincidence or an accident. And even if it had been, the resemblances would still have been there for James and other members of the audience to note. In other words, even if the parallels between Jonson's work and Campion's were entirely fortuitous, those parallels would almost certainly have been part of the king's and others' experience of Jonson's masque. They would probably have heard echoes of Campion and noticed other resemblances whether or not Jonson had deliberately intended them. However, given Jonson's intense awareness of the work and works of his contemporaries, it seems unlikely that the resemblances were entirely accidental.

As Spink has noted, Jonson's work is much more elaborate than the ten songs that survive from Campion's entertainment. If we had a more complete version of Campion's work, particularly the connecting text and some description of the performance, it is possible that even more resemblances between the two compositions would be apparent. As it is, however, the resemblances are numerous enough. Aside from the general structural parallels already reported by Spink, various phrases in Jonson's masque recall similar phrasing from Campion's songs. The main sections of both works, for instance, seem to have been preceded by expressions of welcome. At Burley, the home of James's favorite the Duke of Buckingham and the place where Jonson's masque was initially staged, the King had been greeted by a jocular porter, who had begun by saying that

> If for o[r] thought[s] there could but speeche be found,
> And all that speeche be vttered in one sound,
> So that some Power aboue vs, would afford
> The meanes to make a *Language* of a *word*,
> It should be *Wellcome*. (H&S 7: 565; ll. 1–5)

A little later he continues, exclaiming, "*Wellcome, ö wellcome, then*" (H&S 7: 565; l. 11). Similarly, the song apparently sung at the end of the first day of the King's visit to Brougham Castle (and thus the song that immediately preceded the beginning of the masque proper) begins, "Welcome, welcome, King of guests / With thy princely traine, / With joyfull triumphs and with Feasts / Be welcom'd home again." As if to reiterate the point, Campion also greets James a bit later by calling him "Welcome, welcome as the Sunne / When the night is past" (Davis 465–66). Of course, such a resemblance hardly seems surprising; there are not too many ways to welcome a visiting king other than to say "welcome," and Jonson himself would later use the same technique in welcoming King Charles in the opening of his appropriately named entertainment, *Love's Welcome at Bolsover* (H&S 7: 808; ll. 22–24). Still, the emphatic opening stress on the word "welcome" in both Campion's work and in Jonson's seems simply to have been the first of a series of echoes that might have reminded James, during his visit at Burley, of his earlier visit at Brougham.

Certainly the basic plots of the two works, as Spink has noted, are strikingly similar. Spink summarizes the plot of Campion's entertainment by reporting that at first

> A wandering band of gypsies arrives on the scene—a hallowed spot which they recognize as the dwelling place of Honour and Grace. They break into an 'anticke dance' and then give place to a crowd of country lads and lassies. A ballad is sung, then follows a rustic dance. A gypsy steps forward and sings a song invoking 'a chaine of prophecies.' At this point, or hereabout, the scene may have been transformed, revealing the kingly attributes of Truth, Peace, Love, Honour, Long-life, and Illustrious Posterity, to the accompaniment of a final hymn of praise. (61)

Many of the same elements, and many similar phrases and actions, occur in Jonson's masque. For instance, both masques open by introducing a wandering band of gypsies (whom Campion calls "wandring mates, / Sonnes and daughters of the Fates, / Friends of night"; Davis 466), and both works also bring the gypsies into contact with groups of country yokels. In addition, Jonson's masque, like Campion's, emphasizes a transformation (or "metamorphosis") in the gypsies, and in both works the skills of gypsies as fortunetellers are stressed. Moreover, both works emphasize lively country dances, and both feature long lists of rural names (H&S 7: 592, ll. 814–18; Davis 468). Aside from these larger parallels, however, often the phrasing in the two works is strikingly comparable. For example, one of the introductory songs in which Campion celebrates the King concludes by urging, "Let then that one of all be praised / That hath our fortunes raised" (Davis 465). Jonson also plays with this same idea, calling James "the maker here of all, / Where none doe stand, or sitt in veiwe, / But owe their fortunes vnto you, / At least what they good fortune call" (H&S 7: 576; ll. 336–39). Both works allude to the dancing of fairies to describe the dancing of their own characters (Davis 468; H&S 7: 589; ll. 736–37), and in both works moonlight is prominently mentioned (Davis 465;

H&S 7: 573, 590; ll. 264, 751–52). Similarly (as Spink has noted), both works associate the King with such royal virtues as peace, love, and truth (Davis 469; H&S 7: 574–7; ll. 285, 298, 322).

However, it is in the songs and scenes emphasizing the metamorphoses of the gypsies, as well as their blessings and prophecies, that the most striking parallels can be seen. By the time both works have nearly reached their conclusions, the gypsies have changed both in appearance and in manner; they have become much more seriously prophetic. Jonson signals the shift with a stage direction ("*The Gypses chang'd*"; H&S 7: 608; l. 1289) and with the opening words of the Patrico's next speech:

> Why, now ye behould,
> 'Twas truth that I tould,
> And no deuice:
> They'r changd in a trice . . . (H&S 7: 608; ll. 1292–95)

Campion signals a similar transformation by having one of the gypsies announce that

> The shadowes darkning our intents
> Must fade, and Truth now take her place,
> Who, in our right *Aegyptian* race,
> A chaine of Prophecies presents . . .
> . . .
> . . . heaven-borne Truth our Notes shall guide,
> One by one, while we relate
> That which shall tye both Time and Fate.
> (Davis 469)

The crucial song that then follows in Campion's work seems related to two different sections of Jonson's masque. In the first place, the song—in which various gypsies prophesy the various fortunes that will befall the King—may have helped inspire the memorable scenes early in Jonson's masque, in which various gypsies "one by one" foretell the fortunes of various members of the Jacobean court, including those of James (H&S 7: 574–88). Jonson, in other words, may have taken the germ of an idea from Campion and then greatly expanded it, turning it into one of the central devices and most fascinating sections of his own work. The idea of having gypsies prophesy to the king may at first have belonged to Campion, but Jonson's treatment of the same conceit is developed much more fully, with much greater specificity, topicality, cleverness, and wit. The other section of Jonson's masque that seems reminiscent of the eighth printed song of Campion's entertainment is the section that leads to the masque's conclusion. Here the parallels with Campion's work are often striking. At one point, for instance, Campion has a gypsy prophesy of James,

> Long shall thy three Crownes remaine,
> Blessed in thy long-liv'd raigne.
> Thy age shall like fresh youth appeare,
> And perpetuall Roses beare. (Davis 470)

And then another picks up the same theme:

> Many on earth thy dayes shall be,
> But endlesse thy posteritie,
> And matchless thy posteritie. (Davis 470)

Similarly, Jonson concludes a long and humorous song with the following invocation:

> Bless him, ö blesse him, heau'n, and lend him long
> To be the sacred burthen of all song,
> The Act[s] and yeares of all o^r *Kings* to outgoe,
> And, while hee'is mortal, wee not thinck him so./

In both cases the language and the sentiments are similar, but because Jonson's words are cast in the form of a prayer, they seem a bit less complacent and more contingent. Both poets deal with the issue of the King's mortality, but Jonson is perhaps more frank is facing the certainty of the monarch's inevitable death, despite (or perhaps because of) his expressed desire not to have to think about that prospect.

Both Jonson and Campion repeatedly concur that the King is—and should be—the focus of his subjects' love. Campion, for instance, has one of the gypsies prophesy that "Love, that bindes / Loyall mindes, / Shall make all hearts agree / To magnifie thy state and thee" (Davis 469). A little later, the chorus of gypsies wish that "Truth, Love, Honour, and Long-life attend / Thee, and all those that from thy loynes descend" (Davis 470). Jonson uses some of the same ideas and language when he has his gypsies pronounce that James "is not Lord alone of the Estate, / But of the *Loue* of men, and of the *Empire's* fate, . . . " (H&S 7: 614; ll. 1444–45). A little later he continues, making the Second Gypsy call the King's

. . . Pages *Bountie* and *Grace*, w[ch] many proue.
3. *Gip.* His guardes are Magnanimitie and Loue,
4. *Gip.* His vshers Counsell, truthe, and pietie.
5. *Gip.* And all that followes him, *ffelicitie.*/

(H&S 7: 614; ll. 1452–55)

In both cases the poets personify abstract qualities as royal attendants, but in Jonson's passage there is perhaps more emphasis on the King's own responsibilities (to be bountiful, gracious, etc.) and less emphasis on what he is owed by his subjects. A line from Jonson's masque that is perhaps more strictly in keeping with the spirit of Campion's occurs early in *The Gypsies Metamorphos'd*, when James is called "A Master of men, and that raigne in their hart[s]!" (H&S 7: 575; l. 298). Both poets stress that ideally James's power should be rooted in reciprocal love between the monarch and his people.

As Jonson's masque winds toward its close, one of the gypsies announces that

The sport[s] are done, yet do not let
Yo[r] ioyes in sodaine silence set;
Delight and dumbnes neuer met
In one selfe subiect yet.

(H&S 7: 612; ll. 1394–97)

Similar phrasing can be found in Campion's songs. The last line of the eighth song, for instance (which Spink believes was the last song of the masque proper), has a chorus of gypsies announcing that "Our nightly sports and prophesies wee end" (Davis 470). In addition, the next lyric, entitled "*The Farewell Song*" (which Spink believes was sung at the King's departure), exclaims, "O Joy! too soone thy flowers decay," and then the song laments that after the King's departure, "All will be dimme, all will be dumbe, / And every breast sad hearted" (Davis 470). The parallel references to finished sports, concluding joys, and saddening dumbness may be merely coincidental, but since they may have reminded James and other auditors of Campion's work when they witnessed Jonson's, they seem worth mentioning, whether or not the echoes were intentional. In any case, the conclusion of Campion's "*Farewell Song*," with its emphasis on the general happiness that results from the mutual love between a good king and his subjects, looks forward in phrasing and sentiment to the conclusion of *The Gypsies Metamorphos'd*. Campion writes of James that

Since wee this light must lose,
  Our love expressing,
Farre may it shine, long may it live,
  To all a publique blessing.

Similarly, the Captain of Jonson's gypsies, referring to the King, urges his auditors to

Loue, Loue his fortune then, and *vertues* knowne,
Who is the top of men,
          But make[s] the happinesse o[r] owne:
Since, where the Prince for goodnes is renownd,
The subiect w[th] *felicitie* is Crownd.
          (H&S 7: 614; ll. 1466–70)

Both works, in other words, end (as one might have expected) by emphasizing the harmony and concord between a good prince and his loving people. The ideal was conventional, as was much of the phrasing the passages share, but the totality of the resemblances between Jonson's work and Campion's seems more than a simple coincidence. We have proof, after all, that Jonson paid attention to other works by Campion, and that he responded to them in works of his own. If he did this in *The Gypsies Metamorphos'd*, he would have been doing nothing out of character, either for him or for his age. Imitation and emulation—even rivalry—were central to the experience of many writers during Jonson's time, and Jonson, in this respect as in so many others, seems to have been, in several senses, what Emerson would have called "a representative man." Certainly the impulse to re-present Campion's basic conceit—of gypsies prophesying to a king—seems to have been part of the genesis of one of Jonson's own best and most memorable creations.

It was the very importance of rivalry and competition in Jonson's life that must have made his relations with friends all the more significant and satisfying. We catch glimpses of those relations in many of his works, especially in the nondramatic poems, but evidence of a little-known yet intriguing friendship survives in a relatively unexplored manuscript that sheds interesting light on Jonson's social affiliations and intellectual concerns in the final decade of his career. Jonson's links with Joseph Webbe, examined in my next chapter, are interesting for what they suggest about his conception of poets and poetry at a time when he had already achieved a prominence so unparalleled that it had inevitably begun to fade. Webbe's respect for Jonson must have provided a kind of consolation, but it also suggests how seriously some still regarded the old poet's approval, even in the twilight of his career. As we shall see, Webbe turns to Jonson both as a friend and as an intellectual patron and ally. Even when the issues at hand were as apparently specialized as theories of poetry, grammar, and language, more fundamental matters of power and authority lay just beneath the surface.

7
Jonson, Joseph Webbe, and the Nature and Purpose of Poetry

Jonson's connection with Joseph Webbe is only slightly less well known than Joseph Webbe himself, yet both topics merit further attention. The link between Webbe and Jonson has not been emphasized by Jonson scholars; biographies mention it in passing if they mention it at all, and the standard edition of Jonson's works contains only a few allusions to his connection with Webbe.[1] Webbe himself has been the subject of only sporadic scholarly attention, although his importance has long been recognized by specialists familiar with his works. Thus Foster Watson, perhaps the leading early authority on education in the English Renaissance, devoted an entire article to Webbe and continually emphasized his importance.[2] Similarly, Vivian Salmon, who more than anyone else has enhanced our understanding of Webbe, has called him "one of the most intelligent and perceptive of all scholars working in the field of language in the early seventeenth century."[3] And it is, in fact, chiefly as a linguistic theorist that Webbe has gained his limited renown. His ideas about poetry—and his apparently close friendship with Jonson—are virtually unknown.

The evidence of that friendship and of those ideas is to be found in an epistolary treatise contained in a British Library manuscript, Sloane 1466.[4] Webbe's epistle—addressed to "his deare & louinge frend Mr. Benjamin Johnson" (203^{r})—has never been printed in full, and in fact a separate section of the epistle has previously gone unrecognized. In part the failure of Webbe's treatise to reach print is understandable, since the work's middle section is highly technical; Webbe seems to have had a strong mathematical inclination, and the middle portion is festooned with numbers, charts, and complex calculations. However, the opening and closing sections—the bulk of the work—are lucid and suggestive; their comments about the function and nature of poetry would be of interest even if they had not been addressed specifically to one of England's greatest poets, the man Webbe called his "Deare Brother" and "eldest sonne of our Brittaine muses" (204[r]). Moreover, the fact that Jonson apparently responded to Webbe's ideas increases their significance, although the location of his response is presently unknown. Webbe raises a number of issues that Jonson must have found intriguing, including such concerns as rivalry, misinterpretation, poetic imitation and composition, poetic method and inspiration, memory and reading as sources for writing, reason and enthusiasm, passion, genius, and fame, and a host of technical matters too numerous to mention. Webbe's epistle, in short, must have seemed well worth the consideration that Jonson evidently gave it.

However, before discussing in more detail Webbe's ideas or his links with Jonson, it first seems worth discussing Joseph Webbe himself. His thoughts on poetry were, after all, less central to his thinking and to his contemporary reputation than his broader views on language and linguistic education. He publicized those views in a number of books published in the 1620s, but his ideas had been developing over the course of many preceding years. Webbe seems to have been born shortly before 1560. Although little is known of his early life, he seems to have been educated in Italy, where he received degrees as Doctor of Philosophy and of Medicine. Records preserved in Rome show that as early as 1600 he was a Catholic, while other evidence suggests that he was still a Catholic during the early 1620s. This makes his friendship with Jonson all the more interesting, since the poet had been a Catholic himself during his early maturity.[5] Webbe's first known book, a work on astrology, was published in Rome in 1612, but by the start of the next decade, if not before, he had taken up residence in London.

It was during the 1620s that Webbe seems to have been most active in promoting his linguistic ideas, which centered on a new and even revolutionary method for teaching Latin. He had already published a translation of the *Familiar Epistles of M. T. Cicero* (probably in 1620), but in 1622 he issued his most explicit elaboration of his theories, *An Appeale to Truth*. In this book Webbe assaults the entrenched traditions of teaching Latin that had been codified in England with the publication of Lyly's *Grammar* almost a century earlier. He voices strong objections to the over-reliance on grammars and grammarians, and he sees the latter as having a vested interest in preserving tedious, ineffective, and inefficient methods of instruction. By focusing on individual words as the basic units of language and by drilling students in a plethora of isolated rules, grammarians (according to Webbe) wasted the time, energy, and goodwill of their pupils, who developed little sense of Latin as a living language and little capacity to use it as such. To remedy this educational failure, Webbe advocated a method of instruction much closer to modern "immersion" techniques, in which the student learns a foreign language as he learns his own—by using it and practicing it in concrete ways. Webbe regarded the clause, not the word, as the essential unit of speech, and his various books argue for introducing students to clauses rather than to grammar rules and isolated words.

Webbe was supremely confident that his method would prove successful, both financially and in the classroom.[6] He had already invested a sizable amount of his own money in developing his scheme, and in 1623 he issued *A Petition to the High Court of Parliament*, in which he outlined again the virtues of his methods and requested a patent that would reward his efforts and give him great control over the diffusion and application of his techniques. Details of the proposed patent show that Webbe had given careful thought to the means necessary for protecting and promoting his methods. Moreover, the *Petition* is quick to point out that Webbe had had King James's own "gracious eare and prince-like encouragement," as well as "the assent of many of the nobility, and the fauourable desires and wishes of some of the greatest scholars of this kingdom."[7] Whether Jonson was among this latter group is an interesting question; the fact that Webbe would later turn to Jonson for explicit support of a related project increases the likelihood that the poet, with his connections at court and among the nobility, may also have been a valuable ally of Webbe's earlier efforts.

Yet Webbe was not without antagonists, as well, and his *Petition* alludes to the strong opposition his ideas had aroused (3). Not only was he attacked by schoolmasters and by other intellectuals and educational theorists, but in 1623 he was also accused by John Gee, a militant Protestant, of using his teaching activities as a front for recruiting converts to Catholicism. Gee charged that "D. *Web*, in the *Old Bayly*, . . . pretendeth to teach a new gayne way to learne Languages, and by this occasion may inueigle disciples."[8] Yet Webbe himself seems to have been discreet about his religion, and despite Gee's charges and the other criticism he faced, by the spring of 1626 his patent had been granted.[9] He was now in a position to promote his methods more freely and profitably. Over the next few years, Webbe issued a number of new publications intended to promulgate his linguistic views and pedagogical techniques. Of these, *Usus et Authoritatas*, subtitled *Entheatus Materialis primus* and published in 1626, was the subject of his letter to Jonson.

Usus et Authoritatas was intended to assist students in the composition of Latin poetry. Vivian Salmon has aptly described it as "a list of words in Ovid arranged according to their metrical value, with instructions for combining them, lexically and rhymically [sic], into suitable verses" ("Joseph Webbe," 333). Although such a project might seem strictly unobjectionable, apparently this was not the case. Webbe's letter to Jonson, dated January 1628, alludes to the harsh criticism his project had received, and in the course of defending his views he says a number of intriguing things, not only about poetry and poets in general but also about Jonson in particular.

Webbe's comments about Jonson are interesting for a number of reasons. In the first place, they indicate the kind of reputation Jonson enjoyed in many circles in the late 1620s, a period when his health was failing and when the close connection he had once enjoyed with the Jacobean court seemed less firm now under Charles. Regular masque commissions had ceased, and Jonson had had to return to writing for the stage to supplement his income. Yet Webbe's letter suggests the sort of respect Jonson still enjoyed and the sort of influence his views could be expected to command. In appealing to Jonson for support, Webbe was appealing to a man whose opinions about poetry would carry great weight among the kinds of people to whom Webbe needed to appeal.

The regard Webbe felt for Jonson is suggested not only by the phrases from his pamphlet already quoted, but also by the concluding words of his dedication, in which he "wisheth [Jonson] Bayes; a marble, or some brazen statua; & perpetuall memory" (204ʳ). Webbe's opening words also suggest his close connection with Jonson and the esteem in which he held the poet: "Within yᵉ circuite of my best acquaintance, I find none of Apollo's Judges to grace more yᵉ seate of his Justice either wᵗʰ grauity of person; multiplicitie of reading, or depht [sic] of understanding; than you doe. Nor find I any, from wᵐ I should more ioyfull receiue applause for good, or more patiently tollerate, rebuke for ill;

then from ye doome of yours discretion" (204^{r}). This praise of Jonson must have appealed not only to the poet's self-conception but also to the public image he wished to present. Jonson had always thought of himself not simply as a gifted writer but also as a learned man, and Webbe's opening words—like his pamphlet in general—emphasize the importance of learning and understanding to both the creation and the assessment of poetry. Webbe appeals to Jonson, in other words, not simply as an eminent poet but also as an eminent intellectual, as a *doctus poetus*,[10] and his apparently close friendship with Jonson suggests that he expected that this sort of appeal would indeed prove appealing to the poet.

As a piece of rhetoric, Webbe's epistle exhibits tones and stances that also seem characteristic of Jonson himself. This is particularly true of the epistle's self-defensive posture. In addressing Jonson, Webbe was seeking support from an old veteran of intellectual combat, and Webbe's letter is interesting in part for the light it sheds on the contentious aspects of the intellectual life of his time. Webbe asks Jonson to "Giue mee . . . leaue to intreate none but you to lift ye Bilance betweene my last booke, & some ill Sauouring breath of Malice, now call'd emulation; & to make a iust report of both theyre valewes" (204^{r}). The role of judge was, again, a role that Jonson could have been expected to enjoy, and various circumstances (to be discussed later) suggest that Webbe not only expected but received a basically positive reply.

For the moment, however, it seems worth quoting Webbe more fully, both because his pamphlet has never before been published and also because his early comments are quite suggestive about the social context in which his ideas were developed and received. What Webbe's treatise shows is that even the most technical matters could become issues of heated and personal contention. In appealing to Jonson, Webbe was appealing not only to the poet's learning and judgment but also to his social prestige.

In refuting his unnamed antagonists, Webbe claims that

[204^{r}]

To giue answerres unto all ye Cauills, y^{t} many busy braines suggest as weightie, will neither sort well wth my leysure to write y^{m}, at y^{s} present, nor wth yours to read y^{m}: nor being answered will they much aduantage our present busienes: nor, past wth silence, can they great hinder us. In y^{t}, ye most part, measuringe my future intention, by theyre present capacity therof, mistake my marke & shoote at theyre owne fantasies: choosing rather to gaine opinion of knowledge, by blurting out some thing, nothing to ye purpose; than by patience & mature deliberation & expectance to saue theyre future reputation from ye staine of ignorance.

Many of theyr snarling toothlesse arguments against us are allready answeared in to little English bookes of two howres* reading: & many are by practice & experience daily now confuted; soe y^{t} such as are not herby satisfied, read not, understand not, or seeke not to be satisfied: or else haue other ends y^{n} to be thus satisfied: as in particular may well appeare about our present Entheatus. [204^{r} / 204^{v}]

Some under ye cloake of loue tell mee they are sorie it was euer printed, some cannott endure to looke uppon it because I made it. Others houlde it an idle toy not worth theyre fingering. yet all these confesse they understand it not.

Now good S^{r}. tell me; did equitie or malice make these men iudges or were they of theire owne choosing y^{t} would soe rashly tax a thing y^{t} they y^{m}selues confesse they know not. These men are condemned by their owne confession & their needes noe further proofe against y^{m}: wee will theirefore spend noe longer tyme about y^{m}.

But their are yet others, y^{t} thinke they understand it; & hould it to be a pretty thing but they for sooth can fynd out boyes y^{t} can make ten verses out of theyre owne braines beefore another shall make one out of our booke. Now good S^{r}. aske y^{m} how long their boyes haue beene a learning to make verses: & they will answer you, as a boy of west minster answered mee, y^{t} he hath beene 7 yeares about it. And y^{n} I know you will make some difference betweene 7 daies and 7 yeares of learning any thing.

Next aske y^{m} whither theyr boyes could in 7 weakes after they beganne make soe good a verse as ours shall wth in 7 howres after he hath had our booke.

Aske y^{m} alsoe whither were better for a boy to be trayned up in his owne conceipts [in] words; for wch he hath noe Authoritie, or to bee brought up in Ouid or Virgill whom wee reade in Schooles (as it is thought) to imitate.

Aske y^{m} next whither hast in making verses bee to bee commended: y^{t} they soe much commend ten for one: surely if hast had made good verses, Virgil had beene shamed; who soe many tymes corrected, & blotted one and ye same verse before it passed.

Aske y^{m} yet whither an habitt in verses bred out of Ovids or Virgils authority; would not bee more to ye purpose of those y^{t} seeke perfection therin: y^{n} y^{t} wch is made out of rules, rude wordes, & Childrens fantasies: wch by our booke well understood & frequently used may in farre shorter tyme y^{n} 7 yeares be perfectly gotten.

Several things are of interest here. First is the way Webbe keeps Jonson constantly in mind, continually alluding to that

"Good Sir" and inviting him to take an active role in Webbe's defense. The effect is to increase our sense of the intimate link between the two men, and one wonders whether Webbe would have used this tactic if his connection with Jonson had not in fact been close. Webbe seems to have felt that he could take Jonson's sympathies for granted, and certainly some of the ideas he expresses are thoroughly Jonsonian in spirit and even in phrasing. For instance, his emphasis on poetic imitation as a route to creativity is thoroughly in line with Jonson's own beliefs and practice,[11] while his condemnation of hasty writing and his stress on thoughtful deliberation could easily have come from Jonson's own pen.[12] His concern that learning should be rigorous without being tedious jibes with views Jonson himself expressed in his *Discoveries*,[13] while his impatience with self-indulgent pedantry is an attitude Jonson could be expected to endorse.[14]

Webbe's next few comments can be summarized rather than quoted. He complains that his critics are judging his larger project without full knowledge of it; he defends his book against the charge that its preface is too short, arguing that his aim was clarity, not obscurity; and he explains his decision to write the book in Latin, reminding his critics that his "intent was rather to make y^{m} to make verses, y^{n} discourse of verses" (205^{r}). He continues, asserting that

[205^{r}]

> My desire is to please all men, but that's impossible; & therfore, I am unwillinge y^{t} any thing of mine should come into any hands but such as are of a Candid nature; & will rather make a good construction of y^{t} they cannot, or at least haue not don, y^{m}selues: than bee soe farre transported out of malice or some other passion y^{t} they forgett y^{m}selues and wander as wide as hee did who hauing formerly detracted from mee: & houlding himselfe therby tyed to maintayne his undertaken detraction like a great & religious Schollare slighted Ouids owne (& those of his choiycest) verses as noe way comparable to Ouids uaine onely because hee thought that I had made them. [205^{r} / 205^{v}]
>
> If any one will wth reason Confute mee, I will thanke him, for I hate error as much as any man, yet let him giue mee leaue, to sift & examin y^{t} reason, whether it will hould ye touch or noe: for nothing more deceiueth man; than seeming reason: But if any man that's arm'd wth malice set uppon mee, I must leaue him to his armes. For I hold it prohibited amongst good Christians to play those kind of prises. and I hould y^{m} alsoe unworthie of y^{t} name, y^{t} use y^{t} hatefull & sedi^{ci}ous weapon. yet I shall find a Champion to incounter him mag-

num habet et saluore purgatorium patiens homo, qui suscipiens iniurtas plus dolet de alteriq malitia quam de sua iniuria: vit. Chr:

A number of points in this passage would have struck a sympathetic chord in Jonson. Thus, Webbe's uneasy relationship with his readers, his sense of his susceptibility to malicious interpretation, his singling out of a specific (and foolish) critic, and his appeal to reason as his first defense: these are all, of course, characteristic Jonsonian stances. His allusion to Christ as his champion and his claim to turn the other cheek in the face of detraction are perhaps less typical of Jonson, but there has been little in the treatise so far—either in its substance or its rhetoric—that Jonson would have found objectionable.

Up to this point, Webbe's emphasis has been more on answering his critics than on explicating his own ideas, but now his focus shifts. In the course of explaining his views more fully he makes a number of intriguing assertions about the nature and sources of poetry—assertions that were probably of genuine interest to Jonson. Alluding once more to his critics, Webbe claims to

[205^{v}]

perceiue w^{t} these men looke after, they would but gape & haue verses ready made fall of their owne accords into their mouthes to euery sense y^{t} they but thinke on. nay many would not bee soe much as troubled, wth thinking uppon any sense; but would ye booke turne of it selfe, prompt y^{m} wth sense, poynt out wordes to expresse y^{t} sense, & make these wordes fall out good Latine, & perfect verses. All wch in uery truth it doth if they consider it & had but the perfect use therof.

Now to declare y^{s} use yet further & make it more apparant, Wee are to lay y^{s} ground worke. That all sense is explicable by wordes: as all figures or Images may be fram'd in wax, words therfore are ye Poets wax.

This wax must haue some place to keepe it in, whether ye Artificer may uppon all occasions resort for matter for y^{t} Image hee would worke uppon.

These places are two. Memorie, or Bookes

Of these ye readiest place & nearest ye pea is Memorie. But ye securest place both for us & our posteritie is Bookes: & 'tis a place of greatest Charitie for euery man of poorest memorie may borrow here w^{t} another mans rich memory denyeth him. What am I ye better for Ouids memory or any mans else, if wee can make noe use of it. I confesse a happie memory is a rich store house, but it is like a rose at Christmas for ye rariety; & y^{n} it dures but little for it dwels [205^{v} / 206^{r}] wth in ye man y^{t} owneth it, & cannot be left unto his heyres, but dyes w^{n} ere here [sic] dyes y^{t} lodged it.

And, not ye places of y^{s} matter onely; but the matter it selfe also may bee manyfold, pure, impure, or these mingled. The wax y^{t} our booke affordeth is virgin wax, pure matter, & Ouide: wch subscribe y^{s} affirmation. But y^{t} wch is in memory cannot allwayes bee warranted free from pollution unlesse it were taken from some such fountaine.

Be it w^{t} or where it will bee ye Eye of Reason is Suruayer of ye workes. for first it limitts w^{t} breedth lenght, & thicknes ye whole Image should bee of. As of ye lenght of an Hexameter, Pentameter or any other: of ye bredth of 13 . 14 . 15 . 16 . 17. Syllables if it bee an Hexameter, if a Pentameter of 12 . 13 . 14 . & those Syllables of ye depth of . 3 . 4 . 5 . 6 . 7 . or more wordes And for all those it appoynts modells & formes, of sundry sorts to supply euery diuersity eyther of occasion or Election in ye Artificer. All these diuersities both of formes & matter must bee as well in memory as in my booke & as well in it as in memory otherwise Reason will want matter & tooles to worke wth all, & both these store houses should be defectiue.

Webbe derides those readers who seek a book that will obviate the need for independent thinking; his own book, he makes clear, is not a substitute for thought but an accessory to it—a means of assisting the process of creativity rather than of rendering it obsolete. Webbe assumes, significantly, that all sense is explicable, that whatever can be thought can be expressed. For him, "sense" precedes language; thoughts find *expression* in words. Whereas more modern theorists might insist on the ways that language (as a preexisting system) precedes and shapes thought or "sense," for Webbe the process is just the opposite. His emphasis on the value of books and reading as resources of poetic creativity would very likely have appealed to Jonson, certainly one of the best-read and most learned of English poets.[15] The idea that books preserve for posterity the thoughts that memory is too fragile and evanescent to retain is one with which Jonson may have sympathized, particularly at his current stage of life, when his own memory seemed less dependable than before.[16] Yet Jonson had always shown an appreciation of books and a scrupulous interest in the printing of his own texts, which he obviously viewed as the means by which his own "sense" and "rich memory" could be "left unto his heyres" (205^{v}–206^{r}). Webbe's emphasis on the value of books helps provide a contemporary context for Jonson's very similar assumptions. Webbe's comments on this matter suggest one of the reasons that Jonson seems to have been attracted both to Webbe and to Webbe's treatise.

But what about Webbe's emphasis on Ovid? Would Jonson have empathized with this? We normally think of Jonson as a writer influenced more by the likes of Horace and Martial than by Ovid, but his many borrowings from and allusions to Ovid indicate that he had read this predecessor carefully (H&S 11: 654). According to D. Heyward Brock,

> Like Spenser, Marlowe, and Shakespeare, Jonson was very attracted to Ovid. The young Ovid is a central character in *Poetaster*, and he is frequently referred to in other plays. . . . Ovid's works served as an important source for a number of entertainments and masques. . . . In *Timber* . . . , Jonson alluded to Ovid's comment that there is a god within and we glow when he stirs us, and this inspiration comes from heaven.[17]

As we shall see, this latter point is quite relevant to the conclusion of Webbe's treatise. For the moment, however, it seems safe to say that Jonson would have had little objection to Webbe's focus on Ovid, and certainly he would have sympathized with Webbe's stress on "ye Eye of Reason" as "Suruayer of ye workes" (206^{r}). Here as throughout, Webbe's conception of poetry—like Jonson's—assumes the active exercise of intelligence and judgment. Neither man conceived the poet as merely a passive vehicle for divine inspiration; both emphasized the need for intellectual engagement and discipline.[18] Webbe's book was designed, in part, to help "supply euery diuersity eyther of occasion or Election in ye Artificer" (206^{r}). Such phrasing implies a poet who is responsive both to his circumstances and to his own best judgment.

The next section of Webbe's treatise is far more technical than its predecessors; exposition frequently gives way to charts, lists, figures, and calculations. The gist of Webbe's argument at this point stresses the phenomenal comprehensiveness of his system, with its capacity for generating the maximum possible number of metrical combinations. Webbe justifies this comprehensiveness by arguing that "ye more uniuersall an art is ye lesse it sauoureth of imperfection"—even if this means including verses that make no sense (206^{v}). Webbe's methodology might seem—and to his opponents undoubtedly *did* seem—extraordinarily mechanical, but in fact his point is that his methods are generative, abetting independent creativity precisely because they are so thoroughly comprehensive. Webbe aims for the sort of inclusiveness that no single memory could hope to match. His goal was to provide students with "a pocket booke" (207^{r}), crammed with possibilities, that would inspire individual inventiveness. It is hard to imagine that Jonson would have had much objection.[19]

Not surprisingly, Webbe saves some of his most interesting ideas for last. In his final section, he returns not only to his focus on Jonson but also to the kinds of larger themes with which the treatise began. Much of his thinking here is Jonsonian in spirit and emphasis, even if its phrasing is more metaphorical than Jonson might have fancied. Once again, extensive quotation may be useful:

[209^{r}]

But let me further tell you y^{t} all y^{s} wax or matter of our Image or ye Image it selfe that's made therof; is but ye cloathing of an in ward thing, for whose better expression you shall know that.

Wee haue · 2 · striplings to cloth, ye one of matchlesse beutie; the other a Neger or a Blackamore.

The black a moore is nothing else but humane concept inuention or Imagination: ye best skinne of y^{s} striplinge is alwaies black, as being tainted wth y^{t} night wherin euery man was since his greatest Grandfather, conceiued. But according to ye mould of Reason & y^{e} in-&-out workes therof, he hath his shape eyther perfect or imperfect. for if memorie bee short you, & find y^{s} stripling want a legge or an arme. If ye Imagination bee crooked; hee will haue a poult foot or a crook backe, or a bakers legge, if any of ye senses faile or bee superfluous hee will haue 6 toes uppon one foote & but . 4 . uppon ye other. But if Reason her selfe bee crazed, she in tumbling, falls all in peeces. & y^{n} our stripling is a monster. for sometymes you shall find him borne wth ye head betweene his legges; sometimes ye leggs breast & buttacks; some time ye legge & armes, sometime ye knees & [209^{r} / 209^{v}] elbows; will change places; or else you will find him all head or all body; or nothing in ye world but all confusion: And thus you shall often fynd him in weake boyes & strong fooles, who by their flexible age, & crooked passions, may be wrested & mishaped. If therefore wee desire to mend y^{s} mould of Reason, let us for a time cast away owre owne & put our reason in ye mould of our ancient maisters & w^{n} it hath beene by y^{m} for some yeares better moulded, let us use it.

This black stripling is many times to willing in some men in w^{t} form soeuer to be clothed. And in some other hee is abrode or fast a sleepe, & will not be awaked or clothed till ye stringes of our memorie bee sweetly touched: those sweete stringes of memory are your Topick places wherof Euery page, nay euery word of euery page wthin our Entheatus allready printed is a sweete & shrill sounding string at ye skillfull touche & twange wherof y^{s} stripling if hee bee at home will be soone awake & fall a dauncing for thoughe his reall habitation bee our braine from whence hee seldome wanders; yet now & y^{n} he loues to run a wolle-gathering. And ye dores by wch this boy goes out & coms in are ye senses.

The other beautifull & glorious stripling y^{t} is to be clothed, dwels not in any part of us, but farre aboue us & aboue all other creatures And comes neuer in or goes out but by ye garden gate of our reason: & y^{t} alwaies about midnight, but w^{r}soeuer hee comes into, his presence makes our whole palace more lightsome y^{n} ye poore Sonn. Neyther comes he to euery man, but to some choyce ones & those for ye most part y^{t} are of cleare & pure mindes. And w^{n} hee comes hee will not stay wth any man longer y^{n} he pleaseth: but soe purified himselfe in such sort y^{t} he may take delight in his companie, hee shall haue him often. And he bringes wth him a playne easie booke, of a fayre letter written in euery mans owne character & language, wherin is contained all ye true knowledge, w^{ch} ??? man hath beene in vaine a seeking through all ye Arts & sciences [209^{v} / 210^{r}] inuented since ye fall of Adam. And this booke is redde in an instant & understoode wthout plodding. But you can neuer reade it but by y^{t} light y^{t} y^{s} naked Childe bringes wth him. If you can hansomly win y^{s} Childe & haue his Companie you need not goe to th'Uniuer[si]ties. If any man goe about to clothe y^{s} striplinge, or rather if hee would be cloathed by any man, he appoynts his owne apparell; wth out welt or garde, yet uery desent: And in his choyce hee's neyther superfluous nor deficient; for hee'le not weare a button or a poynt more or lesse, y^{n} w^{t} is needfull. But who soe hath ye fortune or grace to clothe him & bring him to ye vewe of ye world hee makes ye man y^{t} clothed him much admired: for euery man thinks ye pöet made him, but ye truth is otherwise hee made ye Poet. But to speake noe more of y^{s} striplinge wthout his owne light, I will onely name him & leaue him. This is y^{t} true Eutheisiasmus, or Plato's Enthuseasis qui potest capere, capiat.

Though much more may be sayde in ye behalfe of this little booke: yet let this suffice you for ye present. And let report & it bee iudg'd by your opinion. Meane
while I rest

Your deuouted frend
and brother

Glassenburyhouse
in Smithfield: Jan:
20 . 1628 :

Joseph. Webbe.

Webbe's argument in this final passage is more nuanced than his somewhat clumsy imagery might suggest. He shows himself capable of a kind of discrimination that gives his closing thoughts significant precision. On the one hand, he accepts the standard Christian view that the human mind is flawed because of sin, and he stresses—like Jonson himself—the crucial role of Reason.[20] Also like Jonson, he warns against "crooked passions"

(209v)—the kinds of foolish and corrupting humours that the poet so often mocked. Interestingly, Webbe suggests that imitating the best works of the best writers not only promotes the creation of valuable new works but also—more importantly—helps shape the mind of the creator himself.[21] For Webbe as for Jonson, the quality of creativity is intimately connected with the quality (and qualities) of the poet's mind and character.[22] The process and discipline of imitation that Webbe envisages are as much ethical as strictly technical in their purpose and intended results.

Webbe, no less than Jonson, is suspicious of hasty composition, which implies a lack of judgment.[23] At the same time, however, he is critical of mental sloth. His book is meant to provide discipline and direction on the one hand, and incentive and stimulation on the other. Significantly, he envisages his book not as a substitute for memory but as a means of prodding it into action. The earlier emphasis on the distinction between books and memory as sources of creativity is here replaced by a different emphasis on books (or at least on Webbe's books) as tools for strengthening and sharpening mental powers.

Webbe's ensuing discussion of inspiration or enthusiasm might seem at first to make any reliance on books unnecessary, as his comment about not needing to "goe to th'Uniuersities" suggests (210r). However, he also asserts that such inspiration is usually granted to those whose minds are "clear & pure" (209v). Once again Webbe (like Jonson) links intellectual and ethical qualities; surely the word "pure" carries this double meaning, and Webbe builds on this sense by suggesting that the man who has "purified himself" is more often likely to be inspired (209v). Inspiration or "enthusiasm," then, is not merely or entirely a matter of passive receptivity; instead, it is a matter of conscious and deliberate *preparation*. No one, Webbe makes clear, can will himself to be inspired, but the poet can cultivate his mind, talent, and energies in ways that will make inspiration more likely. With all of this Jonson would surely have agreed, as numerous of his writings make clear.[24]

Webbe's closing stress on enthusiasm might seem to conflict with what we normally think about Jonson's poetics, so often associated with classicism, common sense, and sensible restraint. Yet Jonson frequently makes clear his attraction toward such enthusiasm, and he sometimes even claims to be inspired.[25] As several writers have observed, there was an enthusiastic aspect to Jonson's character, both as a man and as a poet; little that Webbe says here would have conflicted with Jonson's own instincts.[26] Besides, Webbe describes enthusiasm in a way that paradoxically emphasizes its balance and measure: in his stylistic "clothing," the "glorious stripling" is "neyther superfluous nor deficient; for hee'le not weare a button or a poynt more or lesse, y^{n} w^{t} is needfull" (210^{r}). Enthusiasm, in other words, produces precisely the kind of stylistic decorum and good sense that Jonson so admired and so often achieved.[27]

Surely Webbe must have felt that Jonson possessed one of those "clear," "pure," and indeed "purified" minds that made poetic inspiration likely.[28] His opening praise of Jonson, to which he returns briefly here, makes this clear. And surely Jonson would have found much more to appreciate in this treatise than simply Webbe's friendly tributes. I have already indicated, in my text and notes, the many points on which Webbe and Jonson were likely to have agreed, and because of this agreement Webbe's ideas help provide an interesting context for Jonson's own. However, what seems worth stressing, in closing, is the evidence Webbe's own text provides of his confidence in Jonson's basic concurrence with his views.

The clearest indication of that concurrence is Webbe's reference, on the title page of his work, to an "an[s]werre" that Jonson had provided. Unfortunately, the poet's reply to Webbe is missing from Sloane 1466, and the standard edition of Jonson's works even suggests that the answer was "torn out" (H&S 11: 359). While this is uncertain, neither is it unlikely. Evidence indicates that the documents in the collection were once arranged differently than at present,[28] and if anything must have seemed worth removing, it would have been Jonson's reply.[29] Even in its absence, however, we can still make safe conjectures about the nature of Jonson's answer. After all, Webbe would have been unlikely to address his treatise to the poet if they had not already discussed its basic contents and if Webbe had not been given some reason to assume Jonson's basic sympathy. His opening praise of Jonson indicates that he expected his treatise to receive a literally friendly reception, while the title page's allusion to the poet's "an[s]werre" suggests that his expectations were not disappointed. Webbe apparently intended to circulate his treatise and Jonson's response among influential readers such as Samuel Hartlib, and he may even have planned to publish both his letter and the poet's reply.[30] All signs point, then, to Webbe's assurance that he and Jonson essentially concurred—a confidence, it seems, that we can confidently share. Everything points in that direction. Webbe's treatise on poetry is a document valuable not only in its own right but also for the light it sheds on Jonson's thinking and intellectual milieu.

However, the defensive tone of Webbe's treatise itself and its appeal for Jonson's support both indicate that ideas, then as now, did not develop in a social vacuum. The history of ideas is necessarily also social history, and Webbe's concern with rivals, as well as his interest in Jonson's intellectual patronage, both resemble key themes in Jonson's own career. As my earlier discussion of his poems to the Earl of Newcastle has already suggested, Jonson's own concern with patrons and patronage was at least as pronounced in his final decade as it had been earlier, and this is an issue to which my final chapter now returns.

8
Jonson, Weston, and the Digbys: Patronage Relations in Some Later Poems

The importance of patronage to Jonson's career has already been suggested, but it is particularly evident from even a cursory glance at any collection of his nondramatic poems. Many if not most of the poems are explicitly addressed to patrons, and all the poems seem fundamentally conditioned by a culture grounded in patronage relations. But while patronage has often been discussed briefly in criticism of Jonson's poems, that discussion has sometimes seemed rather abstract. In fact, it is surprising how little we know about Jonson's flesh-and-blood patrons and about his day-to-day dealings with them. The brief biographical notes provided by most editions inevitably (and necessarily) stick to the most basic details. Even readers who attempt to track down further information will often face frustration: for many of Jonson's patrons only the barest biographical facts are readily available, and determined digging frequently turns up few more. But the more we know or can knowledgeably speculate about his dealings with his patrons, the better we can appreciate his purposes and achievements and the particular accomplishments and complex texture of his works. As this book has tried to demonstrate, information about the social contexts of those works is not so much "background" to Jonson's writings as it is essential to a richer appreciation of their peculiar artfulness.[1]

One of the most important patrons of Jonson's last decade was Richard Weston, for years a highly influential minister in the government of Charles I. More is known about Weston's life than about the lives of many of Jonson's other patrons, but the poems Jonson addressed to Weston have rarely been examined closely. Studying them seems worthwhile for a number of reasons. Not only can doing so provide new insights into the skill and success of these particular works, but it can also suggest significant aspects of Jonson's more general experiences and achievements as a patronage poet. The poems to Weston illustrate, for instance, the crucial importance of such intermediaries at a time when the poet's relations with the King and his status at court were less secure than they once had been. In fact, looking at Jonson's connection with Weston provides an opportunity to look more closely also at his relations with Sir Kenelm Digby, the editor of the 1640 Folio and another highly influential link in Jonson's connection to the Caroline aristocracy. One of the most intriguing poems of patronage Jonson ever wrote was addressed through Digby's wife to Digby, through Digby to Weston, and through Weston to the King and court. Examining the poem can not only give us a glimpse into the complex world of Stuart patronage, with its tangled networks and reciprocities, but can also suggest new facts about the circulation of (and relationships among) Jonson's poems themselves.

The poems to Weston and Digby also illustrate a number of other factors important to Jonson's more general experience as a patronage poet. For example, his willingness to identify himself so closely with Weston—a highly controversial figure—seems unusual for Jonson, and may suggest something about the changed nature of his status at the Caroline court and about the more general changes that had taken place between the court and the "country" during the Caroline period. The poems to Digby and Weston also exemplify how praise of superior patrons could be worked into celebrations of their social inferiors; how complex and uncertain Jonson's relations with his patrons could often be; how that complexity and ambivalence could be reflected in the detailed texture of his works; how various poems to the same patron could be linked in meaning and theme; how distrustful Jonson was of the growing importance of the visual arts at the Caroline court; how the intellectual habits and interests of his patrons may have influenced the kinds of poetry he wrote; how genuinely accomplished many of the poems of his last years are; and how effectively Jonson used his wit (in poems that sometimes discomfit readers who bring romantic and post-romantic critical assumptions to them) to promote himself and his work in the literary and social hierarchies of his day.

I

Wit was always one of Jonson's most potent resources for dealing with his patrons. John Aubrey reports that King James, on the spur of the moment, gave his poet £100 after Jonson delivered a jocular grace in doggerel verse before dinner one evening.[2] Jonson seems to have used his wit most effectively when his need was greatest, especially in his final decade. Through it he was able to communicate some sense of the depth and desperation of his want while still seeming dignified and free of self-pity. When he was most powerless and weak, wit lent the impression that he still had power over himself, that he was still in control. It also gave him license to tease his patrons about their behavior without seeming strictly censorious. A humorous request for help, moreover, was likely to be more persuasive than persistent hectoring, and the potential rejection of a witty request was also easier to accept because less of one's public dignity or "face" had been risked. Jonson's typical approach is illustrated by the poignantly clever "*Epistle Mendicant*" (*Und.* 71) he addressed sometime in the early 1630's "*To the Right Honourable, the Lord high Treasurer of* England," Richard Weston:

> MY LORD;
> POore wretched states, prest by extremities,
> Are faine to seeke for succours, and supplies
> Of *Princes* aides, or *good mens* Charities.
>
> *Disease*, the Enemie, and his Ingineeres
> *Want*, with the rest of his conceal'd compeeres,
> Have cast a trench about mee, now, five yeares;
>
> And made those strong approaches, by *False braies*,
> *Reduicts*, *Halfe-moones*, *Horne-workes*, and such close wayes,
> The *Muse* not peepes out, one of hundred dayes;
>
> But lyes block'd up, and straightned, narrow'd in,
> Fix'd to the bed, and boords, unlike to win
> Health, or scarce breath, as she had never bin,
>
> Unlesse some saving-*Honour* of the *Crowne*,
> Dare thinke it, to relieve, no lesse renowne,
> A *Bed-rid* Wit, then a *besieged* Towne.

Although Jonson claims that his muse is handicapped and incapacitated, the very skill with which he constructs and elaborates the poem's controlling analogy proves otherwise; his indirect description of his disabilities and anxieties renders the poem's success all the more impressive. When, in the final line—after having sustained the comparison of small things to great for such a span (itself an indication of strength and poetic power)—when after all this Jonson finally concedes that he *is* a small thing, merely "A *Bed-rid* Wit," the reader is unwilling to accept the description: the accomplishment of the poem refutes the intended diminishment. The implicit promise of renown that Jonson offers Weston and the King should they come to his aid seems all the more persuasive after the performance just ended: his protest of weakness testifies, paradoxically, to the real and enduring potency of his skills.

Jonson's decision to address his "*Epistle Mendicant*" to the Lord Treasurer was more significant than a first glance might suggest, for Weston's importance at court transcended his role as one of Charles's chief financial officers. Following Buckingham's assassination, Weston had risen to become the single most influential figure at Whitehall beneath the King, and although he never enjoyed the kind of intimacy with Charles that had given Buckingham such sway, his power was still enormous. His control of naval, Irish, financial, and foreign policies was predominant; only in matters of religion and the church did his arch-rival, Laud, exercise more leverage. Although he had been a respected member of the House of Commons while also serving King James as Chancellor of the Exchequer, after 1626 he came to be viewed—somewhat unfairly, it would seem—as one of Buckingham's lackeys.[3]

Certainly Weston was a determined supporter of the Crown; on the famous and fateful day of the parliamentary disorder in March 1629, when members tried to resist the King's decree of adjournment, the House had rung with calls for Weston's impeachment.[4] His appointment to the dual position of Lord Treasurer of England and Treasurer of the Exchequer in July 1628 had helped make him even more widely hated than he had previously been, for Weston took seriously the task of reducing by whatever means possible the Crown's bloated expenditure and debt. One means he hit upon—sharply cutting back the amount paid out in pensions—helped make him as unpopular at court as he was in the country at large.[5] The fact that Weston himself was reaping huge profits from his office while trimming funds for others did not enhance his standing. "Although the Treasurer's official salary was only £365 a year," William Van Cleave Alexander reports, "he received many times that amount through fees and gratuities." According to G. E. Aylmer, "a Lord Treasurer who was watchful of his own interests but not technically corrupt was said to be able to make £ 7000 a year." Alexander estimates that Weston's profits from the office were "in the neighborhood of £ 11,000 or £ 12,000 yearly." Combined with the income he received from his real estate holdings and from other sources, Weston in the early 1630's probably had at his disposal £ 17,000 to £ 18,000 per annum.[6]

Much of this money was spent as soon as it was received, for since 1627 Weston had been building a lavish new family estate in Surrey to advertise and strengthen the power he now enjoyed at court. Painters and other artisans had been put to work decorating the new mansion, which Weston apparently saw as the seat of the family he hoped would soon be raised to membership in the titled aristocracy. His creation in February 1633 as first Earl of Portland fulfilled this ambition, while the marriage of his son and heir the previous year to one of Charles's relatives must have bolstered his confidence that the King's favor would continue. Any such bolstering was welcome, for even a figure as powerful as Weston—or perhaps especially one as powerful as he—had good reason to wonder just how long his fortune would endure. Weston's potent enemies at court would have been delighted by his downfall and were not above attempting to engineer it. These included not only Laud, but even from time to time the Queen. Clarendon describes Weston as being

> of an imperious nature, and nothinge wary in disobligeinge and provokinge other men, and had to much courage in offending and incensinge them, but after havinge offended and incensed them, he was of so unhappy a feminine temper that he was always in a terrible fright and apprehension of them. He had not that application, and submissyon and reverence for the Queene as might have bene exspected from his wisdome and breedinge, and often crossed her praetences and desyres, with more rudeness than was naturall to him; yet he was impertinently sollicitous to know what her Majesty sayd of him in private, and what resentments shee had towards him; and when by some confidents (who had ther ends upon him from those offices) he was informed of some bitter expressions fallen from her Majesty, he was so exceedingly afflicted and tormented with the sense of it, that sometimes by passionate complaints and representations of the Kinge, sometimes by more dutifull addresses and expostulations with the Queene in bewaylinge his misfortunes, he frequently exposed himself, and left his condition worse then it was before. . . . He quickly lost the character of a bold, stoute, and magnanimous man, which he had bene long reputed to be, in worse tymes, and in his most prosperous season, fell under the reproch of beinge a man of bigg lookes, and of a meane and abjecte spiritt. . . .[7]

As long as Weston retained the confidence of the King, however, his enemies could not effectively hurt him, and at the time Jonson addressed his poem to Weston, the Lord Treasurer's power was great and still growing. With his large personal fortune he must have seemed as capable as anyone at court of relieving the poet's financial distress. But to Jonson, temporarily alienated from the King, Weston's ability to influence the "saving-*Honour* of the *Crowne*" (13) must have seemed even more significant.[8]

II

The year after he composed the "*Epistle Mendicant*," Jonson was presented with an opportunity to make the most of his own connection with Weston, and of Weston's connection with the King. Already in 1630 it had been rumored that Weston's son Hierome had become engaged to marry "one of the Blood-royal of Scotland, the Duke of Lennox's sister, and that with his Majesty's consent." But Hierome's wedding to Lady Frances Stuart did not in fact take place until 25 June 1632. Contemporary observers were astonished by the match, since it seemed in most respects "a very unequal one, the young duchess being very much above him in fortune and birth"; but Charles himself intervened to help bring the negotiations to a successful conclusion. Not only did he bestow a present of £ 10,000 upon Lady Frances, but he also showed the couple "extraordinary favour" in agreeing to give away the bride.[9]

Charles's avid interest in promoting the marriage could only serve to confirm and enhance Weston's power at court, but it must also have seemed to bode well for Hierome's future standing there. Weston had hopes that his son would be appointed Secretary of State or Master of the Court of Wards; already he had proven useful to the King on an important diplomatic mission, and he would shortly depart on another. The marriage and the poem it inspired thus offered Jonson the chance to help improve his standing in the eyes of the King and Queen, to strengthen his ties with the King's chief minister, to win the favor and good feelings of a young man whose own favor at court seemed sure to increase, and to display his artistic powers on the occasion of one of the most important social events of the year.[10]

As much a tribute to Weston as to the bride and groom themselves, Jonson's "Epithalamion" (*Und.* 75) also places particular emphasis on the example and role of Charles and his queen. Written in stanzas of eight lines (a number associated with marriage in the Renaissance) and extending over twenty-four stanzas in all (perhaps to suggest the twenty-four hours of the day), the epithalamion addresses the sun, bidding it to stop on its progress in order to witness and lend glory to the wedding. Later, after the ceremony is completed and the newlywedded couple have retired, Jonson is at pains humorously to hasten the sun on its way, so that nightfall and the consummation of the marriage can occur. The address to the sun contributes to the poem's complexity of tone, for while the sun is regarded as a most fitting witness to so glorious an event, Jonson also implies that the sun's splendor seems secondary to the occasion he describes. His attitude toward the sun is alternately respectful and familiar, and helps the poem achieve its delicate balance of good humor and dignity, of wit and decorum, of public festiveness and private delight. Moreover, by figuratively stopping the sun's progress in his poem, Jonson helps call attention to the sense in which the epithalamion does precisely that—the sense in which it stops time, to celebrate, preserve, and commemorate a day whose importance the poem at once mirrors and creates.

Already in the first stanza Jonson indicates the central role Charles and Henrietta Maria will play in this celebration of another couple's marriage. The "Epithalamion" is as much a tribute to the "bountie" of the King and Queen (8), as much a glorification of their own wedded love, as it is a commemoration of Hierome's wedding day. In part Jonson's emphasis on the royal couple simply reflects the cult of married love that had already become a dominant motif of Caroline court culture; in part it reflects his natural impulse to address himself to his most important patrons. But the emphasis is hardly extraneous, not only because Jonson is careful to integrate it thematically with the rest of the work, but also because it was the very participation and interest of the King and Queen that helped make Hierome's wedding such a momentous and memorable event. By stressing the centrality of Charles and his wife, Jonson does not distract attention from the young couple, but instead thereby underscores their importance.

The centrality of the King and the Queen to the "Epithalamion" is more than merely thematic, however. They are quite literally central to the poem—or rather, they share that central position with Weston, the groom's father. The poem's two middle stanzas, the center around which the rest of the work revolves, focus squarely on the grace, favor, and bounty their royal majesties show to Weston, and on the diligent and loyal service he returns. It is as if Jonson suggests that the gap of white space that separates the stanzas and divides the poem is bridged by the reciprocal devotions of the royal couple and their chief minister: what the King and Queen give to Weston in the way of "Dignitie, and Honour" (92)—including the dignity and honor they bestow by participating in this wedding—is returned to them by means of Weston's "Wisdome" and "Counsells deep" (98). The theme of union, which is so obviously crucial to the poem and which appears under such various guises as the union of man and wife, of France and England, of the earth and sun, and the physical union of the two sexes, here takes on still another dimension. In the same way that the love of Charles and Henrietta Maria sets an example for all other marriages, so the link the poem celebrates between Weston and the royal couple becomes a pattern, a standard of ideal reciprocity between ruler and subject, between patron and dependent. The literally central positioning of Weston, Charles, and the Queen thus allows Jonson to underline through the form of the poem one of the chief implications of its content. At the same time, it also allows him to pay his patron Weston a particularly meaningful compliment, for although the concept of a "sovereign centre" was conventional in Renaissance aesthetics, in Jonson's poem the center is shared between the sovereigns and their principal subject.[11]

Harmony is both the subject and the method of the epithalamion, and its importance is reinforced in different ways at different times as the poem proceeds. In the opening stanza, for instance, the balanced reference to the "bountie of a King, and beautie of his Queene" (8) helps emphasize alliteratively how the monarchs bring together and reconcile qualities that seem to have little in common; later Weston himself is praised, with a greater sense of paradox and through effective use of chiasmus, for having led "Mens Loves unto the Lawes, and Lawes to love the Crowne" (104). Similarly, in the stanzas just before the middle of the poem, the King and Queen are hailed as an exemplary bride and groom at the precise moment that Hierome and Frances make their entrance into the chapel. The syntax and subject references in the immediately succeeding lines are so complicated and obscure that it is sometimes difficult to tell at first when one couple and then the other is being referred to. When the sun is asked, for instance, whether in all his days he has seen "that Paire" who "became these Rites so well" (76), the reader can be forgiven for momentarily supposing that Hierome and Frances are intended. In the next line it becomes clear that Jonson means the King and Queen, but the ambiguity here and elsewhere seems deliberate rather than careless. Jonson emphasizes the connection between the royal couple and the newlyweds just as he emphasizes the connection between the Weston family's future and their future service to the Stuart dynasty and British state. The poem celebrates a harmony achieved (at many different levels) at a single moment of history, and then it projects that moment into the future, imagining the continuity of the Weston line, the endurance of the happy marriage, and Hierome's capacity to follow in his father's footsteps as a servant to the Crown. It reconciles youth and age, life and death, night and day, church and state, sexual desire and chaste thought ("The holy perfumes of the Mariage bed" [162]), and all the various elements of the court. In its final stanza, in words that epitomize the gentle humor and delicate decorum of the poem, Jonson wittily uses an economic metaphor involving public exchange to characterize the most private relations possible:

They both are slip'd to Bed; Shut fast the Doore,
  And let him freely gather Loves First-fruits,
Hee's Master of the Office; yet no more
  Exacts then she is pleas'd to pay: no suits,
    Strifes, murmures, or delay,
      Will last till day;
    Night, and the sheetes will show
The longing couple, all that elder Lovers know.

This final image, with its stress on the perfect reconciliation of potentially opposed impulses, captures some of the flavor of the entire work. Although Hierome is credited with superior power and with the right to "Exact" what he desires, Jonson makes it clear that that power is not abused. And more important, he makes it clear that there is no reason for its abuse, since what Hierome might exact, his wife is freely willing to bestow. This image of perfect concord—in which all conflict and opposition are overcome, in which service to one's superior is also identical with the perfect satisfaction of one's own desire—resonates so strongly because it echoes so much that came before it.

The whole epithalamion celebrates, claims to preserve, but (more significantly) attempts to foster and create this kind of unity and accord. The poem is so powerfully appealing precisely because the harmony it exalts is inevitably unstable and could exist perfectly only in a work of fiction. Like many of Jonson's celebratory works, the function of the poem is as much persuasive as festive. It attempts to conjure up (by making so attractive) the harmony it exalts. It betrays an awareness of the fragility of what it commemorates, and yet this awareness makes its commemoration all the more valuable and inviting. Jonson's willingness to admit details into the poem that implicitly or explicitly seem to contradict the harmony it praises is a tribute not only to the work's complex sophistication but also to its pragmatic usefulness. At one point he no sooner praises the bride's beauty than he admits that some spectators had come to rebuke the simplicity of her dress (43–44). Shortly after praising Weston, he refers bitingly to those who envy Weston's good fortune (118–20). Moments after the wedding ends, Jonson projects the marriage's survival in the face of "canker'd Jealousie" and "all corroding Arts" (135–36). He mentions prominently Bishop Laud's participation in the ceremony, although Laud and Weston in real life were often political rivals (132).[12] And he beseeches long life for Weston at a time when Weston's health was in decline (181–84).[13] The poem celebrates Weston's power while subtly indicating its inherent uncertainty. It exalts in his triumph over his enemies, but it never pretends that his enemies do not exist. It praises the Treasurer, but it also attempts to cultivate the favor of the King and of Hierome. And in so doing it promotes the interests of all three men as well as those of the poet. It is in some respects very much a political poem, in both the larger and smaller senses of that term. Far from being a passive record of a day's events, it is an attempt to make the meaning and symbolic significance of those events reverberate into the future. And in all these ways it calls attention to its own utility and accomplishment. One of Jonson's longest lyrics, the Weston epithalamion is also one of the most intriguing, evocative, and richly sophisticated works of his final period. Only a much more detailed analysis could hope to do it justice, but even these remarks may suggest that it is hardly the uninspired product of an old poet's weariness.[14] Even in the final five years of his life, Jonson's poetic powers were far from extinguished. Viewing the epithalamion as a poem of patronage helps us appreciate more fully the complexity of its artistic achievement.

Jonson had more than the usual reasons for wanting to turn in an impressive performance when he came to write this work. His recent disappointments at court, and the news he had received that the King himself was at least momentarily displeased with him for attacking Inigo Jones (the royal architect) must have made him realize that Charles's favor could not be taken for granted. The epithalamion must have seemed an ideal patronage vehicle—not only providing an opportunity to regain the King's admiration and further enhance his standing with Weston, but also thereby repairing any damage done to his reputation and self-esteem. The work is an ambitious undertaking, but superbly carried off. Its success reflects credit on its patrons, and cannot have hurt Jonson's estimation in their eyes.

III

Jonson's concern around this time that Inigo Jones was besting him in the competition for court patronage and prestige seems to have been heightened by his more general misgivings about the growing popularity of the visual arts among the English aristocracy. The social status and financial success of painters grew as more and more of the English ruling class, imitating their Continental counterparts, took an increasing interest in painting. Often the aristocrats who seemed most friendly toward literature and who were the most conscientious patrons of poets were also the ones with the keenest interest in gathering, subsidizing, and displaying paintings. Art collecting and commissioning had become increasingly common activities in the last half of James's reign and in the early years under Charles. The Earl of Arundel—a close friend of Weston—set an example for many of his peers by amassing the first great private collection in England of painting, sculpture, and antiquities, and it was not long before he and Buckingham found themselves in competition for some of the same *objets d'art*. At first Buckingham seems to have begun collecting more because it seemed the thing to do than because of any genuine aesthetic appreciation, but this in itself is of great historical interest. What is particularly fascinating about Buckingham, as Graham Parry has written, "is the cultural style adopted by a man who suddenly found himself equal with princes and endowed with bewildering amounts of money."[15] Much of that money, it would seem, found its way into the hands of visual artists, who could help to magnify—literally—their patron's image at court. By the time of his death the Duke seems to have developed a genuine taste for art, and his own example as a connoisseur was perhaps as important to the developing prestige of painting as the works he commissioned.

Charles himself seems to have had an even surer interest in and eye for art than the royal favorite. He had inherited collections of paintings from his mother and elder brother, and visiting dignitaries and aspiring courtiers presented him with numerous other works over the years. In no time his collection became one of the most renowned in Europe, and such continental masters as Van Dyck, Rubens, and Gentileschi found profitable employment at the English court. Given the monarch's passionate enthusiasm for the visual arts and for painting in particular, it would have been most unusual if Charles's courtiers did not also begin to cultivate and display such tastes. Poetry had always had to compete with painting for aristocratic attention, but by the early 1630s the practical position of the poet in relation to the visual artist must have seemed in some ways far less secure than before.

In "*An Epigram*" to Richard Weston written around this time (*Und.* 77), Jonson emphasizes the superficiality of the visual arts and credits the Lord Treasurer with a taste too sophisticated to be seduced by them. But the compliment may well veil a more critical attitude, for as Jonson knew, Weston had spent or was spending large sums to decorate his new palace. To assist him, he had

> procured the services of Balthasar Gerbier, a Dutchman who had once been associated with Buckingham and was now the accepted arbiter of fashion in the capital. Gerbier made suggestions concerning the design of mantelpieces and balustrades and recommended the hiring of craftsmen, painters, and sculptors. . . . Gerbier also assisted with the layout of Weston's garden and served as an intermediary between him and Hubert Le Sueur, who was commissioned to cast an equestrian statue of Charles I. . . . He was to receive a total of £600 for the statue, which was one of the highest prices paid for a work of art during the 1630's. [16]

Obviously this commission was motivated as much by political considerations as by aesthetic enthusiasm; Le Sueur was one of Charles's favorite artists, and for that reason alone it must have seemed sensible for Weston to patronize him. In 1629, the year before the contract for the statue, Weston had also commissioned a painting from Van Dyck, "which was ultimately presented as a

New Year's gift to the King."[17] At home and at court, then, Weston realized the practical value of the visual arts, but his friendship with Arundel suggests that his appreciation was genuine as well as pragmatic. Jonson's "*Epigram*" eloquently testifies to the importance Weston attached to art, while perhaps also tacitly criticizing that interest:

IF to my mind, great Lord, I had a state,
 I would present you now with curious plate
Of *Noremberg*, or *Turkie*; hang your roomes
 Not with the Arras, but the *Persian* Loomes.
I would, if price, or prayer could them get,
 Send in, what or *Romano, Tintoret,*
Titian, or *Raphael, Michael Angelo,*
 Have left in fame to equall, or out-goe
The old Greek-hands in picture, or in stone.
 This I would doe, could I thinke *Weston* one
Catch'd with these Arts, wherein the Judge is wise
 As farre as sense, and onely by the eyes.
But you I know, my Lord; and know you can
 Discerne betweene a Statue, and a Man;
Can doe the things that Statues doe deserve,
 And act the businesse, which they paint, or carve.
What you have studied are the arts of life;
 To compose men, and manners; stint the strife
Of murmuring Subjects; make the Nations know
 What worlds of blessings to good Kings they owe:
And mightiest Monarchs feele what large increase
 Of sweets, and safeties, they possesse by Peace.
These I looke up at, with a reverent eye,
 And strike Religion in the standers-by;
Which, though I cannot as an Architect
 In glorious Piles, or Pyramids erect
Unto your honour: I can tune in song
 Aloud: and (happ'ly) it may last as long.

By opening the poem as he does, Jonson announces his good intentions while signaling less directly his financial need. If to his "mind" (his intention as well as his intellectual capacity) he had a commensurately impressive "state" (worldly condition; monetary fortune) he would present Weston with costly "plate" and "hang [his] roomes" with rich tapestries and paintings. He would ("if price, or prayer could them get") present Weston with works by the great painters and sculptors of the Italian Renaissance. The similarity in sound of "price" and "prayer" only emphasizes their semantic distinctions, while at the same time suggesting how the second word—and the idea it represents—can be debased and corrupted. "Prayer," which should signify self-abnegation and devotion to higher spiritual ideals, is here associated with the proud pursuit of selfish desire, with a need for the kind of worldly, superficial self-distinction the visual arts can provide. The Italian artists Jonson lists have achieved a kind of personal fame undreamt of by the "old Greek-hands" they have surpassed, whose very anonymity suggests how far they have been outstripped, how much they have been forgotten.

Of course, as the poet slyly suggests, it was in fact Weston who enjoyed the kind of "state" about which Jonson could only surmise; it was Weston who had the money to spend—and who was spending it—on the sorts of items the opening lines detail. What might be called Jonson's "subjunctive generosity" may have been intended to prompt present favors from Weston by reminding this "great Lord" of the poet's slender means. Jonson's avowed inability to carry out his magnanimous wishes not only emphasizes his straitened circumstances but also indicates the high cost of visual art and the kinds of competition for it that existed. The poet's strategy seems to have been not only to make Weston feel a bit guilty about the sums he was spending, but also to cast doubt on the value he was getting for his money.

In fact, in a sudden shift that emphasizes poetry's dynamism in contrast to the static nature of painting and sculpture, Jonson in line 10 begins to take back and undo what he had seemed to promise in the epigram's opening. Using his own artistry to catch his readers by surprise, he claims that even if he were able to present Weston with gifts like those itemized in the opening lines, he would not do so, since Weston is incapable of being "Catch'd with these Arts, wherein the Judge is wise / As farre as sense, and onely by the eyes" (11–12). The verb "Catch'd"—metrically underscored—is significant, suggesting a sort of danger and deceptiveness about these crafty "Arts" (while perhaps also implying something sinister about the motives of some of their practitioners). Jonson credits Weston with the same kind of acute perceptiveness he himself demonstrates in assessing Weston's character: Jonson is able to discern the Treasurer's discernment. Both are well studied in the "arts of life." If Weston is willing to accept the poet's compliments to his acuity, then he must accept as well Jonson's assumptions about the visual arts. Jonson attributes both to himself and to his patron an insight that contrasts implicitly with the merely surface perception he claims those arts at once demand and display.[18]

The fact that Jonson's poem alludes to a similar work by Horace is only another means of testing the acuity of Weston and his other readers: only those sufficiently alert and perceptive will hear the echo. Yet for readers who do, the force of Jonson's poem will be magnified and its tact and power increased. The allusion to Horace helps protect the poem and sanction it, helps make his complaints against the visual arts seem less personal, more insulated from private envy, more enduringly archetypal. It helps suggest the extent to which the conflict between poetry and the visual arts is ageless and impersonal, even as it slyly suggests how Horace both achieved and bestowed a kind of personal fame not won by the artisans with whom he competed. The allusion here is hardly an example of sterile conventionality; instead, it illustrates how Jonson could apply and adapt the work of past writers to very real and specific contemporary situations. Any implied criticism of Weston or of rival artists issues not only from Jonson's pen but from Horace's, too.

Jonson's poem, however, is much more concerned to praise its patron than Horace's had been, just as its tone is much more insistently personal, much more obviously rooted in a deeply felt relationship. For Jonson, the visual arts are inadequate not only because of their superficiality, but because of their static quality, their inability to celebrate Weston's character as reflected in his deeds. Weston "Can doe the things that Statues doe deserve, / And act the businesse, which they paint, or carve" (14–15)—a formulation that implicitly points up the incapacity of statues, paintings, or carvings to imitate such doings, such actions, in the fullest sense. Only the lively art of poetry—in which words, like men, move through time—can do justice to Weston's accomplishments, which are actions informed by contemplation, by a "studied" familarity with the "arts of life" (17). In fact, by describing some of Weston's accomplishments in the immediately ensuing lines, Jonson practices the powers he claims for his art, while depicting Weston himself as a kind of poet, able

> To compose men, and manners; stint the strife
> Of murmuring Subjects; make the Nations know
> What worlds of blessings to good Kings they owe:
> And mightiest Monarchs feele what large increase
> Of sweets, and safeties, they possesse by Peace.[19]

The emphasis throughout this passage is on the verbs, an emphasis that underscores both Weston's deeds and poetry's capacity to render actions as painting cannot. As if to accentuate this point even further, Jonson next describes the same deeds as if they had been rendered visually, as if he were scrutinizing a painting or statue: "These I looke up at, with a reverent eye, / And strike Religion in the standers-by" (23–24). The effect of the lines is complicated: on the one hand they suggest that Weston's deeds are more impressive, in and of themselves, than any statue or painting of them could be; but the lines also imply the inability of a painting or statue to render a full and complete account of any deed that is truly great. Moreover, the syntactical ambiguity of the lines helps emphasize Jonson's potential role in enhancing Weston's reputation. Who or what, precisely, "strike[s] Religion in the standers-by?" When the lines are re-read, it seems clear that the reference is to "These" actions of Weston's. But for a moment the "strik[ing]" can seem to be done by Jonson—as indeed, on further reflection, in one sense it is. One intention of his poem, after all, is to pay striking tribute to Weston, and one of its competitive claims is that it can do this more effectively than the visual arts. The momentary syntactical confusion, which might at first seem merely clumsy (and which might thus exemplify the relative *weakness* of poetry), on second thought seems an instance of the meaningful ambiguity of Jonson's craft.

Although Weston's accomplishments have the potential impact of a powerful icon, the implied comparison only stresses the frozen inertness of the visual arts. It is hardly an accident that Jonson chooses in the last lines to contrast his "song" (a word itself suggesting fluidity and grace) not with painting or with sculpture—which can at least suggest movement and vitality—but with the inescapable solidity of architecture. Yet the contrast has the further effect, paradoxically, of reminding us of the architectonic skill of Jonson's poem.

The concluding reference to "an Architect" (25) seems a double blow—specific and generic. In all probability the poem was written during Jonson's feud with the king's architect, Inigo Jones; but the last few lines suggest indirectly that *no* architect could do what Jonson modestly (if somewhat disingenuously) professes himself incapable of doing. His presentation of himself as a humble songster, modest about the capacities of his own art, comes with a certain irony at the end of a poem that so effectively argues the shortcomings of other artists and their media. But it also serves, perhaps, to balance the slight suggestion of satire in the reference to "glorious Piles, or Pyramids" (26). The poem was, after all, addressed to a man who was just then building or had recently completed the kind of prodigy house to which Jonson objected so strongly in his poem "To Penshurst" (*For.* 3).

The zenith of Weston's power and influence at Charles's court was reached in February 1632/33, when the King himself bestowed on the aging Treasurer the sword and mantle that signified his new rank as Earl of Portland. Jonson wrote an epigram for the occasion, but its purpose was perhaps as much to attack Weston's enemies at court and in the country as to celebrate the Earl himself. Weston by this time had become "the most controversial member of the government, with scores of enemies and detractors as well as friends and supporters."[20] Jonson's allegiance to the Earl—his willingness to risk making himself an enemy of Weston's foes—suggests not only that the Treasurer had already proven a valuable patron but also that Jonson expected his influence to continue. His elevation to the peerage, in fact, meant that his power and social prestige would no longer depend simply on his tenure in appointive office; and it also meant that Hierome was no longer simply the Treasurer's son but was also the prospective successor to his father's Earldom.[21] Thus Jonson's provocative epigram "*To the Envious*" (*Und.* 73) must also have seemed a risk pragmatically worth taking. His willingness to align himself so distinctly with one court faction is a clear measure of his confidence in Weston's staying power in the face of all opposition:

LOoke up, thou seed of envie, and still bring
  Thy faint, and narrow eyes, to reade the *King*
In his great Actions: view whom his large hand
  Hath rais'd to be the *Port* unto his *Land*!
WESTON! That waking man! that Eye of State!
  Who seldome sleepes! whom bad men only hate!
Why doe I irritate, or stirre up thee,
  Thou sluggish spawne, that canst, but wilt not see?
Feed on thy selfe for spight, and shew thy Kind:
  To vertue, and true worth, be ever blind.
Dreame thou could'st hurt it; but before thou wake
  T[o]'effect it, feele, thou'ast made thine owne heart ake.

The epigram not only draws distinctions of character and image between Weston and his detractors—they with their squinting "narrow eyes" that "wilt not see" (2; 8), he the personified "Eye of State" (5)—but it also attempts to depict Weston's enemies as enemies of the King. Indeed, the description of the Lord Treasurer just quoted may have been consciously intended to allude to similar phrasing in the epithalamion composed less than a year earlier. There Weston was depicted—as he is depicted here (5)—as a "waking Man" (111), but in the epithalamion it was Charles who was associated with "That farre-all-seeing Eye" (109). Jonson chooses to emphasize the King's particular role in Weston's elevation, both for the obvious reason of self-interest and in order to make his rebuke of Weston's foes all the more authoritative. The Treasurer's enemies are counseled "to reade the *King* / In his great Actions" (2–3), and although William Hunter glosses the verb "reade" as meaning to "learn from,"[22] clearly another of the word's functions is to help call attention to the action of Jonson's poem itself, which facilitates the kind of "reading" it prescribes. Still, the point of the epigram is less to educate "*the Envious*" than to torment them. Jonson's emphasis on imperative verbs, prominently positioned and metrically stressed, gives the poem a kind of violent energy, while his open and avowed contempt for those he attacks contrasts nicely with their suppressed but seething spite. By the final line one may agree with him that Weston's antagonists have made their own hearts ache, but one recognizes as well the role his poem has played in exacerbating their vexation.

The full skill of the poem does not become obvious until one has a chance to re-read it. Then its underlying logic and patterns of imagery emerge into clearer view. The opening command, for instance—"LOoke up, thou seed of envie"—is variously effective. The first two words not only anticipate the later, more explicit emphasis on Weston's moral and social elevation, they also indicate already the debased status of those who envy him. It is as if Jonson has surprised a nest of vermin by turning over a rock; their "faint, and narrow eyes" wince at the light his poem casts upon them. He commands them (the very first word suggesting the authority the whole poem claims) to "LOoke up"—not only at the King and Weston but implicitly at the poet. The stature he openly ascribes to his patrons he tacitly assumes for himself. Just as the monarch and Earl can look down on the envious, so indeed does Jonson. The opening command is part of a pattern in the poem emphasizing upward movement—a pattern illustrated, most obviously, by the King's "rais[ing]" of Weston. But here the upward movement of the envious creatures' eyes only causes them to sink deeper into jealousy, torment, and discontent, whereas Weston's elevation supposedly makes him less vulnerable (even if more subject) to their hatred.

The creatures Jonson attacks are the "seed" of envy in several senses: they are its seat, its residence; they are its offspring; and they are its source, the infected sperm by which its virulence is spread. Jonson uses a word associated with life, vitality, and healthy procreation precisely for its ironic effect: these seeds represent not life but a kind of death, not generation but corruption, not propagation but a force that is ultimately self-destructive. The word implies the various ironies associated with these creatures, but it also suggests their smallness, their moral insignificance. Nonetheless, Jonson's contemptuous tone cannot quite mask his perception of the threat they pose.

Jonson's emphasis, in line 2, on their "eyes" is significant for several reasons. In the first place, the mention of their squinting eyes not only contrasts with the later reference to Weston as the wide-open "Eye of State" (5) but also links up with the description of him as a "waking man" (5). Indeed, the pattern of images involving sleep, wakefulness, dreaming, closing eyes, and eyes wide open helps organize the entire poem. The envious do squint, but they do not clearly see—unlike the Earl, whose vision serves the King; unlike the King, whose perception has led him to elevate Weston; and unlike the poet, whose insight allows him to appreciate and interpret for others his patrons' greatness. Weston's vision is comprehensive, all-embracing; the fact that this is so implies already that the envious are less a threat to him than they might be to a less observant man. Yet Weston's vision, like the poet's, is ostensibly focused less on his own interests than on the state's. The reference to the "narrow eyes" of the envious might at first suggest their acuity, but in fact Jonson implies how their sight is distorted—unlike his own, which allows him to perform the act of reading and interpretation he calls for in this poem. The King becomes a text within a text: both he and Jonson's poem raise and celebrate the Earl; both he and the poem demand the kind of scrutiny and appreciation the poem itself provides. By reading the King's actions and writing about them, Jonson makes it possible for others to understand them as clearly as he does. The poem offers itself for interpretation even as it interprets for others; it asks to be read, while offering its own reading of Weston and the King.

Jonson claims that Charles has raised Weston to be the "*Port* unto his *Land,*" but the poet's play on the Earl's title, which might at first seem somewhat strained, is not without its merits. Its very playfulness helps contribute to a somewhat light-hearted tone (suggesting strength and self-assurance) that balances both the sneering condemnation and the exclamatory praise that characterize the poem's phrasing elsewhere. Weston is the port—the haven, the source of security and stability in a time of storms—to an England increasingly rocked by political, religious, and economic strife.[23] Of course, to Weston's enemies this claim must have seemed extremely ironic, since they viewed him as one cause of the nation's troubles, or at least as a major impediment to their solution. But Weston was a "port" in the second sense of being a crucial entry-point to the world of power and influence: anyone who sought access to the King and court would have to contend with him.[24] The witty phrase, which at first may seem almost *too* witty, gains added point on reflection.

Jonson's description of Weston as a "waking man"—a phrase that suggests his alertness and vigor—may have seemed somewhat ironic in view of the Earl's declining health, but the phrase also suggests his powers of perception and observation and thus the danger he could still pose to enemies in general and to the envious in particular.[25] The fact that he is someone "whom bad men only hate" (6) testifies both to his power and to their fear. Jonson's phrasing here—especially his placement of the adverb—is typical of a technical skill for which he is still given too little credit. "Only" glances both ways: it can modify the words that precede it as well as the one that follows. The fact that bad men can feel only hate for Weston exemplifies the stunted moral sense that helps to make them bad, and it also reinforces the earlier suggestion (in the reference to their "narrow eyes" [2]) of their constrictions and limitations. But Jonson's phrase can also be read to mean that only bad men hate Weston; good men (such as the King and Jonson) not only value him but exalt the goodness the Earl himself exhibits. Here as so often elsewhere in Jonson's poetry, a single word, exactly placed, resonates with finely tuned artistic and moral implications.

Jonson's stirring up and irritation of the envious "sluggish spawne" (7–8) not only looks back to the phrasing (and develops the implied situation) of the opening lines, it also emphasizes by contrast the constant wakefulness of Weston. The word "spawne" obviously recalls the "seed" mentioned earlier (although the connotations of the later word somehow seem less pleasant), while the adjective "sluggish" highlights by contrast not only the vigor of the Earl and King but also the vitality of Jonson's own poem, with its heavy use of active verbs, its emphasis on clipped monosyllables, its frequent brevity of phrase, and its sprinkled exclamations. The energy of the epigram contrasts with the moral sloth of those it indicts, whose only self-motivated action is an obstinate refusal to act, a perverse determination "not [to] see" Weston's worth. This willed blindness, paradoxically, allows others to see Weston's enemies for the corrupt breed they really are. Their refusal to see and appreciate Weston's true nature reveals their own natures (their own "Kind"); their blindness not only stands opposed to Weston's wakefulness but casts them into a darkness far blacker than the earlier references to their "narrow eyes" and sluggishness had suggested. Of course, Jonson's emphasis on the ways in which they reveal themselves deemphasizes, on one level, the revelatory purpose of his poem, but on another level the phrasing insinuates the poet's role in "shew[ing]" the true natures of those he attacks. The poem's very existence exempts him from the charges of envy and ethical blindness he hurls at others.

Jonson's penultimate injunction—"Dreame thou could'st hurt it" (11)—not only glances back, of course, at the already well-developed pattern of images involving sleep and waking, but also anticipates the final echo of that pattern in the last word of this line ("wake"). The verb "Dreame" implies that Weston's enemies can only fantasize about hurting him, that their power is so limited as to be almost laughable. This, of course, was hardly the case (as Weston well knew and as the epigram's existence suggests); it was in fact the reality of the threats Weston faced that may have made him appreciate a poem such as this.[26] The ambiguity of Jonson's pronoun "it" is not without some point: the momentary confusion it causes forces the reader to puzzle out its referent more intently than might have been true if the word's meaning had been clearer. The word seems to look back to the earlier reference to Weston's "vertue, and true worth" (10), two nouns that Jonson treats as a single quality that transcends Weston yet is embodied in him. To attack Weston, Jonson implies, is to assault Goodness itself.

The poem's final imperative verb—"feele" (12)—is most obviously addressed to the envious and calls attention to the pain they ostensibly have caused themselves. But the verb also helps call attention to the last effect (and to the overall effectiveness) of Jonson's poem: what we as disinterested readers "feele" in the last line is the final twist of Jonson's irony. The poet here is cleverly modest: although he claims that the envious have made their "owne heart[s] ake," the causing of such pain has, of course, been one of the epigram's chief objectives all along. The pain the envious feel is heightened by their sense not only of Weston's but of Jonson's triumph, a triumph that becomes part of the subject of this poem, especially in its final line. Jonson obviously derives a double pleasure from his work: not only the joy of celebrating Weston but the glee of humiliating their mutual enemies. The epigram's sudden, final shift from the anticipated but illusory pain the envious hope to inflict on Weston to the reality of their own suffering underlines, again, the poem's vigor; the turn comes with a stabbing abruptness.

Only in the final line, in the penultimate word, does Jonson raise the possibility that he may have a single envious person in mind: he refers, after all, to a "heart," not "hearts." In retrospect, all the earlier words that could have been read as plurals could also have been read in a singular sense: "*Envious*"; "seed"; "Thy"; "eyes"; "thee"; "spawne"; "thou." Only "heart," almost at the very end of the poem, unambiguously suggests a single target. Of course, the absent "s" may simply have been a slip; if not, it raises intriguing questions about whom Jonson may have had in mind.[27] Perhaps he intended no one in particular, but meant simply to give the finale the force of a highly personal indictment, as if each individual reader should examine his own conscience to see if he might be guilty of envying the Lord Treasurer. Whatever the case, it seems highly appropriate that this poem so stuffed with vigorous verbs should end on one, and that that verb should be "ake" (12). This is a verb that suggests no outward action but merely an inward pain. The "sluggish spawne" will now feel nothing but a prolonged and vexing torment.

IV

Jonson had experienced vexations of his own in the months preceding the composition of the epigram just discussed. His play *The Magnetic Lady*, staged in the fall of 1632, seems to have been more successful than the disastrous *New Inn*, but it still provoked derision from his antagonists. Inigo Jones was apparently present on opening night and found the play hilarious in ways Jonson had not intended, while Alexander Gill—the son of a man Jonson had attacked years earlier—unleashed a satire that elicited the old poet's answering scorn.[28] Jonson's epigram celebrating King Charles's anniversary day in November did not prevent the Queen from selecting another courtier to write the New Year's holiday masque—a decision that made Jonson more dependent than ever for patronage on such second-level figures as Weston and his son.

In an intriguing "*Epigram To my MUSE, the Lady* Digby, *on her Husband, Sir* KENELME DIGBY" (*Und.* 78), Jonson indicates the practical importance he attached to the approval of aristocrats like Weston. The poem also indicates how literary works could be circulated—and how a literary reputation could be built—in a court culture dominated by patronage relations:

THo', happy *Muse*, thou know my *Digby* well,
  Yet read him in these lines: He doth excell
In honour, courtesie, and all the parts
  Court can call hers, or Man could call his Arts.
Hee's prudent, valiant, just, and temperate;
  In him all vertue is beheld in State:
And he is built like some imperiall roome
  For that to dwell in, and be still at home.
His brest is a brave Palace, a broad Street,
  Where all heroique ample thoughts doe meet:
Where Nature such a large survey hath ta'en,
  As other soules, to his, dwell in a Lane:
Witnesse his Action done at Scandero[o]ne;
  Upon my Birth-day the eleventh of *June*;
When the Apostle *Barnabee* the bright
  Unto our yeare doth give the longest light.
In signe the Subject, and the Song will live,
  Which I have vow'd posteritie to give.
Goe, *Muse*, in, and salute him. Say he be
  Busie, or frowne at first; when he sees thee,
He will cleare up his forehead, thinke thou bring'st
  Good *Omen* to him, in the note thou sing'st,
For he doth love my Verses, and will looke
  Upon them, (next to *Spenser*'s noble booke,)
And praise them too. O! what a fame 't will be?
  What reputation to my lines, and me,
When he shall read them at the Treasurers bord,
  The knowing *Weston*, and that learned Lord
Allowes them? Then, what copies shall be had,

What transcripts begg'd? how cry'd up, and how glad,
Wilt thou be, *Muse*, when this shall them befall?
Being sent to one, they will be read of all.

Digby was the son of Sir Everard Digby, a Gunpowder Plot conspirator who had been executed for his role in that attempted treason. Kenelm had remained a Catholic throughout his early years, and although he attended Oxford, his inability to endorse the Thirty-nine Articles meant that he could not be "admitted as a regular resident in a college."[29] Nonetheless he won recognition for his intelligence, and in 1617 was mentioned (along with Jonson) as a potential member of a proposed Royal Academy. Although that plan fell through, Digby's social and intellectual standing continued to grow. In 1621 he toured Italy, where he lectured, collected books, and met Van Dyke (whom he later patronized). In 1623 he was knighted and (around this same time) became a Gentleman to the Privy Council of the Prince. However, Buckingham's antagonism toward Digby's uncle, the Earl of Bristol, clouded the young man's prospects for significant further advancement.[30]

Another complicating factor was his romantic involvement with Venetia Stanley. They had fallen in love at an early age; his first trip to the Continent, in fact, seems to have been viewed by his mother as a means of separating him from Venetia. During his absence, reports may have reached her that Kenelm had died; for this reason or others, she apparently became involved with another courtier. Learning this, Digby determined to forget her, but a chance meeting after his return led, in 1625, to a secret marriage. The hint of scandal that had become attached to Venetia's name was eventually dissipated by her conduct as Digby's wife. By all accounts she was very beautiful, but Digby seems to have admired her as much for her intelligence and understanding as for her physical attractiveness.[31] Thus Jonson's praise of her as his muse is, for several reasons, more than a conventional compliment: it accords well with the image Digby himself liked to present of his wife; it bolsters Digby's efforts to rehabilitate her reputation; and it may in fact reflect Jonson's genuine regard for her intellectual accomplishment. Moreover, in a court that was placing increased stress on the ideal of married love, Jonson's celebration of the Digbys could only reflect well on all concerned.[32]

In the years following his marriage, Digby's own intellectual and social status continued to grow. Late in 1627—realizing, perhaps, that Buckingham's ascendancy limited his prospects at court—he began to equip a small fleet for a voyage of plundering and privateering in the Mediterranean. Official papers commissioning the expedition authorized it as "tending to the service of the realm and the increase of [Digby's] knowledge."[33] In fact the voyage was profitable on practically all counts. Digby's victory over a superior Venetian fleet "furnished the occasion of his earliest feat of public self-propaganda and patriotic posturing, namely 'Relation of a brave and resolute Seafight made by Sir Kenelm Digby . . . to his great Commendation and to the Honour of our English Nation.'"[34] The pamphlet's timing was superb, for after recent military setbacks under Buckingham, Digby's triumph "revived the country's international dignity a little."[35] Buckingham's assassination a short time later removed a potentially troublesome obstacle to Digby's further advancement, and indeed in the next few years—when Jonson's poem was written—his influence at court was at its height. Not long after his return to England he was appointed to a number of official posts, was awarded various monopolies, and was considered a possible candidate for Secretary of State.[36] His friendship with Weston did not prevent him from maintaining close relations with Laud, at whose suggestion he donated many valuable books and manuscripts to the Bodleian Library in 1632.

His interest in literature went beyond book-collecting, however. During his Mediterranean expedition, Digby found time to compose not only a report about his famous battle but also a journal of the voyage; an English translation of Tasso's *Aminta* (now lost); the *Loose Fantasies* (his most famous creative work); and *Observations on the 22 Stanza in the 9th Canto of the 2nd Book of Spenser's Faery Queene*, the first sustained piece of Spenser criticism ever published.[37] The *Observations* present a complicated numerological analysis of one of the most obscure passages in the whole of Spenser's epic. Digby considered the obscurity deliberate and claimed that "were nothing else extent of Spencers writing, yet these few words would make me esteeme him no whit inferior to the most famous men that ever have been in any age: as giving evident testimony herein that he was thoroughly verst in the Mathematicall Sciences, in Philosophy, and in Divinity, to which this might serve for an ample Theme to make large Commentaries upon."[38] Digby's treatise is fascinating in its own right, but it also provides valuable evidence of the kind of assumptions and interests one of Jonson's patrons brought to his reading of literature.

It is even possible that the "lines" and "Verses" Jonson refers to in his poem to Digby were the lines and verses of the numerologically organized Weston epithalamion itself. By a happy coincidence, the date of Jonson's birth seems to have been the same date on which Digby won his famous battle with the Venetians, and by an even more remarkable coincidence, it was also this date—St. Barnabas's Day—on which Spenser, Digby's favorite poet, set his own *Epithalamion*.[39] Jonson may in fact allude to Spenser's work in his poem to Digby, and it hardly seems inconceivable that the "Verses" he passed on to Digby (with the expectation that Digby in turn would pass them on to Weston) may have comprised his own recent effort in the genre Spenser had helped make famous.[40] This assumption helps to explain the otherwise somewhat puzzling prominence Weston enjoys in a poem nominally addressed to Digby and his wife, and it also supports a fairly specific interpretation of Jonson's comment that Digby "doth love my Verses, and will looke / Upon them, (next to *Spenser*'s noble booke,) / And praise them too" (23–25). If the "noble booke" Jonson mentions here is *The Faerie Queene*, one is hard put to imagine which of Jonson's "Verses" would sustain such a comparison. It is possible that Jonson refers to his work as a whole, or to the edition of three of his uncollected plays—*Bartholomew Fair*, *The Devil is an Ass*, and *The Staple of News*—he was "struggling to bring out" in 1631 to raise much-needed money.[41] Or perhaps he refers collectively to the poems, plays, and masques written since the publication of the first folio in 1616. Eventually, it is true, all these works *were* turned over to Digby, who edited them for the posthumous 1640 folio, but contemporary evidence suggests that Digby did not receive the poet's writings *en masse* until "some shorte tyme before [Jonson's] decease" in 1637, while the present poem to Digby could have been written no later than the spring of 1633.[42] It is also possible that the "Verses" Jonson mentions comprise the present poem, although Digby would have to have been quite an egotist indeed not only to have read lines commending himself at Weston's table but to "praise them too."

The simplest explanation may be that "*Spenser*'s noble booke" refers to the small volume in which Spenser published his *Epithalamion* and *Amoretti*, and that the "Verses" of his own that Jonson mentions are the verses he wrote to celebrate the marriage of Weston's son. Digby, with his keen appreciation of both poets, would have been the ideal person to "read" (and point out the accomplishments and subtleties of) Jonson's lines "at the Treasurers bord." The poem's concluding reference to numerous "copies" and "transcripts" (29; 30) reinforces the likelihood that Jonson has in mind a relatively short work (rather than all his "Verses" taken together), while the reference to Weston "Allow[ing]" the lines becomes, on this assumption, a pun—suggesting not only praise but sanction. There is no way to "prove" this supposition (only those immediately involved knew precisely which verses Jonson meant), but the possibility cannot be lightly dismissed. A poem exalting Digby and his wife would provide ideal accompaniment to one praising the recent marriage of the Lord Treasurer's son and heir.

Indeed, the poem's opening line, which refers to Venetia as "happy," implies that the chief source of her happiness is her marriage. In Jonson's writing, even such an apparently simple word can contain reserves of meaning: Venetia is "happy" first in the sense that she takes joy in her husband, secondly in the sense that she is fortunate to be married to such a man, and finally in the sense that both these circumstances contribute to her pleasant disposition. The intimacy between husband and wife celebrated in the poem's first lines is complemented by the poet's own close connection to his patroness; Venetia is a woman important to the lives of both Jonson and Digby, who are drawn even more closely together by the respect they share for her. Although the poem begins by commending Digby's "courtesie," the word also helps call attention to the same quality in Jonson's poem, and although the epigram is ostensibly addressed only to Venetia, it already implicitly addresses the wider audience anticipated at its close. The movement from its first line to its last word is a movement outward, from a tight focus on the happy threesome of poet, patron, and muse to a broader concern with the wider world of "all."

Here as in much of his poetry, Jonson effectively uses lists. The third line lists Digby's virtues as nouns, while the fifth lists them as adjectives. Both catalogues imply the plenitude of his qualities, the potentially inexhaustible tributes he might be paid. Although Digby had won renown for his martial courage, the fifth line emphasizes his qualities of restraint, reason, and judgment, as if to suggest (as Jonson does suggest elsewhere) that mere action does not a hero make. This, surely, is why he spends so much time describing Digby's character before mentioning his physical appearance, and why the description of his body is made to reflect the nature of his spirit and soul. Jonson repeatedly describes Digby in regal terms (6–7; 9), not only to suggest his fitness for service at court but also to magnify his importance there. The poet credits nature with having taken "a large survey" of Digby's being (11), but of course this claim also calls attention to the comprehensive vision of Digby presented by this epigram. It is, after all, the poem itself that so memorably explicates and expresses Digby's qualities—qualities ostensibly obvious to all. Even as he highlights Digby's virtues, Jonson claims that no highlighting is needed.

Yet Jonson's apparent modesty, his willingness to ascribe to "Nature" a central function of his poem, is immediately countered by a reference that at first might seem oddly intrusive—the allusion to his own birth (14). Initially it might seem overbearing to be reminded that Jonson was born on the same day as Digby's great victory, as if the two events were comparable in importance. On reflection, however, the reference seems more defensible. It not only allows Jonson to allude (as has already been suggested) to the date made famous in Spenser's "Epithalamion," but it more significantly suggests that somehow the link between Digby and the two poets was preordained. Surely (Jonson seems to imply) it is no coincidence that he was born on the very day Digby would further ennoble—a day already full of meaning because of its associations with St. Barnaby and with the fullness of light. Surely (Jonson seems to suggest) his connection with Digby was fated; Venetia, his muse, is less the cause of this link than simply one of its instruments. It is as if Jonson has been destined all along to celebrate Digby someday in verse. Of course, in reality the completion of his projected poem on Digby's victory (implied in line 18) would depend less on some mystical fate than on the very practical support he received from his patron. Although Jonson makes his union with Digby seem destined, perhaps he also implies that its full realization would depend on Digby's continued pragmatic encouragement.

By suggesting that Venetia will actually read his verses aloud to her husband (and thus become a singer herself [22]), Jonson not only subtly directs her behavior but also implies a closer connection between poet and muse: it is one thing for a muse to inspire a poet's song, another still for her to sing it. When Jonson further implies that in a sense this singing is unnecessary since Digby already "love[s] my Verses" (23), he once again runs the risk of seeming boastful. But in part this claim merely pays tribute to the breadth of his patron's interests: despite being a great hero and a "Busie" man (20), he still finds time for beauty. Digby's interest in Spenser was apparently well-known, and his thoughtful appreciation of the earlier poet's writing would give his positive assessment of Jonson's work all the more credibility. Jonson's confidence in the worth of his own writings is balanced by his sense that having them read and approved by Digby (and then by Weston) would give them greater social luster. The acceptance of his works, he knew, would affect his own acceptance. Line 26 (with its heavy punctuation) implies an interesting distinction between the poet and his poems: it was not enough for the power of his lines to be acknowledged if that power did not help secure his own. Yet, at least ostensibly, the imprimatur of Digby and Weston will not so much add to the poems' value as merely make that value manifest to "all."

Just as Jonson will win praise if his verses do, so, he suggests, will Venetia. The placement of the phrase "how cry'd up" (30) is suggestively ambiguous. It can look back to the preceding reference to the poems, implying that they will be celebrated, but it can also look forward to the succeeding reference to Venetia, implying that she too will be "cry'd up" (perhaps by others, perhaps by the poet in future verses) for her role in promoting him. One of Venetia's virtues as a muse is her lack of jealousy or envy; she will be genuinely and selflessly "glad" at Jonson's anticipated success (30). Yet his success, of course, will help ratify her own influence, both with her husband and in society at large. Being Jonson's muse when he wins his proper recognition will mean basking in the glow of his triumph. His future devotions to Venetia will be even more valuable to her if his present devotion wins wide social favor. The connections between poet, muse, patron, patron's patron, and chief patron will all be more firmly cemented if Jonson's verses are "Allowe[d]" (29). The subjunctive gladness Jonson attributes to his muse in the poem's closing lines, the pleasure she takes in contemplating his success, looks back to her opening happiness in contemplating her husband. Her joy in the first connection anticipates the satisfaction she also feels in this one.

The poem's closing passage might make it seem as if Jonson is more concerned with exalting himself than with celebrating his patrons; his delight as he imagines the fame their approval will bring him seems at first almost tactlessly blunt, but the lines nonetheless do pay tribute to the pervasive influence the opinions of Weston and Digby enjoyed at Charles's court. At the same time, Jonson's apparent egotism is mitigated even further when one realizes that the last fourteen lines closely paraphrase an epigram by Martial. His self-concern seems less offensive when it becomes clear that he is playing variations on another man's theme. Weston and the Digbys are ennobled even more by being implicitly compared to Martial's patron, and in fact Jonson emphasizes the importance of his patrons far more than Martial does.

The intellectual qualities of both Kenelm Digby and his wife, combined with their financial resources and social prominence, must have made them seem ideal patrons in their own rights. And judging, among other things, by the number and nature of the poems they evoked and the role Digby played in publishing the posthumous 1640 collection of Jonson's works, their interest in the poet in the early 1630's must have been genuine, their encouragement sustained and sustaining. Jonson's "*Epigram*" to Venetia, however, is less important for what it reveals about his contacts with the Digbys than for what it intimates about the network of hierarchical relationships in which, as a practical poet, he had to operate. He passes his work to Venetia in the hope that she will communicate it to her husband, who might then read it in front of Weston, who might then promote the poet's reputation with those around and beneath him, but perhaps especially with those above. In few other poems does Jonson indicate quite so explicitly his awareness of the web of patronage connections or of the influence those contacts had on his status and reputation.

In nearly all his poems, however, to one degree or another, such awareness is implied. Jonson here implicitly concedes that it is not so much the value or success of the poem itself that matters as that value's public recognition by the socially influential. It will be less the work *per se* than Weston's reaction to it that will create the interest Jonson hopes for. Of course, this admission is in part simply another means of complimenting (and influencing) Weston; by attributing such power to him, it helps reinforce the mystique of the power he already holds. Yet the admission is also realistically frank. Jonson knew that no matter how great his merits were as an artist, his opportunities for artistic achievement depended considerably on the support he received from his patrons, and on the support they received from theirs.[43] Every poem attempted in some sense to assert his power, yet few poems express his ultimate dependence as fully or as clearly as the epigram to Venetia, his "*MUSE*." Behind the imaginative conceit of the poem's title stands the real woman and the other real figures on whose support its (and his) success would stand or fall. Like all of Jonson's works, this poem is interesting not only for what it explicitly says but perhaps especially for the complicated social context it simply takes for granted.

Afterword

As many of the preceding pages have shown, throughout his life Ben Jonson inspired both warm tributes and savage attacks, and subsequent critical reactions have often been just as polarized. The reasons for such extreme responses have varied. Champions of Shakespeare have sometimes denigrated Jonson, while his defenders have often proven quite defensive indeed. Jonsonians often identify strongly with their man, while readers who dislike him often take the extra step to disdain. The fact that we know so much more about him than about most of his great contemporaries means that reactions to his art inevitably become entangled with reactions to his personality. Jonson himself, of course, invited this link: much of the most interesting published comment about "Ben" the public figure came from Ben himself. Over the years, Jonson has been depicted both as a principled defender of reason and virtue and as a bullying sycophant. The deeper reasons beneath the often black-and-white, either/or, and strongly moralistic reactions he provokes would be worth exploring, since they are at least as interesting for what they tell us about literary criticism as for what they say about Jonson. Although exploring such reactions fully is not my purpose here, this may be an appropriate place to venture a few final suggestions.

As most critics have acknowledged, moral judgment was central to Jonson's art, and moral judgments of one sort or another have often proven just as central to Jonson criticism. The impulse to judge is strong, and of course Jonson himself saw it as an obligation. He felt confident both of his capacity to judge and of the judgments he delivered. This confidence tends either to attract or repel readers, who then tend either to embrace or reject him, both as a poet and as a person. One measure of his literary force is that he still provokes such warm or such heated response. Since his importance makes him impossible to dismiss or ignore, he simply must be dealt with; but perhaps he is too often dealt with simply. Perhaps it is a weakness of Jonson criticism that we so often adopt his own moralism and assurance, that we so often either side with or attack him, that we so often take on the roles first played by him or his contemporary antagonists. In other disciplines the impulse to champion or denigrate one's subject often seems less urgent than in literary criticism (particularly Jonson criticism), and perhaps this marks our deficiency. A discipline more sure of itself would more readily acknowledge ambiguities and uncertainties. Jonson's ethical, aesthetic, and philosophical confidence seems somewhat old-fashioned today, and in any case it is hard to see how such certitude—and the brisk, assertive rhetoric that so often accompanies it—can help us to a fuller, more complex, more neutral, and thus perhaps more nuanced understanding of this writer and his art. The ethical conviction (both pro and con) that has typified so much commentary on Jonson would puzzle many philosophers, sociologists, historians, anthropologists, and students of comparative religion, or even those who honestly ponder the ambiguities of their own lives or the lives of others around them.

The tendency of much traditional Jonson criticism has been to take Jonson pretty much as he presented himself, and to the extent that this tendency helps us appreciate his intentions, it is a good antidote to criticism that simply denigrates his character or passes quick judgment on his morals. Perhaps neither approach, however, can give us a poet as complicated as Jonson himself—the kind of artist who emerges, for instance, in David Riggs's recent biography or even in the concluding pages of the biography by Rosalind Miles. Theirs is a messy Jonson, a person not wholly in control of his life or his writing, a person (like most of us) caught between contending impulses and conflicting social forces, a person whose career and works could not be neatly arranged or precisely patterned. We can get closer to this Jonson partly through detailed historical study of his life and writings, and the more we study them, the more messy, ambiguous, and fascinatingly complex they can seem. The Jonson who emerges from such study may not be the culture-hero we so often seem to seek, and the art we examine through such a lens may not always seem consoling, inspiring, or "humane" in any simple sense. But it *will* be recognizably human, since it will be an art tangled in all the diverse motives and circumstances that characterize the lives most people live.

It seems precisely this complexity that gives Jonson's art much of its interest and richness. Perhaps it is less important that literary critics boost, protect, or apologize for the art and authors they study than that they attempt to understand and explain them to the fullest possible degree. Any approach that helps us to such a fuller understanding is welcome. No single approach, of course, can do complete justice to the full complexity of Jonson's career and works, but the very value of different readings is that they can complicate our understanding. Such complication, ultimately and paradoxically, may help us to a vision more humane and ethical (because less instantly judgmental and assured). Although Jonson's circumstances frequently seemed to compel him to pronounce clear and certain judgments, we can view his situation with more neutrality and distance, with no need to take sides, and certainly with no need to reeenact the various battles he waged with such vigor. We have the luxury of feeling confident, as Jonson himself never quite could, that his place in literary history is distinguished and assured, and that there is consequently no longer any need to feel defensive when we discuss him. Attempting to view him in the contexts of his times is one way, perhaps, to help us better appreciate his continuing interest, impact, and importance.

Notes

Chapter 1. Jonson and Historical Criticism

1. See, for example, comments by Michael McCanles in response to *Ben Jonson and the Poetics of Patronage* and to David Riggs's recent biography of Jonson (*Criticism* 32 [1990]: 129–32). In referring to McCanles's remarks, I will cite relevant page numbers parenthetically in the body of my text. The objections McCanles raises are thoughtful and serious and are therefore worth a serious response; I do not wish to personalize my reaction anymore than circumstances make this somewhat inevitable. I sympathize with Gerald Graff's puzzlement at "the overheated polemical atmosphere of cultural discussion"; see his essay "Co-optation" in H. Aram Veeser, ed., *The New Historicism* (New York and London: Routledge, 1989), 168–81; 180.

I find it difficult to respond to large objections to "new historicism" because I am not exactly sure what this term means. Reading Veeser's anthology quickly makes clear how difficult it is to define either the term or the movement. In fact, one of the few things on which the essayists agree is that the term is "a phrase without an adequate referent" (Vesser, "Introduction," x). I will return frequently to these essays because they provide many responses to the topic as well as a comprehensive sense of previous work and of the issues at stake. The relation between my earlier book and the work of various "new historicists" is not simple, as I suggested more than once (see 18, 270), but I freely acknowledge the family resemblance. In the body of my response I will limit my reactions to the specific issues McCanles raises; in my notes, I will offer some broader thoughts about the "new historicism" in general. In so doing, I will respond especially to Edward Pechter's cogent essay, "The New Historicism and Its Discontents: Politicizing Renaissance Drama," *PMLA* 102 (1987): 292–303, which I have found very useful as a compendium of constructive objections. See also M. D. Jardine, "New Historicism for Old: New Conservatism for Old?: The Politics of Patronage in the Renaissance," *The Yearbook of English Studies* 21 (1991): 286–304.

2. For this reason I sympathize with the resistance to polarities outlined, for instance, in Theodore Leinwand's "Negotiation and New Historicism," *PMLA* 105 (1990): 477–90. See also the first chapter of Stephen Greenblatt, *Shakespearean Negotiations: The Circulation of Social Energy in Renaissance England* (Berkeley and Los Angeles: University of California Press, 1988). I also sympathize with Greenblatt's comments on "new historicism" in the first half of his essay "Resonance and Wonder" in *Literary Theory Today*, ed. Peter Collier and Helga Geyer-Ryan (Ithaca: Cornell University Press, 1990), 74–90. I wish to thank Ted Leinwand for

several helpful discussions on the whole issue of "negotiation." For more on this issue, see note 15 below.

Jongsook Lee discusses the implications of "new historicism" for Jonson criticism in the final chapter of her book *Ben Jonson's Poesis: A Literary Dialectic of Ideal and History* (Charlottesville: University Press of Virginia, 1989). At one point she sums up her argument by saying that Jonson's poems of praise articulate "the individual voice of a poet fiercely guarding his intellectual independence against those that make it precarious. In that sense, and to that extent, they show the ways in which he confronts and transforms his immediate circumstances" (81). I would emphasize the qualifying phrases with which the second sentence begins, and I would add others, saying that Jonson "attempts to guard" and "attempts to confront" and "attempts to transform." Such phrases would emphasize the rhetorical nature of Jonson's poetry, its constant awareness of the need to appeal to an audience. For further comment on Lee's approach, see my earlier book, 281.

3. In this sense I see my earlier book as an attempt to overcome one of the limitations Pechter finds in "new historicism": "its detachment from the text" (298). On this issue, see also Anthony Low, "Donne and the New Historicism," *John Donne Journal* 7 (1988): 125–31. My previous book offered numerous close readings; it attempted to show how historical awareness could offer new ways of reading texts in detail. Although Pechter rightly sees "new historicism" as reacting against extreme versions of formalism (292), own book attempted to combine the strengths of formalist close reading with a sensitivity to historical nuance. Pechter contends that "new historicism" "systematically deprives the text of its capacity to surprise" (302). However, in other fields a theory's ability to explain numerous data is considered a strength, not a weakness. And besides, "new historicist" readings often prove offensive precisely for emphasizing surprising aspects of texts—aspects we might prefer to ignore.

4. My reference to the "universality and inevitability of micropolitics" might seem open to Pechter's charge that the "knowledge [new historicists] furnish of 'present concerns' in the Renaissance is [presented as] a universal knowledge, good for all concrete situations" (297). This would make me guilty of "essentialism" (see Graff, "Co-optation," 174), which the new historicism is supposed to undermine (see Veeser, "Introduction" xi). However, the "universals" to which I allude seem arguably to be rooted in biological evolution and (more immediately) in issues of practical survival. Indeed, two aspects of "new historicism" that appeal to me are its emphasis on "matters that deeply affect people's practical lives" and its interdisciplinary emphasis (Veeser, "Introduction," ix). It seems odd that recent literary theory, with its strong interdisciplinary tendencies, has shown such little interest in the implications of recent developments in the biological sciences. Theories of evolution, for instance, would seem to be greatly relevant to current debates about "power" and "new historicism."

5. I also make this point in "'Games of Fortune, Plaid at Court': Politics and Poetic Freedom in Jonson's Epigrams," in *"The Muses Common-weale: Poetry and Politics in the Seventeenth Century*, ed. Claude J. Summers and Ted-Larry Pebworth (Columbia: University of Missouri Press, 1988), 48–61; 49, 60. This volume, incidentally, prints comments on the new historicism by Richard Strier, Leah Marcus, Richard Helgerson, and James G. Turner (207–17).

6. Another instance of the same tendency occurs in Pechter's comment on Greenblatt's claim that in all the texts he examined, "there were, *so far as I could tell*, no moments of *pure, unfettered* subjectivity; indeed, the human subject itself

began to seem *remarkably* unfree, the ideological product of the relations of power in a particular society." Pechter responds: "In this view, human power to shape the world, even to fashion that small part of the world called the self, turns out to be *illusory*. There is *no* free space in Greenblatt's conception of culture, not in the theater, not for the self" (300; emphasis added in each case). However, this glosses over Greenblatt's sensible qualifications. The fact that "new historicism" often provokes extreme reactions helps undermine Pechter's further claim that "new historicism," by "trying to see the text as essentially generated from and directed toward the politics of a historically remote period . . . cannot help draining [literary works] of much of their potential to involve an audience. One aspect of this draining strategy is the new historicists' tendency to deemphasize passages whose affective power seems unusually great" (Pechter 299). This presumes, first, that "politics" is macropolitics (i.e., ideological), whereas my earlier book emphasized instead the importance of power relations among individuals. Emphasizing micropolitics has great potential to involve an audience since most persons will recognize the relevance of such issues to their own lives. My book attempted to show how works and passages that might seem conventional and derivative were once charged with social energy and can still strike sparks if discussed from a power perspective. (On this point, see Greenblatt, *Shakespearean Negotiations*, 6–7.) Note how Pechter's own phrasing inadvertently concedes the usefulness of conceiving of texts this way: the "affective power" he prizes is a power possessed not by the text alone but also by its creator; *literary* power can augment *social* power. As I will suggest again later, a "power approach" to literature can accommodate and incorporate most other approaches (indeed, it is enriched by them), whereas not all other approaches can accommodate an emphasis on power, and some are frankly hostile to it.

7. Like many, Pechter associates "new historicism" with an emphasis on a "will to power" (301) or "desire to dominate" (301) or "*libido dominandi*," which he calls "the most problematic aspect of the new historicism" (292). However, my earlier book stressed power as a prerequisite for social *security*, as a necessary precondition for achieving "loftier," more "impersonal" goals, as a requirement for attaining some measure of personal peace, serenity, and (limited) autonomy and freedom. This not only does better justice to the complexity of "power" as a social phenomenon, but it also makes it seem less malign, less threatening, and more recognizable. To see "the will to power as the defining human essence," as Pechter says new historicists do (301), does indeed seem narrow-minded, unless one claims that possessing (relative) power helps make possible the pursuit of practically any other human aspiration.

8. If critics focused less on a menacing-sounding "will to power" and more on such a will's effects and effectiveness, debate might be more productive. Similarly, if this "will" were simply renamed "competition," then many specific objections would seem answerable. For instance, Pechter does "not find it useful to believe that human activity is essentially determined by the will to power, because it is hard to base much of a future on that belief" (301). However, competition has arguably been an engine of human progress, and the future has arguably been brighter for systems embracing competition than for those nominally committed to cooperation. At one point Pechter wonders how, without some notion of benevolence, "we can imagine a community of any kind, let alone 'genuine' community?" (301). One might respond that power relations do not preclude benevolence, cooperation, and community but in fact can help promote and explain them: individuals unite and cooperate in order to compete,

both among themselves and with other groups, and such groups in turn cooperate to compete among themselves and with others. This balancing or diffusion of powers is thoroughly familiar—in business, politics, foreign relations, and team sports. Pechter says that "new historicism" is rooted in the cliché that "it's a jungle out there." To this he opposes another cliché, "love makes the world go round," which is rooted in "kindness, or at least tolerance, and benevolence, or at least cooperation" (301). However, the crucial difference (as he implies [301]), is that the first cliché can swallow the second. That is, benevolence, et al., can all be explained in terms of power relations, but it isn't clear that the reverse is true. Calling such an analysis "reductive" merely concedes its explanatory power; any good theory (e.g., evolution) is "reductive" in the same way.

9. Leinwand quotes many analysts who accept this view, which he summarizes as follows: "Power . . . is relational—from top down and from bottom up" (481). The notes to the first and second chapters of my earlier book cite numerous other writers in various disciplines who make the same (it seems to me, reasonable) assumption; see, for instance, 275–76.

10. I sympathize with Greenblatt: "If the textual traces in which we take interest and pleasure are not sources of numinous authority, if they are the signs of contingent social practices, then the questions we ask of them cannot profitably center on a search for their untranslatable essence. . . . The idea is not to strip away and discard the enchanted impression of aesthetic autonomy but to inquire into the objective conditions of this enchantment, to discover how the traces of social circulation are effaced" (*Shakespearean Negotiations* 5). Anthony Low makes a similar point (130). See also Deborah C. Payne, "Patronage and the Dramatic Marketplace under Charles I and II," *Yearbook of English Studies* 21 (1991): 137–52, esp. 137.

11. On the complexities of "subjectification," see Louis A. Montrose, "Professing the Renaissance: The Poetics and Politics of Culture," in Veeser, *The New Historicism* 15–36; 21. Graff refers to the "traditional type of critical sentimentality which locates the defining characteristic of literature . . . in its supposed independence of the realm of material circumstances," a view in which the definition of literature "comes to be determined by a logic of agoraphobia: literature is anything and everything that the marketplace is *not*—disinterested, autonomous, a communicative mode that does not 'mean' but simply 'is,' and so forth" ("Co-optation," 176; 177).

12. Pechter quotes Foucault on "The omnipresence of power: not because it has the privilege of consolidating everything under its invincible unity, but because it is produced from one moment to the next, at every point, or rather in relation from one point to another. Power is everywhere; not because it embraces everything, but because it comes from everywhere" (297). Like Pechter, I find this analysis attractive. In fact, far from criticizing "new historicism" for emphasizing the "relational" nature of power, Pechter attacks it for viewing power in terms that are not relational enough. To my own way of thinking, power isn't possessed "by no one," but rather by everyone *to one degree or another*. On this point, see Leinwand (480).

Interestingly, while Pechter sees new historicists as being too influenced by "the early Foucault" and not enough by such later works as *The History of Sexuality*, Graff in "Co-optation" writes that "the new historicism is particularly indebted to the work of Michel Foucault, especially the later Foucault of such works as. . . . *The History of Sexuality*" (169).

13. In "Towards a Poetics of Culture," Greenblatt notes the "effacement of contradiction" as typical of much recent theory (in Veeser, *The New Historicism*,

1–14; 5). Similarly, Catherine Gallagher argues that the "new historicist, unlike the Marxist, is under no nominal compulsion to achieve consistency"; see "Marxism and the New Historicism" in Veeser, *The New Historicism*, 37–48; 46. Greenblatt and Gallagher obviously do not mean to defend logical contradiction or inconsistency; rather, they mean to resist the impulse to impose a simplistic logic on complex phenomena.

14. On the implications for literary analysis see (for instance) Leinwand and also Greenblatt, *Shakespearean Negotiations*. Arthur Marotti speaks of the pre- and early-modern periods as eras "in which literature was more obviously implicated in immediate social relations" and in which "the relationships of writers, publishers, patrons, and readers were habitually the subject of explicit negotiation." See his article "Patronage, Poetry, and Print," *Yearbook of English Studies* 21 (1991): 1–26. The quoted passage is from his opening paragraph. Lest it be thought that I am simply mimicking current jargon, I should mention that my earlier book (e.g., 54) and the 1983 dissertation on which it was based had already argued for a view of Jonson's poems as instances of negotiation, compromise, and accommodation.

15. See, for instance, the data presented in chapter five of my earlier book.

16. Frank Lentricchia, in "Foucault's Legacy—A New Historicism?" (in Veeser, *The New Historicism*, 321–42), argues that there is "a self-subversive tug in historicist discourse," a need to believe "that there is a secret recess of consciousness as yet unmanipulated, some hiding place where we do not feel ourselves to be utterly just entities who have been enabled by vast, impersonal systems" (241). This tension between acknowledging outside powers and desiring to escape them seems to replicate a tension central to many of the texts that "new historicists" study. Such influences can never be totally escaped, but total escape isn't necessary. Relative freedom can possess its own attractions and satisfactions. In fact, assuming that freedom is (or can always be) compromised can make it seem all the more precious.

17. Lentricchia also sees paranoia in some "new historicist" discourse; see "Foucault's Legacy," 235, 242. Among the rhetorical advantages of raising the issue of paranoia, not the least is that any response to the charge can be interpreted as confirming it. In his "Introduction," Veeser writes that "new historicism" assumes that "selves and texts are defined by their relation to hostile others. . . ." (xiii). As it applies to my earlier book, I would simply amend this description by inserting "potentially" before "hostile."

18. Besides, if Jonson's perceptions of threat were in fact paranoid, they would be even more worthy of study as influences on his life and writing.

19. Interestingly, very few book-length discussions of Jonson contain sustained analyses of this admittedly important poem, which may be one more justification for analyzing it at some length here. Wesley Trimpi argues that the work fails: "Since the occasion of the poem is only nominally related to its subject, there is no real situation, either stated or implied, from which to take details or to derive feelings, and the extended discussion becomes the most arid didacticism. . . . The result is repetitious and strained moralizing on the art of giving, with an occasional magnificent line. . . ." See *Ben Jonson's Poems: A Study in the Plain Style* (Stanford: Stanford University Press, 1962), 276. This reaction depends, I think, on seeing the poem chiefly as a restatement of classical commonplaces rather than as a work intimately relevant to Jonson's own experience. I am more in sympathy with Alexander Leggatt's brief comment that in this poem "we are aware of the tension and insecurity of the writer's position"; see *Ben Jonson: His Vision and His Art* (London and New York: Methuen, 1981), 205.

However, it seems to me that these tensions are not resolved as easily or simply as Leggatt implies.

20. On micropolitics in Seneca's own life and writings see, for instance, J. P. Sullivan, *Literature and Politics in the Age of Nero* (Ithaca and London: Cornell University Press, 1985). To ignore this context would confirm a charge that Pechter alleges against the "new historicists"—that they exhibit "indifference to the particular social and cultural setting for which [a] text is designed," including such "particular circumstances" as "author, audience, chronology" (297). For a fuller discussion of the similarities between the careers of Jonson and Seneca and of Jonson's reading of the Roman moralist, see my essay "Jonson's Copy of Seneca," *Comparative Drama* 25 (1991): 257–92.

21. For the text of this poem, see *Ben Jonson*, ed. C. H. Herford and Percy and Evelyn Simpson, 11 vols. (Oxford: Clarendon Press, 1925–52), 8: 153–58. On the scatalogical pun in the final quoted couplet, see my "Jonson's 'Epistle to Sir Edward Sacvile,'" *The Explicator* 43, no. 3 (1985): 7.

When citing collections of Jonson's verse, I will abbreviate their titles as follows: *Epigrammes* (*Ep.*); *The Forrest* (*For.*); *Under-wood* (*Und.*); *Ungathered Verse* (*U.V.*).

22. On one aspect of the poem's debt to its sources, see George Parfitt, *Ben Jonson: Public Poet and Private Man* (London: Dent, 1976), 109–10.

23. Leggatt also comments on Jonson's humility in this poem (217–18), but his analysis stops short of my conclusions.

24. Stanley Fish, in a valuable article that contains helpful comments on this poem, also notes the pun on "prevent"; see "Authors-Readers: Jonson's Community of the Same," *Representations* 7 (1984): 26–58; 50. Fish writes that "It is as if Jonson never asked for anything at all but was simply the object of a gesture so spontaneous that it seemed to have no cause, no *occasional* stimulus, except for the recognition by one noble nature of another" (50). However, as my comments already have suggested (and as Fish's own conditional phrasing seems to concede), both the act and the poem that celebrate it were in fact responsive to a variety of occasional stimuli. For my general response to Fish's reading of Jonson, see Evans, *Ben Jonson and the Poetics of Patronage*, 274.

25. For this possible reading, see the *OED*, s.v. "Beast," 6.

Chapter 2. Rivals and Patrons: Early and Late

1. For a brief discussion of the poetomachia in these terms, see Evans, *Ben Jonson and the Poetics of Patronage* (Lewisburg, PA: Bucknell University Press, 1989), 146–48. See also Kathleen E. McLuskie, "The Poets' Royal Exchange: Patronage and Commerce in Early Modern Drama," *Yearbook of English Studies* 21 (1991): 53–62, esp. 60–61. Other recent discussions of the conflict include David Riggs, *Ben Jonson: A Life* (Cambridge, MA: Harvard University Press, 1989), 72–84; George E. Rowe, *Distinguishing Jonson: Imitation, Rivalry, and the Direction of a Dramatic Career* (Lincoln: University of Nebraska Press, 1988), 68–70, 81–82, 132–33, 173–76; and James P. Bednarz, "Representing Jonson: *Histriomastix* and the Origin of the Poet's War," *Huntington Library Quarterly* 54.1 (1991): 1–30. Helpful previous discussions of the skirmish include Roscoe Addison Small, *The Stage-Quarrel Between Ben Jonson and the So-Called Poetasters* (Breslau: M & H Marcus, 1899); Robert Boies Sharpe, *The Real War of the Theaters* (Boston: C. C. Heath, 1935); Ralph W. Berringer, "Jonson's *Cynthias's Revels* and

the War of the Theatres," *Philological Quarterly* 22 (1943): 1–22; and especially W. David Kay, "Ben Jonson, Horace, and the Poetomachia: The Development of an Elizabethan Playwright's Public Image" (Diss., Princeton, 1968). See also Kay's article "The Shaping of Ben Jonson's Career: A Re-examination of Facts and Problems," *Modern Philology* 67 (1970): 224–37.

2. All references to *Satiromastix* will cite the text printed in the first volume of *The Dramatic Works of Thomas Dekker*, ed. Fredson Bowers, 4 vols. (Cambridge: Cambridge University Press, 1953–61). Citations will be given parenthetically by act, scene, and line numbers. Although Dekker was primarily responsible for *Satiromastix*, it has usually been assumed (in Roscoe Small's words) that "Marston was at Dekker's elbow during the composition" (122). I sometimes refer to the play as a collaborative effort only to indicate that it presents a defense of both men against Jonson's earlier attacks in *Poetaster*.

3. Cyrus Hoy quotes Swinburne's judgment that the incongruity exhibited by *Satiromastix* is both "monstrous" and "perverse"; see his *Introduction, Notes, and Commentaries to Texts in* The Dramatic Works of Thomas Dekker *Edited by Fredson Bowers*, 4 vols. (Cambridge: Cambridge University Press, 1980): 1: 180–81n. Hoy himself considers the work a "dramatic medley" in which satire and romance are blended at some cost to "dramatic congruity" (1: 180). George R. Price speaks of "incongruities of tone or dramatic method that vitiate the play" and says that Dekker must be blamed "for the discord between the serious and comic plots, which seem quite devoid of thematic relation to each other"; see his book *Thomas Dekker* (New York: Twayne, 1969), 59–60. Small writes that the "Celestine-Terrill story . . . has absolutely no connection with the Horace-plot except that the names Crispinus and Demetrius are applied to two mute courtiers, and that, after the Celestine-story is ended, the King is made judge over Horace" (119). For similar comments about the play's defects of structure, see M. T. Jones-Davies, *Un Peintre de la Vie Londonienne: Thomas Dekker*, 2 vols. (Paris: Librairie Marcel Didier, 1958), 44, and also Morse Allen, *The Satire of John Marston* (New York: Haskell House, 1965), 67–68.

4. See, for instance, Thomas M. Greene, "Spenser and the Epithalamic Convention," in *The Prince of Poets: Essays on Edmund Spenser*, ed. John R. Elliott, Jr. (New York: New York University Press, 1968), 152–69, esp. 155.

5. For the view that Jonson's presentation of Augustus is not wholly unambiguous, see John Gordon Sweeney III, *Jonson and the Psychology of Public Theater* (Princeton: Princeton University Press, 1985), 44. Still, as Sweeney himself points out, the momentary questioning of Augustus's judgment is not given much emphasis; certainly there is nothing in Jonson's play like the thoroughgoing criticism of the king in *Satiromastix*.

6. Larry S. Champion calls the work "a notoriously ill-constructed play in which [Dekker] apparently in great haste utilizes the sketch of an unfinished play as a frame upon which to hang his satiric counterattack." He says that *Satiromastix* "has probably done more to damage Dekker's reputation as a playwright than any other single work," and he calls it an "incongruous conflation of topical material." See *Thomas Dekker and the Traditions of English Drama* (New York: Peter Lang, 1985), 28. Julia Gasper suggests part of the importance of *Satiromastix* when she notes that it is "one of the very earliest examples of tragicomedy to appear on the English stage"; see *The Dragon and the Dove: The Plays of Thomas Dekker* (Oxford: Clarendon Press, 1990), 12.

7. "In the final analysis," according to Champion, "*Satiromastix* suffers from a kind of artistic schizophrenia. . . . the matter of the poetomachia is inserted almost randomly throughout the play" (34). Gasper, in *The Dragon and the Dove*,

notes that the play combines "a potentially tragic plot with contemporary satire" (178), but she does not explore the links between the two.

8. One of the best studies of the poetry Jonson produced in his final period is John Lemly, "Masks and Self-Portraits in Jonson's Late Poetry," *ELH* 44 (1977), 248–66. Yet even Lemly speaks of Jonson's "fawning performances before Charles and his court, which, despite their pluck, verge on bathos and literal cries for help" (254). Similarly, of the famous "Ode to Himselfe" and its concluding reference to the king, Lemly remarks that "Jonson seems unable to maintain his defiant stance without a wishful appeal to an unworthy champion" (254). Other valuable recent studies of the later works include especially Anne Barton, *Ben Jonson: Dramatist* (Cambridge: Cambridge University Press, 1984), which argues for the importance and quality of the final plays, and Annabel Patterson, *Censorship and Interpretation: The Conditions of Writing and Reading in Early Modern England* (Madison: University of Wisconsin Press, 1984), which includes a chapter on the social circumstances of the later poems. In a recent article on these poems ("Jonson, Marvell, and Miscellaneity?" in *Poems in Their Place: The Intertextuality and Order of Poetic Collections*, ed. Neil Fraistat [Chapel Hill and London: University of North Carolina Press, 1987], 95–118), Patterson contends that "The evidence as presented in [the 1640 folio] argues that [Jonson's] idealism was not empty, his venality and servility not unselfconscious, his stand, finally, not without courage" (106).

9. One of the best short treatments of Jonson's circumstances in this and other periods of his life remains the biographical overview provided in the first volume of H&S, which also reprints Jonson's letters to Newcastle; volume 11 contains many other relevant documents.

10. For fuller discussion of this poem, see chapter 8 below.

11. For data about Newcastle's life, see Thomas P. Slaughter, *Ideology and Politics on the Eve of Restoration: Newcastle's Advice to Charles II* (Philadelphia: American Philosophical Society, 1984); [Cavendish], Margaret, Duchess of Newcastle, *Life of William Cavendish*, ed. C.H. Firth (London: George Routledge, n.d.); Thomas Longueville, *The First Duke and Duchess of Newcastle-Upon-Tyne* (London: Longmans, 1910); Henry Ten Eyck Perry, *The First Duchess of Newcastle and Her Husband as Figures in Literary History* (Boston: Ginn & Co., 1918); the article in the *Dictionary of National Biography* [*DNB*]; and the documents reprinted in David Nichol Smith, *Characters from the Histories and Memoirs of the Seventeenth Century* (Oxford: Clarendon Press, 1918).

For Wotton's assessment, see *The Life and Letters of Sir Henry Wotton*, ed. Logan Pearsall Smith, 2 vols. (Oxford: Clarendon Press, 1907), 2:4; 2. For Clarendon's comment, see Nichol Smith, *Characters*, 117. On Newcastle as a patron, see chapter 2 of Perry's book. I discuss one of the poems written on a relative of Cavendish in "Jonson's Epitaph on the Countess of Shrewsbury," *The Explicator* 44, no. 3 (1986), 15–17.

12. See Nichol Smith, *Characters*, 116.

13. On the association between the horse and fleshly passions in medieval literature, see D. W. Robertson, Jr., *A Preface to Chaucer: Studies in Medieval Perspectives* (Princeton: Princeton University Press, 1962), 30; 194; 253–55; 394; 476. For comment on this association in Renaissance iconography, see George Ferguson, *Signs and Symbols in Christian Art* (New York: Oxford University Press, 1954), 18. See also, for instance, Edgar Wind, *Pagan Mysteries in the Renaissance*, rev. ed. (New York: Norton, 1968), 145–48, and the fine note in Ian Donaldson, *Ben Jonson* (Oxford: Oxford University Press, 1985), 699–700.

Interestingly enough, Cavendish himself, in one of his later published treatises on horsemanship, uses the centaur image in much the same way Jonson uses it in the poem: "What can be more Comely or Pleasing, than to see *Horses* go in all their several *Ayres*? and to see so Excellent a Creature, with so much Spirit, and Strength, to be so Obedient to his *Rider*, as if having no Will but His, they had one Body, and one Mind, like a *Centaur*?" See William Cavendishe, *A New Method and Extraordinary Invention, to Dress Horses . . .* (London: Thomas Milbourn, 1667), 13.

14. Sir Philip Sidney, *An Apology for Poetry*, ed. Geoffrey Shepherd (Manchester: Manchester University Press, 1973), 95. The *Apology* opens by recounting Sidney's journey to the continent with Sir Edward Wotton; interestingly, Newcastle himself later made a similar journey with Sir Henry Wotton, Edward's half-brother. This biographical connection would only enhance the possibility that Newcastle would recognize—and appreciate the aptness of—Jonson's allusion.

15. Donaldson, ed., *Ben Jonson*, 700.

16. On this point, see especially Stanley Fish, "Authors-Readers: Jonson's Community of the Same."

17. The second part of the poem may have had the effect of reminding readers of Jonson's own youthful prowess, and perhaps even of the fact that he had killed two men. He was clearly proud of his bravery and boasted about it to William Drummond of Hawthornden. One of his favorite taunts against his rival Inigo Jones concerned the latter's alleged cowardice. In this poem, then, Jonson speaks as someone who knows what it means to use a sword, and whose endorsement of virtuous patience is therefore more credibly effective.

18. Judith Kegan Gardiner discusses Jonson's concepts of valor in this and other poems in *Craftsmanship in Context: The Development of Ben Jonson's Poetry* (The Hague: Mouton, 1975), 92.

19. Sara J. van den Berg notes that Jonson's "definition of valor applies equally to Newcastle's heritage and Jonson's art"; see *The Action of Ben Jonson's Poetry* (Newark: University of Delaware Press, 1987), 170.

20. For an eloquent statement of this view of the late poems, see ibid., 181.

Chapter 3. Thomas Sutton: Jonson's Volpone?

1. An exception to this silence is R. B. Parker's valuable Revels Plays' edition (Manchester: Manchester University Press, 1978), although Parker disputes any connection between Sutton and Volpone by noting that Sutton "was certainly rich and was indeed courted by people hoping to inherit his wealth, but there the parallel ends: he was a rather admirable person, with no other resemblance to Volpone's character or situation. The source for the legacy hunting plot has to be sought in Jonson's reading, not in contemporary London life" (12–13). In discounting the possibility of personal satire, Parker is echoing the standard edition, which contends that "a knowledge of the true facts of [Sutton's] life completely refutes the imputation" that he was Jonson's target (H&S 9: 682). In support of this argument, Herford and the Simpsons refer readers to a still earlier edition, *The Works of Ben Jonson with . . . a Memoir by William Gifford*, ed. Francis Cunningham, 3 vols. (London: Chatto and Windus, 1897), xxxii–xxxiii. Although all the editors mentioned stress Sutton's exemplary character, another student of the period, the historian Lawrence Stone, has called Sutton "the greatest blood-

sucker of the aristocracy"; see his article "The Anatomy of the Elizabethan Aristocracy," *Economic History Review* 18 (1948): 12n. Given such a wide divergence of opinion, it seems all the more justifiable to re-open the issue here.

Herford and the Simpsons mention John Aubrey's "quite untrue" account of the Volpone-Sutton connection (9: 681), although they do not cite other early evidence that supports Aubrey's claims (for instance, see notes 12 and 16 below). Margaret Hotine has recently provided an additional bit of evidence that supports such claims and that also strengthens the argument of this chapter; see her note "Ben Jonson, Volpone, and Charterhouse," *Notes and Queries*, n.s. 38 (1991): 79–81.

2. Perci Burrell, *Sutton's Synagogue or, The English Centurion* (London, 1629). Although not printed until later, the sermon was actually delivered in 1614, three years after Sutton's death.

For other accounts of Sutton's life see, for instance, William Winstanley, *England's Worthies* (London, 1660); Samuel Herne, *Domus Carthusiana* (London, 1677); Philip Bearcroft, *An Historical Account of Thomas Sutton Esq. And of His Foundation in Charter-House* (London: E. Owen, 1737); [Wilford, John], *Memorials and Characters* (London: J. Wilford, 1741); R. Smythe, *Historical Account of Charter-House* (London: C. Spilsbury, 1808); *Charter-House: Its Foundations and History* (London: M. Sewall, 1849); William Haig Brown, *Charterhouse: Past and Present* (Godalming: H. Stedman, 1879); Dom Lawrence Hendriks, *The London Charterhouse: Its Monks and Martyrs* (London: Kegan Paul, 1889); E. P. Eardley Wilmot and E. C. Steatfeild, *Charterhouse: Old and New* (London: John C. Nimmo, 1895); William F. Taylor, *The Charterhouse of London: Monastery, Palace, and Thomas Sutton's Foundation* (London: J. M. Dent, 1912); Gerald S. Davies, *Charterhouse in London: Monastery, Mansion, Hospital, School* (London: John Murray, 1921). See also the article in the *Dictionary of National Biography* (*DNB*).

3. "Thomas Sutton," *Carthusiana* 20, no. 1 (October 1948): 2–8; for the quoted passage, see 2.

4. See "Thomas Sutton; Tudor-Stuart Moneylender," *Business History Review* 50 (1976): 456–76; for the quoted passage, see 458n. For instance, the account of Sutton by Gerald S. Davies, on which Herford and the Simpsons place such great reliance, denies that Sutton was in any ordinary sense a moneylender. Shipley's scrupulous investigation of Sutton's detailed financial records shows just how important an activity his money-lending was.

5. All quotations in this paragraph are from Trevor-Roper, 2–3.

6. Trevor-Roper, 4.

7. All preceding quotations in this paragraph are from Trevor-Roper, 4–5.

8. Shipley, 463.

9. All quotations in this paragraph are from Trevor-Roper, 6–7. For discussion of the new evidence from Charterhouse concerning the Sutton-Harington relationship, see my article "Sir John Harington and Thomas Sutton: New Letters from Charterhouse," *John Donne Journal* 7 (1988): 213–38.

10. Trevor-Roper, 7.

11. Shipley, 462.

12. Interestingly enough, Herne does not mention the account of Sutton offered by William Winstanley in his *England's Worthies*, published seventeen years before Herne's book. Winstanley's account (see 268–73) corroborates Herne's in many important respects—including its discussion of the Jonson connection—but contains none of Herne's more serious inaccuracies. Herne's book has been the source of many subsequent accounts of Sutton, despite the fact that

Winstanley's (admittedly briefer) depiction of Sutton has fewer flaws and was published almost two decades closer to the events it describes. Winstanley (unlike Herne) does not attempt to deny that Jonson satirized Sutton; he simply reports the charges in passing: "I have conversed with some of the Wits, who credibly informed me, that *Ben. Jonsons* Play of the Fox under the name of *Vulpone,* had some allusion to Mr. *Suttons* maner of treating of his Kindred. But to pass by such impertinences . . ." (270).

As early as 1737, Philip Bearcroft had called attention to Herne's various inaccuracies; see his *Historical Account,* ix–x.

13. British Library (hereafter BL) Lansdowne MS. 1198, fol. 1[v]. The identity of the manuscript's author is unknown, although a reference on fol. 5[v] to "us his relations" implies that the author may have had some familial connection to Sutton.

Brackets and parentheses appear in the original manuscript; any insertions or emendations of mine are indicated by [ ] marks, except where I have silently expanded contractions. XXX marks indicate portions of the manuscript which have been heavily inked over. When a word or phrase is overscored but is still legible, I have reproduced this effect by marking a line through it.

Hebrews 7: 4 deals with Melchizedek, a "priest of the Most High God," to whom Abraham gave "the tenth of the spoils."

A notation in the manuscript's left margin (running alongside the passage that begins with "by the *warre*" and ends with "ours by the") reads as follows: "d: Grot. / jun. / belli et / pacis- / [???] / 1:"—alluding to Hugo Grotius, *De Jure Belli ac Pacis Libri Tres* (*The Law of War and Peace*; see the translation by Francis W. Kelsey (Indianapolis: Bobbs Merrill, 1925). Book I, chapter 1 deals with the questions, "What is War? What is Law?"; Book I, chapter 2 asks "Whether it is ever Lawful to wage War" (and answers affirmatively); Book I, chapter 3 deals with the "Distinction between Public and Private War."

14. BL Lansdowne MS. 1198, fol. 2[r].

For the cited statutes, see *Statutes of the Realm,* ed. A. Luders et al., 11 vols (London: 1810–28). Matthew 25: 14–28 recounts the famous parable of the talents. Luke 19: 1–23 offers another version of this parable, along with the story of Zacchaeus, a rich tax collector. The citations from Genesis deal with various exploits of Joseph under the Pharoah.

A notation in the manuscript's left margin (running alongside the passage that begins with "and *bite*" and ends with "aequitable consideration"), reads as follows: "Kesch[?]ch / biting usury—." I have been unable to determine what this refers to.

Later, another notation in the left margin (running from "for money" to beyond "to 23"), reads as follows: *a quae ipso: / usu consu= / =muntur / noq naturali / rationis neq / civil / recipiunt / usu / frutum. / Just; Instit: / lib: 2. tit: 4. /-----------/ Plut: ab de usuru-: / in: Cic: de offic: / lib: 2 ad finem. / Plato de leg: dial. 5. / Salmas: de foen: / trapez: p. 227. 228– / Panormit: in Greg: / de ent: l. 5: tit: 19. / c. 5."

The first citation refers to Justinian's *Institutes,* a highly influential legal text. See the edition translated and introduced by Peter Birks and Grant McLeod (Ithaca: Cornell University Press, 1987). The cited passage occurs in section 4 of book 2, a discussion of "usufruct." The cited words (italicized here to distinguish them from their context) are translated as follows: "There can be a usufruct in slaves, beasts, and other things, as well as land and buildings. *But not in things used up by being used. Logic and law argue against the possibility of a usufruct in these.* . . ." (60–61).

"Plut: ab de usuru[m]:" apparently refers to Plutarch's essay *De Vitando Aere Alieno*, part of his *Moralia*. Wilibald Pirckheimer's Latin translation, issued in Nuremberg in 1515, was entitled *De vitanda usura*. Plutarch's ideas are summarized by Thomas Wilson in his *Discourse Upon Usury* (1572); see R. H. Tawney's edition (New York: Augustus M. Kelley, 1965), 332–33.

The exact nature of the reference to Cicero's *De Officiis* is unclear. Book II deals with "those kinds of duty which have to do with the comforts of life, with the means of acquiring the things that people enjoy, with influence, and with wealth." See the translation by Walter Miller in the Loeb Classical Library (Cambridge, Mass.: Harvard University Press, 1975), 169. At the very end of the book, Cicero relates an anecdote of Cato's which compares the respectability of money-lending to that of murder (265–67).

For the cited comments by Plato on usury in *The Laws*, Book 5, see *The Dialogues of Plato*, trans. B. Jowett, 2 vols. (New York: Random House, 1937), 2: 508. The reference to "Salmas" is to a work by Claude de Saumaise (1588–1653?), *Dissertatio de feonore trapezitico, in tres libros dursa* (1640).

"Panormit: in Greg:" refers to Panormitanus, a name given to Nicolaus de Tudeschis (or Niccolò de' Tudeschi), a canonist and Archbishop (1386–45), whose commentaries on the decretals of Pope Gregory IX are important in the history of ecclesiastical law; see John T. Noonan, *The Scholastic Analysis of Usury* (Cambridge, MA: Harvard University Press, 1957), 70–71.

15. BL Lansdowne MS. 1198, fols. 3^v - 4^r.

16. BL Lansdowne MS. 1198, fols. 4^v - 5^r. The reference to "Broome" is to Richard Brome, Jonson's one-time servant who later became a playwright himself. As newly discovered evidence shows, Brome was indeed a resident at Charterhouse in the final months of his life. See Robert C. Evans, "Richard Brome's Death," *Notes and Queries*, n.s. 36 (1989): 351. The quotation from Cicero is from the oration "Pro C. Rabirio Postumo," section 3. I am grateful to my friend Ron Romanov and to Professor Edward Courtney of Stanford University for their help in tracing this and some of the classical sources I have cited. I have been unable to trace either of the translations the MS ascribes to Jonson, nor are they reported in H&S.

Further evidence that *Volpone* was assumed to refer to Sutton exists in a Bodleian Library manuscript, Rawlinson B 158. Its date and authorship are unknown, but its contents (referring to figures and events from the Interregnum) and handwriting suggest that it must have been written in the latter seventeenth or perhaps early eighteenth centuries. In any case, on fol. 178 the following passage occurs: "Tis said that Ben Johnson in his Volpone: / = personated, Master Sutton the founder of / Suttons Hospitall, for whose Estate very / many persons gapeing, and he makeing / use of their Hopes got divers advantages."

17. BL Lansdowne MS. 1198, fol. 2^v

18. BL Lansdowne MS. 1198, fols. 5^r–5^v. A notation in the manuscript's left margin, (running alongside the passage that begins with "plea of" and ends with "*him*"), reads as follows: "a / Testamen= / ta et or= / bos tan= / quam / indagi= / ne capi: / Tacitus / de Sen= / =eca: /—." Tacitus recounts the accusations of Suillius against Seneca: "Romae testamenta et orbos velut indagine eius capi, Italiam et provincias inmenso faenore hauriri . . ." ("In Rome his nets were spread for the childless and their testaments: Italy and the provinces were sucked dry by his limitless usury"); see *The Annals*, trans. John Jackson, Loeb Classical Library, 4 vols. (Cambridge, MA: Harvard University Press, 1962), 4: 74–75.

19. *The Letters and Epigrams of Sir John Harington*, ed. Norman Egbert McClure (Philadelphia: University of Pennsylvania Press, 1930), 140.

20. For a helpful discussion of the issue of personal satire, especially as it relates to Jonson, see David McPherson, "The Origins of Overdo," *Modern Language Quarterly* 37 (1976): 221–33.

21. As R. W. Ingram notes, "The theater is particularly suited to satirize a person without necessarily giving any clear indication of it in the text of the play. On the stage, a physical mannerism, a trick of gait, a gesture with the hand, a manner of talking, an unusual inflection or pronunciation can be quite enough to direct attention to a comparison with a living person"; see his book *John Marston* (Boston: Twayne, 1978), 46.

22. *Censorship and Interpretation*, 57.

23. The dedication is printed primarily in italic type, with only highlighted words in Roman; to make reading easier, I have reversed this.

24. The Latin reads as follows: "*—Sibi quisq; timet, quanquam est intactus, & odit.*" For the source in *Poetaster*, see H&S 4: 259.

25. The note occurs on the folio's page 391.

Chapter 4. Political Contexts of *The Devil is an Ass*

1. *Ben Jonson, Dramatist* (Cambridge: Cambridge University Press, 1984), 234. For a contrasting view and for a good distillation of some previous complaints about the play, see Robert E. Knoll, *Ben Jonson's Plays: An Introduction* (Lincoln: University of Nebraska Press, 1964), 162–72. See also John J. Enck, *Ben Jonson and the Comic Truth* (Madison: University of Wisconsin Press, 1957), 210–15. For a more positive assessment, see Larry S. Champion, *Ben Jonson's "Dotages": A Reconsideration of the Late Plays* (Lexington: University Press of Kentucky, 1967), 22–44.

2. See her discussion of the play in *The Politics of Mirth: Jonson, Herrick, Milton, Marvell and the Defense of Old Holiday Pastimes* (Chicago: University of Chicago Press, 1986), 85–105.

3. For this information, see H&S 2: 151. Act, scene, and line references to *The Devil is an Ass* will be given parenthetically, preceded by the abbreviation "DA."

4. See *The Letters of John Chamberlain*, ed. Norman Egbert McClure, 2 vols. (Philadelphia: American Philosophical Society), 2: 9.

5. See Jesse Franklin Bradley and Joseph Quincy Adams, *The Jonson Allusion-Book* (New Haven: Yale University Press, 1922), 94.

6. See *Alderman Cockayne's Project and the Cloth Trade: The Commercial Policy of England in Its Main Aspects 1603–1625* (London: Oxford University Press, 1927). L. C. Knights mentions the Cockayne project in passing in his discussion of *The Devil is an Ass*; see *Drama and Society in the Age of Jonson* (New York: Norton, 1968), 210–18.

7. See *Commercial Crisis and Change in England 1600–1642: A Study in the Instability of a Mercantile Economy* (Cambridge: Cambridge University Press, 1959), 51.

8. See *The Narrative History of King James, for the first fourteen Years* (London, 1651). In *A Collection of Scarce and Valuable Tracts . . .*, ed. Walter Scott, 13 vols. (London: T. Cadell and W. Davies, 1809–15), 2: 280. See also Menna Prestwich, *Cranfield: Politics and Profits Under the Early Stuarts* (Oxford: Clarendon Press, 1966), 168n.

9. On these points see Evans, *Ben Jonson and the Poetics of Patronage*, 108–9.

10. See *The Works of Francis Bacon*, ed. James Spedding, et al., 14 vols. (London: Longmans, Green, 1862–1901), 12: 171. Subsequent references to material in this edition will cite Spedding's name plus appropriate volume and page numbers.

11. See Gardiner's *History of England from the Accession of James I. to the Outbreak of the Civil War, 1603–42*, 10 vols. (New York: AMS Press, 1965), 2: 154.

12. See the notes in Donaldson, ed., *Ben Jonson*, 765.

13. See Great Britain, Historical Manuscripts Commission, *Report on the Manuscripts of His Grace the Duke of Portland*, 10 vols. (London: HMSO, 1891–1923), 9: 14, 28–29.

14. See Edmund Gosse, *The Life and Letters of John Donne*, 2 vols. (London: William Heinemann, 1899): 2: 40.

15. See R. C. Bald, *John Donne: A Life* (New York: Oxford University Press, 1970), 314.

16. See *The Correspondence of Sir Robert Kerr, First Earl of Ancram and His Son William, Third Earl of Lothian*, 2 vols. (Edinburgh: [R. and R. Clark], 1875), 1: ix–x.

17. See the *Calendar of State Papers . . . Venice*, 38 vols. (London: HMSO, 1864–1947), 14: 245. Hereafter I will abbreviate this particular volume as *CSPV* and will cite appropriate page numbers.

18. See Great Britain, Public Record Office, *Calendar of State Papers Domestic, James I, 1611–18*, ed. Mary Anne Everett Green (London: Longman, 1858), 291–92. Hereafter I will cite this particular volume as *CSPD*.

19. See *The Changing Fenland* (Cambridge: Cambridge University Press, 1983), 62.

20. See H. C. Darby, *The Draining of the Fens* (Cambridge: Cambridge University Press, 1940), 32–38.

21. See *Dudley Carleton to John Chamberlain, 1603–1624*, ed. Maurice Lee, Jr. (New Brunswick, NJ: Rutgers University Press, 1972), 35.

22. Sir James Balfour Paul, ed., *The Scots Peerage*, 9 vols. (Edinburgh: David Douglas, 1904–14), 1: 348. See also David Masson, ed., *The Register of the Privy Council of Scotland* (Edinburgh: H. H. General Register House, 1877), 10: lv. For further information on Argyll's life see, for instance, the entry for him (under "Archibald Campbell") in the *Dictionary of National Biography*.

23. See John Willcock, *The Great Marquess . . .* (Edinburgh: Oliphant, Anderson & Ferrier, 1903), 8.

24. William Anderson, *The Scottish Nation*, 3 vols. (Edinburgh: A. Fullarton, 1863), 1: 555.

25. See Paul, 1: 348 and Masson, 10: xcix.

26. See Paul, 1: 350 and also *Letters from George Lord Carew to Sir Thomas Roe*, ed. John Maclean (London: Camden Society, 1860): 21.

27. See Willcock, 9.

28. See Maurice Lee, Jr., *Great Britain's Solomon: James VI and I in His Three Kingdoms* (Urbana: University of Illinois Press, 1990), 218.

29. Great Britain, Historical Manuscripts Commission, *Report on the Manuscripts of the Marquess of Downshire*, 4 vols. (London: HMSO, 1924–40), 2: 216.

30. Great Britain, Historical Manuscripts Commission, *The Manuscripts of the Marquess of Abergavenny . . .* (London: HMSO, 1887), 84.

31. Ibid.

32. See the entry on Sackville in the *Dictionary of National Biography*.

33. See Samuel Wells, *A Collection of the Laws Which Form the Constitution of the Bedford Level Corporation* (London: R. Pheney, 1828), 60–70.

34. Interestingly, evidence suggests that at either or both of the times when Jonson may have penned satire of Scots, he may also have been living in the household of a Scottish nobleman—Esme Stuart, Seigneur of Aubigny. Jonson thus seems to have felt no prejudice against Scotsmen as such; indeed, his own ancestors seem to have been Scottish (H&S 1: 139), and he would soon be well received during his walking tour of Scotland. It is possible that his mocking of particular Scotsmen may in fact have been partly encouraged by rivals from their own country. It would be interesting to know, for instance, what Aubigny's relations were with the Scotsman who complained about *Eastward Ho*, or how he felt about Carr or Argyll. Unfortunately, the full facts of Jonson's relations with Aubigny are tantalizingly uncertain; see H&S 11: 576–77. For further discussion of factional politics as it relates to Jonson's satire, see Evans, *Ben Jonson and the Poetics of Patronage*, 69–72 *et passim*.

35. See Johnson's edition of *The Devil is an Ass* (New York: Henry Holt, 1905), xviii.

36. See [Thomas Frankland], *The Annals of King James and Charles the First* (London, 1681), 372.

37. See section V, below, which discusses George Ruggle's comedy *Ignoramus* as a possible source for Jonson's play and for its satire on Coke.

38. See *Acts of the Privy Council of England, 1615–1616* (London: HMSO, 1925), 601–5.

39. Ibid., 609.

40. See Camden's *Annals . . . of King James I*, printed in *A Complete History of England*, ed. White Kennet, 3 vols. (London: 1706), 2: 646.

41. See Wilson's *Life and Reign of King James, the First*, printed in *A Complete History of England*, ed. White Kennet, 3 vols. (London: 1706), 2: 706. See also Anne C. Little, "Jonson's Poetry and the Star Chamber Speech," *Notes and Queries* 238 (1993): 212-14.

42. See Kittredge's article "King James I and *The Devil is an Ass*," *Modern Philology* 9 (1911): 195–209.

43. For the full text of James's Star Chamber speech, see *The Political Works of James I*, ed. Charles Howard McIlwain (New York: Russell and Russell, 1965), 326–45. For the specific quotation just cited, see 328. Hereafter I will cite material from this volume by using the abbreviation "James."

44. See Thomas Birch, ed., *The Court and Times of James the First*, 2 vols. (London: Henry Colburn, 1849): 1: 430.

45. See the Records of Early English Drama volumes dealing with *Cambridge*, ed. Alan H. Nelson, 2 vols. (Toronto: University of Toronto Press, 1989), 750. Nelson prints many relevant documents. Hereafter I will cite his volumes as "Nelson."

46. See James Bass Mullinger, *The University of Cambridge*, 3 vols. (Cambridge: Cambridge University Press, 1884), 2: 543.

47. See the introduction to E. F. J. Tucker's facsimile edition of a manuscript of Ruggle's *Ignoramus* (Hildesheim: Georg Olms, 1987), 4. Hereafter I will cite this text as "Tucker edition."

48. See the introduction to the Tucker edition, 5. See also Nelson, Appendices 4 and 5.

49. Tucker edition, 9.

50. Tucker edition, 4.

51. See his article "*Ignoramus* and Seventeenth-Century Satire of the Law," *Harvard Library Bulletin* 19 (1971): 314–30, esp. 319. Hereafter I will abbreviate this as "Tucker, 'Satire.'"

52. Within a few years Jonson would remark to his friend William Drummond that "he wished" that in order "to please the King, that piece of Forth-Feasting [one of Drummond's poems] had been his owne" (H&S 1: 135).

53. See his study *"Ignoramus" . . . An Examination of Its Sources and Literary Influence* (Lancaster, PA: New Era Printing, 1906), 70.

54. See Thomas L. Berger and William C. Bradford, Jr., *An Index of Characters in English Printed Drama to the Restoration* (Englewood, CO: Microcard Editions Books, 1975), 86. For a general discussion of the relations between Jonson's play and earlier dramas other than Ruggle's, see Robert N. Watson, *Ben Jonson's Parodic Strategy: Literary Imperialism in the Comedies* (Cambridge, MA: Harvard University Press, 1987), 172–209.

55. Tucker, "Satire," 316.

56. Ibid., 317.

57. Ibid., 318.

58. Ibid., 320.

59. For much more extensive summaries of the play's plot, see Mullinger, 529–40, and the Tucker facsimile edition, 10–17. On pages 7–8, Tucker offers a helpful discussion of printed editions and translations of the play. At present, the closest thing to a scholarly edition of Ruggle's comedy remains the heavily annotated version prepared by John Hawkins (London: Ginger, 1787). My act and scene references to *Ignoramus* will be keyed to this edition; no line numbers are printed. Robert Codrington issued a fairly literal English translation (London, 1662).

60. On the possible symbolic significance of the ring in Jonson's play, see C. G. Thayer, *Ben Jonson: Studies in the Plays* (Norman: University of Oklahoma Press, 1963), 156–77, esp. 175–76.

61. On this aspect of Jonson's play, see Peter Hyland, *Disguise and Role-Playing in Ben Jonson's Drama* (Salzburg: Institut für Englische Sprache und Literatur, 1977), 146–59.

62. On the significance of clothing in Jonson's work, see James E. Savage, *Ben Jonson's Basic Comic Characters and Other Essays* (n.p.: University and College Press of Mississippi, 1973), 165–75.

Chapter 5. "Other Men's Provision": Jonson's Parody of Robert White in *Pleasure Reconciled to Virtue*

1. For the texts of the masques, see H&S 7: 475–510; for commentary and documents, see 10: 573–96. Also useful are the documents printed in *Inigo Jones: The Theatre of the Stuart Court*, ed. Stephen Orgel and Roy Strong, 2 vols. (Berkeley: University of California Press, 1973); see 1: 276–93.

2. For a useful summary of contemporary reactions and of modern explanations of them, see Riggs, *Ben Jonson: A Life*, 250–54. Stephen Orgel stresses the sophisticated nature of the masque's artistic innovations as a reason for the audience's reaction; see the introduction to his edition, *Ben Jonson: The Complete Masques* (New Haven: Yale University Press, 1969), esp. 24 and 30–31. On this point, see also Richard S. Peterson, "The Iconography of Jonson's *Pleasure Reconciled to Virtue*," *Journal of Medieval and Renaissance Studies* 5 (1975): 123–51, esp. 150. The political and satirical implications of *Pleasure Reconciled* are developed most fully by Leah S. Marcus in *The Politics of Mirth: Jonson, Herrick, Milton, Mar-*

vell and the Defense of Old Holiday Pastimes, 106–27. Other valuable commentary on the work includes Orgel's discussion in *The Jonsonian Masque* (Cambridge, MA: Harvard University Press, 1965), 149–85.

3. Peter Walls, "Jonson's Borrowing," *Theatre Notebook* 28 (1974): 80–81.

4. See "*Cupid's Banishment*: A Masque Presented to Her Majesty by Young Gentlewomen of the Ladies Hall, Deptford, May 4, 1617," edited by C. E. McGee, in *Renaissance Drama*, n.s. 19 (1988): 226–64. All subsequent references to White's masque will be to this edition and will cite the line numbers McGee provides. Parenthetical references to McGee's introduction, commentary, or apparatus will cite his name and the appropriate page number(s).

5. See Olive and Nigel Hamilton, *Royal Greenwich: A Guide and History to London's Most Historic Borough* (London: The Greenwich Bookshop, 1969), 212–17. For further information on Jones's role, including records of payment, see George H. Chettle, *The Queen's House, Greenwich: Being the Fourteenth Monograph of the London Survey Committee* (Greenwich: Trustees of the National Maritime Museum, [1937]), 25–28. An appendix prints records of the payments Jones received in connection with this project; see 97–103.

6. Evidence survives of a "*Masque of Amazons, or The Ladies' Masque*," sponsored by Lady Hay, which was projected for performance a few days before *Pleasure Reconciled* but which was mysteriously cancelled, despite the fact that it had been completely prepared and rehearsed. John Chamberlain wrote that although the prospective performers "had taken great paines in continuall practising, and were almost perfet and all theyre implements provided, . . . whatsoever the cause was, neither the Quene nor King did like or allow of yt and so all is dashed." Sir Gerard Herbert noted, "The Masque of Ladies at Lord Hay's given up, from some remark of the King or Queen, &c." (See Gerald Eades Bentley, *The Jacobean and Caroline Stage*, 7 vols. [Oxford: Clarendon Press, 1941–68], 5: 1288–89.) One wonders whether White, perhaps commissioned by Lady Hay, may have had anything to do with the preparation of this work, and whether its cancellation may have had anything to do with complaints by Jonson. Certainly White, having recently written a successful masque for young women, would have been a logical candidate to write one for court ladies.

Interestingly enough, one of Jonson's main sources of information about Hercules—the central figure in his masque and, I shall argue, in some senses a representative of the poet—was Diodorus's *Bibliotheca*, which stresses Hercules's conflicts with the Amazons and his ultimate triumph over them. See the translation by C. H. Oldfather in the Loeb Classical Library, 12 vols. (London: Heinemann, 1946–67), 2: 429–33. I shall have more to say later about the possible significance of Jonson's allusions to Diodorus.

7. Bentley, 5: 1258.

8. McGee, noting Bentley's suggestion that White may have been the school's master (228), raises the further possibility that he may have been "the Robert White who received his B.A. from Merton College, Oxford, in 1608" (236). It may be worth mentioning that references to various Robert Whites living in the Deptford area may be found in the article on "The Greenwich Parish Registers, 1615–1636–7," printed as vol. 2 of the *Transactions of the Greenwich and Lewisham Antiquarian Society* (London: Blackheath Press, 1920). An entry for 22 May 1628 records the marriage of a "Robert Whit and Elizabeth Wickcome" (64); an entry for 14 January 1629/30 records the marriage of a "Robert White and Cicely Reade" (66); an entry for 4 October 1629 records the burial of "Elizabeth White wife of Robert White" (108).

9. For the figure, see Orgel and Strong, 1: 282.

10. For a recent overview of Lucy's life and of her connections with Jonson, see Barbara Lewalski, "Lucy, Countess of Bedford: Images of a Jacobean Courtier and Patroness," in *Politics of Discourse*, ed. Kevin Sharpe and Steven N. Zwicker (Berkeley: University of California Press, 1987), 52–77, esp. 65–67. See also Jennifer Reynolds Taylor, "Lucy Countess of Bedford, Jonson, and Donne," Ph.D. diss., McMaster University, 1979.

11. On the whole issue of rivals and of Jonson's reactions to them, see Evans, *Ben Jonson and the Poetics of Patronage*, 145–91.

12. For a fuller discussion of this poem and its circumstances and significance, see *ibid.*, 40–53.

13. See David McPherson, *Ben Jonson's Library and Marginalia: An Annotated Catalogue*, in *Studies in Philology* 71, no. 5 (1974): 11.

14. See Evans, *Ben Jonson and the Poetics of Patronage*, 59; 146–48; 167; 181–91; 210–12.

15. On this point, see *ibid.*, 233–35.

16. On this point, see *ibid.*, 158–59; 232.

17. Orgel and Strong, 1: 283.

18. As the note in H&S indicates, this last reference alludes to a story recorded in Diodorus's *Bibliotheca*: "And since these Atlantides excelled in beauty and chastity, Busiris the king of the Egyptians . . . was seized with the desire to get the maidens into his power; and consequently he dispatched pirates by sea with orders to seize the girls and deliver them into his hands. About this time Heracles, while engaged in the performance of his last Labour, slew in Libya Antaeus. . . . Meanwhile the pirates had seized the girls while they were playing. . . . Heracles came upon the pirates . . . [and] slew the pirates to a man and brought the girls back to Atlas their father. . . ." See the translation by C. H. Oldfather, 2: 429–31. Interestingly, whereas Diodorus repeatedly mentions "pirates," Jonson specifies a single "pirate." Might he have intended White?

19. See Orgel and Strong, 1: 283. As Orgel suggests elsewhere, this "goddess" was probably Virtue; see *The Jonsonian Masque*, 150. She would thus have been comparable not only in her appearance but also in her connotations to White's Diana.

20. See Marcus, 124.

21. For discussion of such motives as they affect the plays, see Evans, *Ben Jonson and the Poetics of Patronage*, 246–68, and also Robert N. Watson, *Ben Jonson's Parodic Strategy: Literary Imperialism in the Comedies* and George E. Rowe, *Distinguishing Jonson*.

Chapter 6. Jonson, Campion, and *The Gypsies Metamorphos'd*

1. See Richard S. Peterson, *Imitation and Praise in the Poems of Ben Jonson* (New Haven: Yale University Press, 1980); Katharine Eisaman Maus, *Ben Jonson and the Roman Frame of Mind* (Princeton: Princeton University Press, 1984); Robert N. Watson, *Ben Jonson's Parodic Strategy: Literary Imperialism in the Comedies*; and George E. Rowe, *Distinguishing Jonson: Imitation, Rivalry, and the Direction of a Dramatic Career*.

2. See, for instance, my articles entitled "Jonson's Copy of Seneca"; "More's *Richard III* and Jonson's *Richard Crookback* and *Sejanus*," *Comparative Drama* 24

(1990): 97–132; "Ben Jonson's Chaucer," *English Literary Renaissance* 19 (1989): 324–45, and other articles cited therein.

3. Most of my comments about Campion's life will be based on the information contained in the "Introduction" to Percival Vivian's edition of *Campion's Works* (Oxford: Clarendon Press, 1909). Material from this edition will be cited parenthetically as "Vivian." Where necessary or appropriate, I will supplement the information Vivian provides with data from other sources. Information about Jonson's life is available in the first volume of H&S.

4. See Franklin and Adams, *The Jonson Allusion Book*, 33.

5. On this point, see David Lindley, *Thomas Campion* (Leiden: E. J. Brill, 1986), 66. Lindley's book is one of the most helpful of recent works on Campion; I will cite it parenthetically simply as "Lindley" to distinguish it from other works by the same author.

6. On this point see Walter R. Davis, ed., *The Works of Thomas Campion* (Garden City, NY: Doubleday, 1967), 212. When quoting from Campion's works, I will cite the Davis edition, citing Davis's name and the appropriate page number(s) in parentheses.

7. See Edward Lowbury, Timothy Salter, and Alison Young, *Thomas Campion: Poet, Composer, Physician* (London: Chatto & Windus, 1970), 92. Subsequent parenthetical references to this book will cite "Lowbury" and the appropriate page number(s).

8. On this point see Catherine W. Peltz, "Thomas Campion, An Elizabethan Neo-Classicist," *Modern Language Quarterly* 11 (1950): 3–6, esp. 4.

9. See Frederick W. Sternfeld, "Song in Jonson's Comedy: A Gloss on *Volpone*," in *Studies in English Renaissance Drama in Memory of Karl Julius Holzknecht*, ed. Josephine W. Bennett, et al. (New York: New York University Press, 1959), 310–21, esp. 315–16 and 320. On this topic see also Gordon Braden, "*Vivamus mea Lesbia* in the English Renaissance," *English Literary Renaissance* 9 (1979): 199–224.

10. See Roger L. Clubb, "The Paradox of Ben Jonson's 'A Fit of Rime Against Rime,'" *CLA Journal* 5 (1961): 145–47.

11. See Stephen Orgel and Roy Strong, eds., *Inigo Jones*, 1: 241, 244. See also Lindley, 197, 203.

12. On this point see David Lindley, "Embarrassing Ben: The Masques for Frances Howard," *English Literary Renaissance* 16 (1986): 343–59, esp. 358. I will cite this parenthetically as "Lindley, 'Embarrassing.'"

13. See Orgel, ed., *Ben Jonson: The Complete Masques*, 484 and H&S 10: 543–44.

14. See John Orrell, "The Agent of Savoy at *The Somerset Masque*," *Review of English Studies* 28 (1977): 301–5.

15. See Spink's "Campion's Entertainment at Brougham Castle, 1617," in *Music in English Renaissance Drama*, ed. John H. Long (Lexington: University Press of Kentucky, 1968), 57–74.

16. For exhaustive treatment of the question of sources and of just about every other aspect of the Jonson's masque, see Dale B. J. Randall's extremely valuable book *Jonson's Gypsies Unmasked: Background and Theme of The Gypsies Metamorphos'd*" (Durham, NC: Duke University Press, 1975). However, Randall mentions the Brougham Castle *Ayres* only very briefly in passing in a footnote (124), but he does not comment on the Campion connection, nor does he cite Spink's article. For a valuable recent discussion of the work, see Martin Butler, "'We are one mans all': Jonson's *The Gipsies Metamorphosed*," *Yearbook of English Studies* 21 (1991): 253–73. Butler argues for a closer connection between Jonson and Buckingham than Randall's thesis would suggest.

Chapter 7. Jonson, Joseph Webbe, and the Nature and Purpose of Poetry

1. See H&S 11: 358–59 and also 1: 114, 2: 419. For a quick reference to Webbe by a recent biographer of Jonson, see Rosalind Miles, *Ben Jonson: His Life and Work* (London and New York: Routledge & Kegan Paul, 1986), 243. Webbe is also discussed briefly by William Dinsmore Briggs; see "On Certain Incidents in Ben Jonson's Life," *Modern Philology* 11 (1913): 279–88, esp. 285–87. In addition, Webbe is also mentioned by Bradley and Adams in *The Jonson Allusion Book*, 142.

2. See "Dr. Joseph Webbe and Language Teaching (1622)," *Modern Language Notes* 26 (1911): 40–46. Elsewhere, Watson says of Webbe that "it would be difficult to cite the name of a more incisive and competent critic of grammar-teaching in the 17th century." See *The English Grammar Schools to 1660: Their Curriculum and Practice* (Cambridge: Cambridge University Press, 1908), 285. Chapter 17 of this book contains a helpful overview of "The Grammar War."

3. See her article on "Problems of Language-Teaching: A Discussion Among Hartlib's Friends," *Modern Language Review* 59 (1964): 13–24, esp. 14. Other relevant articles by Salmon include "An Ambitious Printing Project of the Early Seventeenth Century," *The Library*, 5th ser., 16 (1961): 190–96, and "Joseph Webbe: Some Seventeenth-Century Views on Language-Teaching and the Nature of Meaning," *Bibliothèque d'Humanisme et Renaissance* 23 (1961): 324–40. In the latter essay, Salmon argues that Webbe's ideas "were inspired by a good deal of common sense, and foreshadowed some linguistic theories to which full expression was not given until the twentieth century" (324). Salmon's articles on Webbe and other topics are reprinted in her book *The Study of Language in 17th-Century England* (Amsterdam: Benjamins, 1979).

4. Sloane 1466 is a large collection and contains a number of interesting papers, including letters and treatises by Webbe and by William Brooks that debate the merits of Webbe's theories. As Briggs notes (287), the collection also contains one other brief reference to Jonson; for the text of this, see H&S 11: 359–60. Many of the papers in Sloane 1466 were written for Samuel Hartlib, the intellectual and later the friend of Milton. Webbe was eager to attract Hartlib's support for his ideas. For more on this connection see note 30, below. Webbe's letter to Jonson is dated "Jan: 20. 1628." In the *Jonson Allusion Book*, Bradley and Adams (probably following Briggs, 286) interpret this as an Old Style dating—i.e., as January 1629 in modern terms. However, there seem good reasons for accepting the earlier dating. For one thing, the book Webbe was defending was published in 1626; would he have been likely to let so much time pass before responding to criticism? Whatever the case, the precise date is of small importance to my argument.

In transcribing portions of Sloane 1466 I have tried to follow the manuscript as closely as possible. However, where Webbe uses capital J for capital I, I have substituted the latter, and where he uses the abbreviation "g" to represent the prefixes "con" or "com" (as in "gfuted"), I have expanded his abbreviation.

5. For these and the following biographical details, see Salmon, "Joseph Webbe," esp. 325–26. Additional information on Webbe's life is available in the Wellcome Library of the Royal College of Physicians in London. The Library's typescript translation of the *Third Book of Annals* of the College, covering the years 1608–47, contains a number of details about Webbe. For instance, the entry for 6 December 1616 notes that Webbe was one of several doctors examined by the College's censors. The entry notes that "Dr. Webb, of Padua twelve years

before, was required to be incorporated here but was approved for the first time" (91). This suggests that Webbe had moved to London rather recently, since he had not yet been incorporated as a physician by an English university. However, a later entry—for 7 April 1626—notes that "Dr. Webb of Padua in the year 1603 (as he claimed) [said] he had already been examined here some time before: but it does not appear in the records. A fine was therefore imposed upon him of an annual payment of four pounds beginning at the next feast of St. John the Baptist: this the Censors reported to the President" (203). Apparently, then, Webbe had failed to become incorporated but was practicing nonetheless. Interestingly, an entry for 29 March 1626 lists "Dr. Webb in old Bailie black and white courte" as "among the men practising medicine or pharmacy about London . . . suspected of papistry" (202). This entry valuably confirms evidence available from another source (see note 8 below). Finally, Webbe's name appears in a list of persons affiliated with the College in 1628; he is listed as one of those "making payment on account of fines" (244). All these data are summarized by William Munk in his *Roll of the Royal College of Physicians of London*, 2nd ed. (London: Royal College of Physicians, 1878), 1: 169. In the Wellcome Library's interleaved copy of Munk's *Roll*, Munk has added additional information in his own hand to his entry about Webbe. Most of the additional data are available in other sources (see, for instance, the *Dictionary of National Biography*), but one item of value that I have not seen mentioned elsewhere reads as follows: "On the 21 July 1637 being then 60 years of age he was at Leyden and entered his name in the Album Studiosorum." I have not been able to trace this information further, but if Munk's assertion is accurate it provides evidence that Webbe was still alive in the year Jonson died. Salmon had suggested that Webbe "must have died fairly soon after 1629" ("Joseph Webbe," 337).

6. On this point see Salmon, "An Ambitious Printing Project."

7. Joseph Webbe, *A Petition to the High Court of Parliament* (London, 1623), 2.

8. John Gee, *The Foot Out of the Snare*, 4th ed. (London, 1624), sig. X^v.

9. Salmon, "An Ambitious Printing Project," 191.

10. On this point see particularly Joyce Monroe Simmons, "A Study of the Influence of Martial in the Renaissance Upon the Epigrams of Ben Jonson," Ph.D. diss., Duke University, 1980, esp. 4–10.

11. See, for instance, Richard S. Peterson, *Imitation and Praise in the Poetry of Ben Jonson* and the chapter on Jonson in Thomas M. Greene, *The Light in Troy: Imitation and Discovery in Renaissance Poetry* (New Haven: Yale University Press, 1982).

12. In his *Discoveries*, Jonson notes that "when it was told to *Alcestis*, that *Euripides* had in three daies brought forth but three verses, and those with some difficultie, and throwes; *Alcestis*, glorying hee could with ease have sent forth a hundred in the space; *Euripides* roundly repl[i]'d, Like enough. But, here is the difference; Thy verses will not last those three daies; mine will to all time. Which was, as to tell him, he could not write a verse" (H&S 8: 638). Another note in the *Discoveries* advises that one should "take care in placing, and ranking both matter, and words, that the composition be comely; and to doe this with diligence, and often. No matter how slow the style be at first, so it be labour'd, and accurate: seeke the best, and be not glad of the forward conceipts, or first words, that offer themselves to us, but judge of what wee invent; and order what wee approve" (H&S 8: 615).

The value of the *Discoveries* as a clue to the links between Jonson's thinking and Webbe's is enhanced when one recalls that the *Discoveries* were probably compiled mainly during the last decade or so of Jonson's life (H&S 11: 213)—that is, during the period when he seems to have been friendly with Webbe.

13. Thus he notes that "change is a kind of refreshing in studies, and infuseth knowledge by way of recreation. Thence the Schoole it selfe is call'd a Play, or Game: and all Letters are so best taught to Schollers. They should not be affrighted, or deterr'd in their Entry, but drawne on with exercise, and emulation" (H&S 8: 614).

14. Although Jonson himself composed an English grammar, passages in the *Discoveries* suggest that he may have shared Webbe's disdain for the officiousness of many grammarians. Thus he notes the "extreame anxieties, and foolish cavils of *Grammarians*," and later he notes the "diseases" of "*Grammarians*," contrasting the latter with the "true *Critick*, or *Censor*" (H&S 8: 642). Foster Watson sees Jonson's own grammar as an example of "the new direction of grammar teaching" and quotes a passage indicating Jonson's impatience with intellectual dogmatism; see *The Beginnings of the Teaching of Modern Subjects in England* (London: Isaac Pitman, 1909), 29–31.

15. In the *Discoveries*, Jonson notes that "*For* a man to write well, there are required three Necessaries. To reade the best Authors, observe the best Speakers: and much exercise of his owne style" (H&S 8: 615). Later he notes that what is especially required of a poet is "exactnesse of Studie, and multiplicity of reading" (H&S 8: 639).

16. In the *Discoveries*, Jonson (imitating the elder Seneca) notes that "*Memory*, of all the *powers* of the mind, is the most *delicate*, and *fraile*: it is the first of our *faculties* that Age invades" (H&S 8: 578).

17. See *A Ben Jonson Companion* (Bloomington: Indiana University Press, 1983), 206.

18. In his *Discoveries*, Jonson notes that the poet must "so . . . master the matter, and Stile, as to shew, hee knowes, how to handle, place, or dispose of either, with *elegancie*, when need shall bee. And not thinke, hee can leape forth suddainely a *Poet*, by dreaming hee hath been in *Parnassus*, or, having washt his lipps (as they say) in *Helicon*. There goes more to his making, then so. For to Nature, Exercise, Imitation, and Studie, *Art* must bee added, to make all these perfect. And, though these challenge to themselves much, in the making up of our Maker, it is Art only can lead him to perfection, and leave him there in possession, as planted by her hand" (H&S 8: 639).

19. In the *Discoveries*, Jonson notes that in developing as a stylist, "as it is fit for grown and able Writers to stand of themselves, and worke with their owne strength, to trust and endeavour by their owne faculties: so it is fit for the beginner, and learner, to study others, and the best" (H&S 8: 616).

20. In the *Discoveries*, for instance, Jonson notes that "*Opinion* is a light, vaine, crude, and imperfect thing, settled in the Imagination; but never arriving at the understanding, there to obtaine the tincture of *Reason*" (H&S 8: 564).

21. In the *Discoveries*, Jonson notes that "the mind, and memory are more sharpely exercis'd in comprehending an other mans things, then our owne; and such as accustome themselves, and are familiar with the best Authours, shall ever and anon find somewhat of them in themselves, and in the expression of their minds, even when they feele it not, be able to utter something like theirs, which hath an Authority above their owne" (H&S 8: 616).

22. Thus in the Dedication to *Volpone*, Jonson asserts "*the impossibility of any mans being the good Poet, without first being a good man*" and argues that "*so diuine a skill*" as poetry "*should not bee attempted with vncleane hands.*" He also asserts

that he himself had *"euer trembled to thinke toward the least prophanesse"* (H&S 5: 17–18).

23. The most memorable comment in the *Discoveries* on hasty writing is, of course, the famous passage on Shakespeare: "*I remember*, the Players have often mentioned it as an honour to *Shakespeare*, that in his writing, (whatsoever he penn'd) hee never blotted out line. My answer hath beene, Would he had blotted a thousand. Which they thought a malevolent speech. I had not told posterity this, but for their ignorance, who choose that circumstance to commend their friend by, wherein he most faulted" (H&S 8: 583). Elsewhere, Jonson notes that "Ready writing makes not good writing; but good writing brings on ready writing: Yet when wee thinke wee have got the faculty, it is even good to resist it: as to give a Horse a check sometimes with [a] bit, which doth not so much stop his course, as stirre his mettle" (H&S 8: 616). Later still, he notes that "The common Rymers powre forth Verses, such as they are, (*ex tempore*) but there never come[s] from them one Sense, worth the life of a Day" (H&S 8: 638).

24. In the *Discoveries* Jonson, after first emphasizing the need for natural poetic talent, then notes the need to cultivate and develop that talent: "To this perfection of Nature in our *Poet*, wee require Exercise of those parts, and frequent. If his wit will not arrive soddainly at the dignitie of the Ancients, let him not yet fall out with it, quarrell, or be over-hastily Angry: offer, to turne it away from Study, in a humor; but come to it againe upon better cogitation; try an other time, with labour. If then it succeed not, cast not away the Quills, yet: nor scratch the Wainescot, beate not the poore Deske; but bring all to the forge, and file, againe; tourne it a newe. There is not Statute *Law* of the Kingdome bidds you bee a Poet, against your will; or the first Quarter. If it come, in a yeare, or two, it is well" (H&S 8: 637–38).

25. An extended passage in the *Discoveries* discussing poetic enthusiasm begins by noting that "whereas all other Arts consist of Doctrine, and Precepts: the *Poet* must bee able by nature, and instinct, to powre out the Treasure of his minde; and, as *Seneca* saith, *Aliquando secundum Anacreontem insanire, jucundum esse*: by which hee understands, the *Poeticall Rapture*" (H&S 8: 637). For examples of Jonson claiming or calling on poetic inspiration see, for instance, *Under-woods* 23 and 25.

26. William Drummond, in his summary of his famous conversations with Jonson, noted that the latter was "oppressed with fantasie, which hath ever mastered his reason, a generall disease jn many poets" (H&S 1: 151). Among more recent observers, Anne Barton notes, for instance, that the "rage for order which shapes [Jonson's] work is almost always met and, in a way, substantiated by an equally powerful impulse towards chaos and license." See her book *Ben Jonson: Dramatist*, x.

27. Previous commentary on Sloane 1466 has not noted the existence of a separate section of Webbe's treatise; this occurs on fols. 297r-298v of the manuscript and was apparently designed to amplify Webbe's thinking about his two "striplings." Since this section was not included in the main body of the text, and since it is uncertain that Jonson read this section, I have not included it in the body of my chapter. However, its inherent interest and its obvious relevance make it worth reprinting here. This portion of Webbe's text is much less clearly written than the main section, and in several instances the phrasing has proven indecipherable.

[297r]

But first giue mee leaue to vse a familiar Similie for the better vnd[er]standing of the branches of our practike Poetrie.

We haue 2 striplings to clothe the one of matchles beautie; the other a Neger or a blackamore.

The Clothes that wee would put upon them are either at the maisters readie mad, as the dublet et hose at the tailors the gloves at the glovers the stockinges at the hosiers et the shoes at the shoemakers, vpon their seueral [indecipherable] forms measures et patterns. Or else wee will get the materials at the drapers, silke-men skinners et the like, et make these cloths ours. cutting them many times out of the whole cloth or peece at random rudely without all measure or p[ro]portion much misshapen.

The drapers et silke-men are content to take these materials from their Weauers, who were guided by theire frames, bredths, thicknes et Exampils.

Now if wee should be constrained to goe downe so lowe as to weaue our owne stuffes, et should doe it without thes artificers frames et exa[m]pels; I doubt wee should make the piece now to broade then to narrow, sometimes w[th] puckers et uneuennes et nowhere look et as it should bee; et so difform our naked [297[r]/297[v]] boyes by clothing them, than they would no longer seem well-limmed children but ugly monsters.

This simile holdeth in our Practise of Poetrie For wee haue also forms upon w[ch] the matter of our whole peeces are wouen.

These first et furthest forms are the quantities of our words et are either Temporal or Numeral as u- uu. u-.--.-uu.---. for exampel sake being numerally examin'd u. .-. are forms of words of one syllable a peece uu u- -.- are forms of words of 2 syllables a peece. And -uu.---. of 3: a peece. But if they bee temporally examind so u. is of 1. tyme [&] - of 2, uu of 2. u- of 3, [&] -.-. of 4. So is -uu of 4 [&] -.-.-. of 6 tymes although by number they are but 3.

Our Matter wouen upon these formes or frames in the whole peece are sometimes of silke satin or ueluet, as our whole peece of substa[n]tiues, under the figure 1. Sometimes of wolle as our whole class or kersey of Adjectiues under the figure 2. sometimes of haire as our grograine of verbes whose whole peece is marked with 3. [297[v]–298[r]]

And sometymes Linnin as our Cambrick Holland bockram or Canvace of Indeclined parts marked w[th] 4. All w[ch] if any man haue a minde thertoo let him cal them fustians so hee will but und[er]stand them all authentical.

The Patterns or measures by w[ch] wee cut our Clothes out of this Matter are of 2. sortes of workmen eyther of bot[c]hers or or good et allowed artificers. These allowed Artificers are our best Àuthors et the bot[c]hers yong beginners or such as leaue the paths of Authoritie.

Bot[c]hers would but make us bot[c]h et therf. wee will leaue their Patterns unto those whose Spirits sore no higher than to become botchers.

Proclaymed workemen as ouid Virgil et their Equals that helpe vs to patterns et these bee our second or newer forms of clothing; et wee call them the formes of Clauses; w[ch] yeeld vs not only p[er]fect grases of speech, but p[er]fect collocutio[n] or distribution of wordes, whereby wee flie sole [indecipherable], et are made Harmonical; as also p[er]fect Gramar, though wee ours. at first conceiued it not.

These patternes of Clauses are as the patternes [298[r]-298[v]] of a Collar, back-peece fore-peeces, winges, sleeues et skirts of a doublet, w[ch] being layde upon the whole cloth, et it punctually cut out according to the p[re]sident wee haue all the parcels of an entire principal garment. W[ch] if wee kn. not how to put together, let vs again obserue our learned maisters; et they will in euery place giue vs compositiue formes of solid vestures; whose threds of reason if we follow, wee shall not sow the sleeue to the collar nor the skirt, where the wing should bee, but euery part shal haue his true peculiar et proper posture, et the whole garment finished shall make the world confesse that wee were bound apprentises to cunni[n]g maisters, not to botchers. And by this time wee kn. how to make a garment for our striplinges.

28. Sloane 1466 has obviously been carefully rebound. One indication of a different prior arrangement of its contents is that ink "bleeding" on fol. 216[v] corresponds to what appears on the present fol. 224[r]. Thus the material in between seems to have been inserted at a later stage.

29. Parts of Sloane 1466 seem to have belonged, at one time, to Samuel Hartlib, most of whose papers are now housed in the Sheffield University Library. A check of the catalogue of those papers kept at the Royal Commission on Historical Manuscripts unfortunately turned up no indication that Jonson's "Answer" is now among them. However, the National Register of Archives report on the collection notes that "It is fairly conclusive . . . that many of the papers have not survived, and it is suggested that [John] Worthington [Hartlib's friend] extracted papers during his arrangement in 1667." See Royal Commission on Historical Manuscripts, *Report on the correspondence and papers of Samuel Hartlib* (London, 1980), 1. This is NRA report # 23591.

30. Certainly the provision of an elaborate and separate title page for the treatise (which is not true of many of the other documents in the collection) suggests this. Also, the English version of the treatise is a relatively clean copy, from which type could easily be set, whereas the Latin version (also included in Sloane 1466) is sprinkled with marginal annotations and insertions (in English) that correspond to phrases in the English version. Perhaps the Latin version was prepared first, and perhaps the English version is a translation of it. The remote but intriguing possibility that the marginal annotations in the Latin version were made by Jonson must remain a possibility merely, although there are some similarities between the handwriting used in making these notes and Jonson's own penmanship. The more likely annotator, however, is Webbe himself. In any case, these annotations seem not to have been mentioned in previous discussions of Sloane 1466.

Chapter 8. Jonson, Weston, and the Dibgys: Patronage Relations in Some Later Poems

1. For fuller discussion of these issues, see Evans, *Ben Jonson and the Poetics of Patronage*. My thinking about Jonson and patronage has been stimulated by the work of a number of previous writers, especially Richard Helgerson, Annabel Patterson, Don Wayne, Leah Marcus, and Stanley Fish. My book offers fuller acknowledgments and citations than I have space for here.

2. See H&S 1: 180. Aubrey provides no independent confirmation of the incident, but the mere fact that he found the report of it credible says a great deal about the nature of Renaissance patronage.

3. See Michael Van Cleave Alexander, *Charles I's Lord Treasurer* (London: Macmillan, 1975), 130–31. On Weston, see also David Nichol Smith, *Characters from the Histories and Memoirs of the Seventeenth Century*, 21–29, and Edward [Hyde], Earl of Clarendon, *The History of the Rebellion and Civil Wars in England*, ed. W. Dunn Macray, 6 vols. (Oxford: Clarendon Press, 1888), 1: 59–67.

4. For a superb account of the whole episode see Samuel R. Gardiner, *History of England from the Accession of James I to the Outbreak of Civil War*, 7: 67–69.

5. See Alexander, 161.

6. Alexander, 128–29 and 167–69; Aylmer, *The King's Servants: The Civil Service Under Charles I, 1625–1642*, 2nd ed. (New York: Columbia University Press, 1974), 203.

7. See Nichol Smith, 27–28. Alexander suggests (173) that Clarendon's harsh estimate may have been influenced by his regard for Laud, Weston's rival. However, the dispatches of various Venetian representatives at Charles's court also reflect the essential ambivalence of Weston's status and attitudes reported in Clarendon's account; see volumes 22 and 23 of the *Calendar of State Papers . . . Venice*, ed. Allen B. Hinds (London: HMSO, 1919–21)—hereafter cited as *CSPV*. These reports make it clear that although Weston enjoyed more influence than any other courtier, he also feared a fall. His preoccupation with the machinations of his rivals is a recurrent theme in the Venetian dispatches, and clearly he had good reason to worry. For instance, a report dated 27 July 1629 indicates the Queen's displeasure with Weston (*CSPV* 22: 142). Another, dated 7 September 1629, reports Weston's fears of falling and the likelihood of his eclipse (*CSPV* 22: 177). At one point a friendly courtier warned Weston that he would be held responsible for all that went wrong with a particular government policy, and the warning seems to have had some impact (*CSPV* 22: 184). A particularly interesting report indicates that, at least at one point, even Charles seems to have grown jealous of Weston's power and disdained seeming too dependent on him (*CSPV* 22: 204–5); yet, another report written just a few weeks later asserts that Weston was highly esteemed by Charles (*CSPV* 22: 218). This ambivalence is typical of the Venetian comments on Weston's fortunes during his years of greatest prosperity: even when (or perhaps especially when) his power seemed at its height, it never was (and never could be) entirely secure. The Lord Treasurer had too many natural antagonists and personal enemies for that to be the case. Thus various reports throughout the years of his preeminence indicate tensions with the Queen, who saw him as a rival for influence with Charles (*CSPV* 22: 450; 464); with the Puritans, who suspected him of Catholic sympathies (*CSPV* 22: 309); with the Catholics, who also distrusted him (Clarendon, 1: 63); with the French ambassador, who tried to stir up trouble for Weston in the English court (*CSPV* 22: 331; 510; 585); with various members of the Privy Council, who distrusted his power (*CSPV* 23: 220); with Archbishop Laud, one of Weston's most persistent foes (*CSPV* 23: 226); and with the people in general (*CSPV* 23: 315). The list of Weston's enemies could easily be extended; see Clarendon, 1: 62.

Powerful though he was, Weston knew that he could not ignore his rivals; the Venetians frequently report his worries about his security and his attempts to ensure it (*CSPV* 22: 538; 546; 598; 607). Evidence abounds that Charles favored Weston, and that as long as he did, the Treasurer's status was relatively secure (*CSPV* 22: 177; 218–20; 592; 623; 626; 637; *CSPV* 23: 80). Weston may have feared his rivals, but as long as he retained the King's support, his rivals also had reason to fear (*CSPV* 23: 87). Conflict with Weston or his kin might threaten ruin, even for powerful aristocrats (*CSPV* 23: 100). Much of the court's business inevitably passed through his hands (*CSPV* 22: 610). Moreover, Weston knew how to use his influence with the King to his own advantage and against his foes (*CSPV* 22: 464; 588). Yet when pretexts for attacking him arose, his rivals did not fail to exploit them (*CSPV* 23: 221–22). At times even Charles seemed to be growing distant (*CSPV* 23: 294–95). Usually, however, the King's support remained firm, helping Weston to weather several crises (*CSPV* 23: 223–24). Charles seems to have been genuinely afflicted by his old servant's death, and he assured Weston during his final illness that the interests of his family would be protected. Thus one of the last of the Venetian reports on Weston epitomizes their typical ambivalence, mentioning both the support he enjoyed and the protection he craved. Even in his last days he could not escape the anxiety about his power (now viewed as the prospective yet uncertain power of his heirs) that had bedevilled him throughout his life (*CSPV* 23: 350–51). For a humorous example of such anxiety, see Clarendon, 1: 66–67.

8. On Jonson's circumstances in his last decade see H&S 1: 89–102; Marchette Chute, *Ben Jonson of Westminster* (New York: Dutton, 1953), 305–36; and Riggs, *Ben Jonson: A Life*, 295–350. After an early period of what Jonson seems to have interpreted as neglect in the first years of the new reign, he regained some of his old status at court, but then risked annoying Charles with his increasingly bitter attacks on his old rival, Inigo Jones; see Evans, *Ben Jonson and the Poetics of Patronage*, 182–85.

9. For the passages cited, see Alexander, 170.

10. Shirley and Davenant also wrote poems to celebrate the marriage; Davenant's final lines show his awareness that his contribution would inevitably be compared to those of other writers: "He that in strength of wishes, next shall trie, / T' increase your blessings with his Poetry / May shew a fiercer Wit, and cleaner Art; / But not a more sincere, and eager Heart." Interestingly enough, Davenant's poem is addressed not to Hierome, but to his father; the poem praises the marriage as "A mixture of two Noble bloods"—language that must have appealed to the recently ennobled Weston. See *The Works of Sir William Davenant* (New York: Benjamin Blom, 1968), 1: 230–31. Shirley's first stanza also suggests his expectation that his poem would be compared with other gifts and tributes. See *The Dramatic Works and Poems of James Shirley*, ed. Alexander Dyce (London: J. Murray, 1833), 6: 438–39.

11. See Alastair Fowler, *Triumphal Forms: Structural Patterns in Elizabethan Poetry* (Cambridge: Cambridge University Press, 1970), 22–33.

12. Alexander reports (169) that Weston made "occasional friendly, albeit unsuccessful gestures" to Laud. One, a month before Hierome's wedding, also involved officiating at a religious service: Weston invited Laud to dedicate the newly-completed chapel of his new estate. Could Jonson's prominent reference to the Bishop be in any way related to such conciliatory motives?

13. The state of Weston's health may help to answer Annabel Patterson's question about why, through a classical allusion in the poem's last lines, "the question of decay was raised at all"; see *Censorship and Interpretation: The Conditions of Writing and Reading in Early Modern England*, 138. By subtly reminding Weston of his frail health, Jonson also reminds him of the poem's ability to give him a kind of immortality, not only by celebrating him personally but also by helping him to cement the public status of his family. (On Weston's ambitions for his family, see, for instance, Clarendon, 1: 63.) Patterson implies some ambivalence in Jonson's attitude toward Weston (136–38).

14. "At some points," writes Virginia Tufte, "the tone suggests that the poet

is weary at the idea of saying again all the things that are customarily said about weddings, but here and there Jonson is at his best." See *The Poetry of Marriage: The Epithalamium in Europe and Its Development in England* (Los Angeles: Tinnon-Brown, 1970), 217.

15. See *The Golden Age Restor'd: The Culture of the Stuart Court, 1603–42* (Manchester: Manchester University Press, 1981), 136. Parry valuably discusses Arundel and Buckingham as patrons (108–45).

16. Alexander, 169.

17. Alexander, 179.

18. Jonson's view of painting was probably not as uniformly negative as this poem suggests. For instance, a passage in the *Discoveries* proclaims that "Picture is the invention of Heaven: the most ancient, and most a kinne to Nature." Only a few lines earlier, however, Jonson writes that while both poetry and painting are concerned with imitation, "the Pen is more noble than the Pencill. For that can speake to the Understanding; the other, but to the Sense." And a little later he writes (in a passage inspired by Possevino) that "*Picture* tooke her faining from *Poetry*," and then lists painting's indebtedness to various other arts and sciences. See H&S 8: 609–12. In "Ben Jonson: The Poet to the Painter" (*Texas Studies in Literature and Language*, 18 [1976–77]: 381–92), Mary Livingston argues that almost all of Jonson's comments about the visual arts include the idea that they are incapable of adequately rendering universal truths (383).

When possible, we should try to place each of Jonson's pronouncements about the visual arts within its immediate context—especially its immediate patronage context—rather than generalizing very broadly about them. His expressed attitudes may have been affected by the seriousness of the threat he perceived at any given time from the visual arts (or, more precisely, from visual artists, such as Inigo Jones). On his disdain for the visual arts in his last years, see John Lemly's valuable article, "Masks and Self-Portraits in Jonson's Late Poetry," 248–66.

19. The *OED* records no use of the verb "compose" in connection with painting before 1655, whereas the word's associations with writing seem much older (in fact, the *OED* cites one of Jonson's uses of it in this latter sense).

In addition to linking the patron and the poet, the word "compose" (with its etymology of "bring together" and its associations with pacification) puns on Weston's political role and his vigorous support for a policy of peace. Ironically, Weston's actual effect on the English politics of his day was the opposite of "composing": his policies were decidedly controversial.

On an echo of Horace in "compose," and for other helpful comments on the poem's classical allusiveness, see Richard S. Peterson, *Imitation and Praise in the Poems of Ben Jonson*, 99–101.

20. Alexander, 172.

21. After his father's promotion, Hierome came to be called "Lord Weston." In addition to cultivating his attention in the "Epithalamion," Jonson in early 1633 addressed a very beautiful "*Ode gratulatorie*" to him to celebrate his return from an important mission abroad; see H&S 8: 250–51. The poem's full title celebrates Hierome's own elevation by addressing him as "L. Weston."

22. *Complete Poetry of Ben Jonson* (New York: Norton, 1963), 229n.

23. For other relevant meanings of "port," see the note in Ian Donaldson, ed., *Ben Jonson*, 705.

24. On Weston's central role at court, see (for instance) *CSPV* 22: 608.

25. On other courtiers' fears of Weston, see (for instance) *CSPV* 23: 87.

26. During a high point in his unpopularity in 1634, Weston sought to affect

public opinion by having his dependents advertise his merits; see *CSPV* 23: 223–24.

27. One possibility is John Eliot, who (in one poem) had mocked Weston's patronage of Jonson and who (in another) may have had Weston in mind when he attacked Jonson for flattering "e'en the worst of men" (H&S 11: 406). Jonson replied to the first poem with spirited invective (H&S 8: 408–9). Ironically, one of Weston's own fiercest opponents was the parliamentarian Sir John Eliot.

28. Gill claims that "*Inigo* w[i]th laughter ther grewe fatt / That thear was Nothing worth the Laughing att." Significantly, Gill seems as much interested in embarrassing Jonson socially as in attacking his play (H&S 11: 346–48). Jonson's response was a small masterpiece of invective. Like Gill's poem, it seeks to embarrass its target socially, dredging up Gill's conviction a few years before for slandering the dead Buckingham, as well as Charles and James. Its ending epitomizes Jonson at his sardonic best: "A Rogue by Statute, censur'd to be whipt, / Cropt, branded, slit, neck-stockt; go, you are stript" (H&S 8: 410–11). The last four words epitomize the poem's own effect.

Donald Lemen Clark, in *John Milton at St. Paul's School* (New York: Columbia University Press, 1948), recalls that Jonson had also been suspected of endorsing Buckingham's death, and suggests that his attack on Gill may have been partly designed to distance himself further from these allegations (96).

29. See R. T. Peterson, *Sir Kenelm Digby: The Ornament of England, 1603–1665* (Cambridge, MA: Harvard Univ. Press, 1956), 35. Also valuable on Digby's life is the preface to Vittorio Gabrieli's edition of Digby's *Loose Fantasies* (Rome: Edizioni di Storia e Letteratura, 1968).

30. R. T. Peterson, 54; 66.

31. See Gabrieli, 6.

32. R. T. Peterson (among others) argues that Digby wrote the *Loose Fantasies* to vindicate his wife's reputation (43). Gabrieli cautions that there is no evidence that Digby's manuscript ever circulated (xvii), but it seems difficult to believe that Digby wrote it with no intention of having it read.

33. Gabrieli, xxiii.

34. Gabrieli, xxv.

35. R. T. Peterson, 82.

36. R. T. Peterson, 83–84.

37. Gabrieli, xxiii.

38. See *The Works of Edmund Spenser*, ed. Edwin Greenlaw, et al. (Baltimore: Johns Hopkins University Press, 1933), 2: 472.

39. On 11 June as Jonson's birthday, see Miles, *Ben Jonson: His Life and Work*, 280–81.

40. Ian Donaldson cautions that although the phrase "Barnabee the bright" (15) also occurs in Spenser's poem, it was traditional as well. See his edition, *Ben Jonson*, 707.

41. Chute, 326.

42. H&S 11: 98.

43. In short, the poem assumes the "relational" nature of power discussed in my Introductory chapter. For another view of Jonson's relations with the powerful, see Bruce Thomas Boehrer, "Renaissance Overeating: The Sad Case of Ben Jonson," *PMLA* 105 (1990): 1071–82.

Bibliography

Manuscripts

Bodleian Library, Oxford; MS Rawlinson B 158.

British Library, London; MS Lansdowne 1198.

British Library, London; MS Sloane 1466.

Wellcome Library, Royal College of Physicians, London; Third Book of Annals (1608–47); typescript.

National Register of Archives, London. Royal Commission of Historical Manuscripts. Report of the correspondence and papers of Samuel Hartlib. NRA Report no. 23591; typescript. 1980.

Books, Articles, and Notes

Alexander, Michael Van Cleave. *Charles I's Lord Treasurer*. London: Macmillan, 1975.

Allen, Morse. *The Satire of John Marston*. New York: Haskell House, 1965.

Anderson, William. *The Scottish Nation*. 3 vols. Edinburgh: A. Fullarton, 1863.

Anonymous. *Charter-House: Its Foundations and History*. London: C. Spilsbury, 1808.

———. "The Greenwich Parish Registers, 1615–1636–7." Vol. 2 of *Transactions of the Greenwich and Lewisham Antiquarian Society*. London: Blackheath Press, 1920.

———. *The Narrative History of King James, for the first fourteen Years*. London: 1651.

Aylmer, G. E. *The King's Servants: The Civil Service Under Charles I, 1625–1642*. 2d ed. New York: Columbia University Press, 1974.

Bacon, Francis. *The Works of Francis Bacon*. Edited by James Spedding et al. 14 vols. London: Longmans, 1862–1901.

Bald, R. C. *John Donne: A Life*. New York: Oxford University Press, 1970.

Barton, Anne. *Ben Jonson, Dramatist*. Cambridge: Cambridge University Press, 1984.

Bearcroft, Philip. *An Historical Account of Thomas Sutton Esq. And of His Foundation in Charter-House*. London: E. Owen, 1737.

Bednarz, James P. "Representing Jonson: *Histriomastix* and the Origin of the Poets' War." *Huntington Library Quarterly* 54.1 (1991): 1–30.

Bentley, G. E. *The Jacobean and Caroline Stage*. 7 vols. Oxford: Clarendon Press, 1941–68.

Berger, Thomas L. and William C. Bradford, Jr. *An Index of Characters in English Printed Drama to the Restoration*. Englewood, CO: Microcard Editions, 1975.

Berringer, Ralph W. "Jonson's *Cynthia's Revels* and the War of the Theaters." *Philological Quarterly* 22 (1943): 1–22.

Birch, Thomas, ed. *The Court and Times of James the First*. 2 vols. London: Henry Colburn, 1849.

Boehrer, Bruce Thomas. "Renaissance Overeating: The Sad Case of Ben Jonson." *PMLA* 105 (1990): 1071–82.

Braden, Gordon. "*Vivamus mea Lesbia* in the English Renaissance." *English Literary Renaissance* 9 (1979): 199–224.

Bradley, Jesse Franklin and Joseph Quincy Adams. *The Jonson Allusion-Book*. New Haven: Yale University Press, 1922.

Briggs, William Dinsmore. "On Certain Incidents in Ben Jonson's Life." *Modern Philology* 11 (1913): 279–88.

Brock, D. Heyward. *A Ben Jonson Companion*. Bloomington: Indiana University Press, 1983.

Brown, William Haig. *Charterhouse: Past and Present*. Godalming: H. Stedman, 1879.

Burrell, Perci. *Sutton's Synagogue or, The English Centurion*. London: 1629.

Butler, Martin. "'We are one mans all': Jonson's *The Gipsies Metamorphosed*." *Yearbook of English Studies* 21 (1991): 253–73.

Camden, William. *Annals . . . of King James I*. In *A Complete History of England*, edited by White Kennet, 2:361-65a. 3 vols. London: 1706.

Campion, Thomas. *Campion's Works*. Edited by Percival Vivian. Oxford: Clarendon Press, 1909.

———. *The Works of Thomas Campion*. Edited by Walter R. Davis. Garden City, NY: Doubleday, 1967.

Carew, George. *Letters from George Lord Carew to Sir Thomas Roe*. Edited by John Maclean. London: Camden Society, 1860.

Carleton, Dudley. *Dudley Carleton to John Chamberlain, 1603–1624*. Edited by Maurice Lee, Jr. New Brunswick, NJ: Rutgers University Press, 1972.

[Cavendish], Margaret, Duchess of Newcastle. *Life of William Cavendish*. Edited by C. H. Firth. London: George Routledge, n.d.

Cavendishe, William. *A New Method and Extraordinary Invention, to Dress Horses*. London: Thomas Milbourn, 1667.

Chamberlain, John. *The Letters of John Chamberlain*. Edited by Norman Egbert McClure. 2 vols. Philadelphia: American Philosophical Society, 1939.

Champion, Larry S. *Ben Jonson's "Dotages": A Reconsideration of the Late Plays*. Lexington: University Press of Kentucky, 1967.

———. *Thomas Dekker and the Traditions of English Drama*. New York: Peter Lang, 1985.

Chettle, George H. *The Queen's House, Greenwich: Being the Fourteenth Monograph of the London Survey Committee*. Greenwich: Trustees of the National Maritime Museum, [1937].

Chute, Marchette. *Ben Jonson of Westminster*. New York: Dutton, 1953.

Cicero. *De Officiis*. Translated by Walter Miller. Loeb Classical Library. Cambridge, MA: Harvard University Press, 1975.

Clarendon, Edward [Hyde], Earl of. *The History of the Rebellion and Civil Wars in England*. Edited by W. Dunn Macray. 6 vols. Oxford: Clarendon Press, 1888.

Clark, Donald Lemen. *John Milton at St. Paul's School*. New York: Columbia University Press, 1948.

Darby, H. C. *The Changing Fenland*. Cambridge: Cambridge University Press, 1983.

———. *The Draining of the Fens*. Cambridge: Cambridge University Press, 1940.

Davenant, William. *The Works of Sir William Davenant*. 2 vols. New York: Benjamin Blom, 1968.

Davies, Gerald S. *Charterhouse in London: Monastery, Mansion, Hospital, School*. London: John Murray, 1921.

Dekker, Thomas. *The Dramatic Works of Thomas Dekker*. Edited by Fredson Bowers. 4 vols. Cambridge: Cambridge University Press, 1953.

Dictionary of National Biography. Edited by Leslie Stephen and Sidney Lee. 22 vols. Oxford: Oxford University Press, 1885–1913.

Digby, Kenelm. *Loose Fantasies*. Edited by Vittorio Gabrielli. Rome: Edizioni di Storia e Letterature, 1968.

Diodorus. *Bibliotheca*. Translated by C. H. Oldfather. Loeb Classical Library. 12 vols. London: Heinemann, 1946–67.

Enck, John J. *Ben Jonson and the Comic Truth*. Madison: University of Wisconsin Press, 1957.

Evans, Robert C. *Ben Jonson and the Poetics of Patronage*. Lewisburg, PA: Bucknell University Press, 1989.

———. "'Games of Fortune, Plaid at Court': Politics and Poetic Freedom in Jonson's Epigrams." In *"The Muses Common-weale": Poetry and Politics in the Seventeenth Century*, edited by Claude J. Summers and Ted-Larry Pebworth, 48–61. Columbia: University of Missouri Press, 1988.

———. "Jonson's Copy of Seneca." *Comparative Drama* 25 (1991): 257–92.

———. "Jonson's 'Epistle to Sir Edward Sacvile.'" *The Explicator* 43, no. 3 (1985): 7.

———. "Jonson's Epitaph on the Countess of Shrewsbury." *The Explicator* 44, no. 3 (1986): 15–17.

———. "Richard Brome's Death." *Notes and Queries*, n.s. 36 (1989): 351.

———. "Sir John Harington and Thomas Sutton: New Letters from Charterhouse." *John Donne Journal* 7 (1988): 213–38.

Ferguson, George. *Signs and Symbols in Christian Art*. New York: Oxford University Press, 1954.

Fish, Stanley. "Authors-Readers: Jonson's Community of the Same." *Representations* 7 (1984): 26–58.

Fowler, Alastair. *Triumphal Forms: Structural Patterns in Elizabethan Poetry*. Cambridge: Cambridge University Press, 1970.

[Frankland, Thomas]. *The Annals of King James and Charles the First*. London: 1681.

Friis, Astrid. *Alderman Cockayne's Project and the Cloth Trade: The Commercial Policy of England in Its Main Aspects 1603–1625*. London: Oxford University Press, 1927.

Gallagher, Catherine. "Marxism and the New Historicism." In *The New Historicism*, edited by Aram Veeser, 37–48. New York and London: Routledge, 1989.

Gardiner, Judith Kegan. *Craftsmanship in Context: The Development of Ben Jonson's Poetry*. The Hague: Mouton, 1975.

Gardiner, Samuel R. *History of England from the Accession of James I to the Outbreak of Civil War*. 10 vols. New York: AMS Press, 1965.

Gaspar, Julia. *The Dragon and the Dove: The Plays of Thomas Dekker*. Oxford: Clarendon Press, 1990.

Gee, John. *The Foot Out of the Snare*. 4th ed. London: 1624.

Gosse, Edmund. *The Life and Letters of John Donne*. 2 vols. London: William Heinemann, 1899.

Graff, Gerald. "Co-optation." In *The New Historicism*, edited by Aram Veeser, 168-81. New York and London: Routledge, 1989.

Great Britain. *Acts of the Privy Council of England, 1615–1616*. London: HMSO, 1925.

———. Historical Manuscripts Commission. *The Manuscripts of the Marquess of Abergavenny*. London: HMSO, 1887.

———. Historical Manuscripts Commission. *Report on the Manuscripts of His Grace the Duke of Portland*. 10 vols. London: HMSO, 1891–1923.

———. Historical Manuscripts Commission. *Report on the Manuscripts of Lord De L'isle and Dudley*. 6 vols. London, 1925–66.

———. Historical Manuscripts Commission. *Report on the Manuscripts of the Marquess of Downshire*. 4 vols. London, 1924–40.

———. Public Record Office. *Calendar of State Papers Domestic, James I, 1611–18*. Edited by Mary Anne Everett Green. London: Longman, 1858.

———. Public Record Office. *Calendar of State Papers, Venetian*. 38 vols. London, 1864–1947.

———. Royal Commission of Historical Manuscripts. *Report on the correspondence and papers of Samuel Hartlib*. London, 1980. National Register of Archives Report no. 23591.

Greenblatt, Stephen. "Resonance and Wonder." In *Literary Theory Today*, edited by Peter Collier and Helga Geyer-Ryan, 74-90. Ithaca: Cornell University Press, 1990.

———. *Shakespearean Negotiations: The Circulation of Social Energy in Renaissance England*. Berkeley and Los Angeles: University of California Press, 1988.

———. "Towards a Poetics of Culture." In *The New Historicism*, edited by Aram Veeser, 1-14. New York and London: Routledge, 1989.

Greene, Thomas M. *The Light in Troy: Imitation and Discovery in Renaissance Poetry*. New Haven: Yale University Press, 1982.

———. "Spenser and the Epithalamic Convention." In *The Prince of Poets: Essays on Edmund Spenser*, edited by John R. Elliott, Jr., 152-69. New York: New York University Press, 1965.

Grotius, Hugo. *The Law of War and Peace*. Translated by Francis W. Kelsey. Indianapolis: Bobbs-Merrill, 1925.

Hamilton, Olive, and Nigel Hamilton. *Royal Greenwich: A Guide and History to London's Most Historic Borough*. London: The Greenwich Bookshop, 1969.

Harington, John. *The Letters and Epigrams of Sir John Harington*. Edited by Norman Egbert McClure. Philadelphia: University of Pennsylvania Press, 1930.

Hendriks, Dom Lawrence. *The London Charterhouse: Its Monks and Martyrs*. London: Kegan Paul, 1889.

Herne, Samuel. *Domus Carthusiana*. London, 1677.

Hotine, Margaret. "Ben Jonson, Volpone, and Charterhouse." *Notes and Queries*, n.s. 38 (1991): 79–81.

Hoy, Cyrus. *Introductions, Notes, and Commentaries to Texts in 'The Dramatic Works of Thomas Dekker'*. 4 vols. Cambridge: Cambridge University Press, 1981.

Hyland, Peter. *Disguise and Role-Playing in Ben Jonson's Drama*. Salzburg: Institut für Englische Sprace und Literatur, 1977.

Ingram, R. W. *John Marston*. Boston: Twayne, 1978.

James I, King. *The Political Works of James I*. Edited by Charles Howard McIlwain. New York: Russell and Russell, 1965.

Jardine, M. D. "New Historicism for Old: New Conservatism for Old?: The Politics of Patronage in the Renaissance." *Yearbook of English Studies* 21 (1991): 286–304.

Jones-Davies, M. T. *Un Peintre de la Vie Londonienne: Thomas Dekker*. 2 vols. Paris: Librairie Marcel Didier, 1958.

Jonson, Ben. *Ben Jonson*. Edited by C. H. Herford and Percy and Evelyn Simpson. 11 vols. Oxford: Clarendon, 1925–52.

———. *Ben Jonson*. Edited by Ian Donaldson. New York: Oxford University Press, 1985.

———. *The Complete Poetry of Ben Jonson*. Edited by William B. Hunter, Jr. New York: Norton, 1963.

———. *The Devil Is an Ass*. Edited by William Savage Johnson. New York: Henry Holt, 1905.

———. *Volpone*. Edited by R. B. Parker. The Revels Plays. Manchester: Manchester University Press, 1978.

———. *The Works of Ben Jonson*. Notes and a memoir by William Gifford. Edited by Francis Cunningham. 3 vols. London: Chatto & Windus, 1903.

Kay, W. David. "Ben Jonson, Horace, and the Poetomachia: The Development of an Elizabethan Playwright's Public Image." Ph.D. diss., Princeton University, 1968.

———. "The Shaping of Ben Jonson's Career: A Reexamination of Facts and Problems." *Modern Philology* 67 (1970): 224–37.

Kerr, Robert. *The Correspondence of Sir Robert Kerr, First Earl of Ancram and His Son William, Third Earl of Lothian*. 2 vols. Edinburgh: [R. and R. Clark], 1875.

Kittredge, G. L. "King James I and *The Devil is an Ass*." *Modern Philology* 9 (1911): 195–209.

Knoll, Robert E. *Ben Jonson's Plays: An Introduction*. Lincoln: University of Nebraska Press, 1964.

Lee, Jongsook. *Ben Jonson's Poesis: A Literary Dialectic of Ideal and History*. Charlottesville: University Press of Virginia, 1989.

Lee, Maurice, Jr. *Great Britain's Solomon: James VI and I in His Three Kingdoms.* Urbana: University of Illinois Press, 1990.

Leggatt, Alexander. *Ben Jonson: His Vision and His Art.* London: Methuen, 1981.

Leinwand, Theodore. "Negotiation and New Historicism." *PMLA* 105 (1990): 477–90.

Lemly, John. "Masks and Self-Portraits in Jonson's Late Poetry." *ELH* 44 (1977): 248–66.

Lentricchia, Frank. "Foucault's Legacy—A New Historicism?" In *The New Historicism,* edited by Aram Veeser, 321-42. New York and London: Routledge, 1989.

Lewalski, Barbara. "Lucy, Countess of Bedford: Images of a Jacobean Courtier and Patroness." In *Politics of Discourse,* edited by Kevin Sharpe and Steven N. Zwicker, 52–77. Berkeley: University of California Press, 1987.

Lindley, David. "Embarrassing Ben: The Masques for Frances Howard." *English Literary Renaissance* 16 (1986): 343–59.

———. *Thomas Campion.* Leiden: E. J. Brill, 1986.

Little, Anne C. "Jonson's Poetry and the Star Chamber Speech." *Notes and Queries* 238 (1993): 212-14.

Livingston, Mary L. "Ben Jonson: The Poet to the Painter." *Texas Studies in Literature and Language* 18 (1976): 381–92.

Longueville, Thomas. *The First Duke and Duchess of Newcastle-Upon-Tyne.* London: Longmans, 1910.

Low, Anthony. "Donne and the New Historicism." *John Donne Journal* 7 (1988): 125–31.

Lowbury, Edward, Timothy Salter, and Alison Young. *Thomas Campion: Poet, Composer, Physician.* London: Chatto & Windus, 1970.

Luders, A., et al. *Statutes of the Realm.* 11 vols. London: 1810–28.

McCanles, Michael. Review of David Riggs, *Ben Jonson: A Life* and Robert C. Evans, *Ben Jonson and the Poetics of Patronage. Criticism* 32 (1990): 129–32.

McLuskie, Kathleen E. "The Poets' Royal Exchange: Patronage and Commerce in Early Modern Drama." *Yearbook of English Studies* 21 (1991): 53–62.

McPherson, David. "Ben Jonson's Library and Marginalia: An Annotated Catalogue." *Studies in Philology* 71, no. 5 (1974): i–xii, 1–100.

———. "The Origins of Overdo." *Modern Language Quarterly* 37 (1976): 221–33.

Marcus, Leah S. *The Politics of Mirth: Jonson, Herrick, Milton, Marvell, and the Defense of Old Holiday Pastimes.* Chicago: University of Chicago Press, 1986.

Marotti, Arthur. "Patronage, Poetry, and Print." *Yearbook of English Studies* 21 (1991): 1–26.

Masson, David, ed. *The Register of the Privy Council of Scotland.* Edinburgh: H. H. General Register House, 1877.

Miles, Rosalind. *Ben Jonson: His Life and Work.* London: Methuen, 1986.

Montrose, Louis A. "Professing the Renaissance: The Poetics and Politics of Culture." In *The New Historicism,* edited by Aram Veeser, 15–36. New York and London: Routledge, 1989.

Mullinger, James Bass. *The University of Cambridge.* 3 vols. Cambridge: Cambridge University Press, 1884.

Munk, William. *Roll of the Royal College of Physicians of London*. 2d ed. 3 vols. London: Royal College of Physicians, 1878.

Nelson, Alan, ed. *Cambridge*. 2 vols. Records of Early English Drama. Toronto: University of Toronto Press, 1989.

Noonan, John T. *The Scholastic Analysis of Usury*. Cambridge, MA: Harvard University Press, 1957.

Orgel, Stephen, ed. *Ben Jonson: The Complete Masques*. New Haven: Yale University Press, 1969.

———. *The Jonsonian Masque*. Cambridge, MA: Harvard University Press, 1965.

——— and Roy Strong. *Inigo Jones: The Theatre of the Stuart Court*. 2 vols. Berkeley: University of California Press, 1973.

Orrell, John. "The Agent of Savoy at *The Somerset Masque*." *Review of English Studies* 28 (1977): 301–5.

Parfitt, George. *Ben Jonson: Public Poet and Private Man*. London: Dent, 1976.

Parry, Graham. *The Golden Age Restor'd: The Culture of the Stuart Court, 1603–42*. Manchester: Manchester University Press, 1981.

Patterson, Annabel. *Censorship and Interpretation: The Conditions of Writing and Reading in Early Modern England*. Madison: University of Wisconsin Press, 1984.

———. "Jonson, Marvell, and Miscellaneity?" In *Poems in Their Place: The Intertextuality and Order of Poetic Collections*, edited by Neil Fraistat, 95-118. Chapel Hill and London: University of North Carolina Press, 1987.

Paul, Sir James Balfour, ed. *The Scots Peerage*. 9 vols. Edinburgh: David Douglas, 1904–14.

Payne, Deborah C. "Patronage and the Dramatic Marketplace Under Charles I and II." *Yearbook of English Studies* 21 (1991): 137–52.

Pechter, Edward. "The New Historicism and Its Discontents: Politicizing Renaissance Drama." *PMLA* 102 (1987): 292–303.

Peltz, Catherine W. "Thomas Campion, An Elizabethan Neo-Classicist." *Modern Language Quarterly* 11 (1950): 3-6.

Perry, Henry Ten Eyck. *The First Duchess of Newcastle and Her Husband as Figures in Literary History*. Boston: Ginn & Co., 1918.

Peterson, R. T. *Sir Kenelm Digby: The Ornament of England, 1603–1665*. Cambridge, MA: Harvard University Press, 1956.

Peterson, Richard S. "The Iconography of Jonson's *Pleasure Reconciled to Virtue*." *Journal of Medieval and Renaissance Studies* 5 (1975): 123–51.

———. *Imitation and Praise in the Poems of Ben Jonson*. New Haven: Yale University Press, 1981.

Prestwich, Mina. *Cranfield: Politics and Profits Under the Early Stuarts*. Oxford: Clarendon Press, 1966.

Price, George. *Thomas Dekker*. New York: Twayne, 1969.

Randall, Dale B. J. *Jonson's Gypsies Unmasked: Background and Theme of* The Gypsies Metamorphos'd. Durham, NC: Duke University Press, 1975.

Riggs, David. *Ben Jonson: A Life*. Cambridge, MA: Harvard University Press, 1989.

Robertson, D. W., Jr. *A Preface to Chaucer: Studies in Medieval Perspectives*. Princeton: Princeton University Press, 1962.

Rowe, George E. *Distinguishing Jonson: Imitation, Rivalry, and the Direction of a Dramatic Career*. Lincoln: University of Nebraska Press, 1988.

Ruggle, George. *Ignoramus*. Translated by Robert Codrington. London, 1662.

———. *Ignoramus*. Edited by John Hawkins. London: Ginger, 1787.

———. *Ignoramus*. Edited by E. F. J. Tucker. Hildesheim: Georg Olms, 1987.

Salmon, Vivian. "An Ambitious Printing Project of the Early Seventeenth Century." *The Library*, 5th ser., 16 (1961): 190–96.

———. "Joseph Webbe: Some Seventeenth-Century Views of Language-Teaching and the Nature of Meaning." *Bibliothèque d'Humanisme et Renaissance* 23 (1961): 324–40.

———. "Problems of Language-Teaching: A Discussion Among Hartlib's Friends." *Modern Language Review* 59 (1964): 13–24.

———. *The Study of Language in 17th-Century England*. Amsterdam: Benjamins, 1979.

Savage, James E. *Ben Jonson's Basic Comic Characters and Other Essays*. N.p.: University and College Press of Mississippi, 1973.

Sharpe, Robert Boies. "Jonson's 'Execration' and Chapman's 'Invective': Their Place in Their Authors' Rivalry." *Studies in Philology* 42 (1945): 555–63.

Shipley, Neal R. "Thomas Sutton; Tudor-Stuart Money-Lender." *Business History Review* 50 (1976): 456–76.

Shirley, James. *The Dramatic Works and Poems of James Shirley*. Edited by Alexander Dyce. London: J. Murray, 1833.

Sidney, Sir Philip. *An Apology for Poetry*. Edited by Geoffrey Shepherd. Manchester: Manchester University Press, 1973.

Simmons, Joyce Monroe. "A Study of the Influence of Martial in the Renaissance Upon the Epigrams of Ben Jonson." Ph.D. diss., Duke University, 1980.

Slaughter, Thomas P. *Ideology and Politics on the Eve of the Restoration: Newcastle's Advice to Charles II*. Philadelphia: American Philosophical Society, 1984.

Small, Roscoe. *The Strange Quarrel Between Ben Jonson and the So-Called Poetasters*. New York: AMS Press, 1966.

Smith, David Nichol. *Characters from the Histories and Memoirs of the Seventeenth Century*. Oxford: Clarendon, 1918.

Smythe, R. *Historical Account of Charter-House*. London: C. Spilsbury, 1808.

Spenser, Edmund. *The Works of Edmund Spenser*. Edited by Edwin Greenlaw, et al. 10 vols. Baltimore: Johns Hopkins University Press, 1932–58.

Spink, Ian. "Campion's Entertainment at Brougham Castle, 1617." In *Music in English Renaissance Drama*, edited by John H. Long, 57-74. Lexington: University Press of Kentucky, 1968.

Sternfeld, Frederick W. "Song in Jonson's Comedy: A Gloss on *Volpone*." In *Studies in English Renaissance Drama in Memory of Karl Julius Holzknecht*, edited by Josephine W. Bennett, et al., 310-21. New York: New York University Press, 1959.

Sullivan, J. P. *Literature and Politics in the Age of Nero*. Ithaca and London: Cornell University Press, 1985.

Supple, B. E. *Commercial Crisis and Change in England 1600–1642: A Study in the Instability of a Mercantile Economy*. Cambridge: Cambridge University Press, 1959.

Sweeney, John Gordon, III. *Jonson and the Psychology of Public Theater*. Princeton: Princeton University Press, 1985.

Tacitus. *The Annals*. Translated by John Jackson. Loeb Classical Library. 4 vols. Cambridge, MA: Harvard University Press, 1962.

Taylor, Jennifer Reynolds. "Lucy Countess of Bedford, Jonson, and Donne." Ph.D. diss., McMaster University, 1979.

Taylor, William F. *The Charterhouse of London: Monastery, Palace, and Thomas Sutton's Foundation*. London: J. M. Dent, 1912.

Thayer, C. G. *Ben Jonson: Studies in the Plays*. Norman: University of Oklahoma Press, 1963.

Trevor-Roper, Hugh. "Thomas Sutton." *Carthusiana* 20, no. 1 (October, 1948): 2–8.

Trimpi, Wesley. *Ben Jonson's Poems: A Study in the Plain Style*. Stanford, CA: Stanford University Press, 1962.

Tucker, E. F. J. "*Ignoramus* and Seventeeth-Century Satire of the Law." *Harvard Library Bulletin* 19 (1971): 314–30.

Tufte, Virginia. *The Poetry of Marriage: The Epithalamium in Europe and Its Development in England*. Los Angeles: Tinnon-Brown, 1970.

van den Berg, Sara J. *The Action of Ben Jonson's Poetry*. Newark: University of Delaware Press, 1987.

Van Gundy, J. L. "*Ignoramus*" . . . *An Examination of Its Sources and Literary Influence*. Lancaster, PA: New Era Printing, 1906.

Veeser, Aram, ed. *The New Historicism*. New York and London: Routledge, 1989.

Walls, Peter. "Jonson's Borrowing." *Theatre Notebook* 28 (1974): 80–81.

Watson, Foster. *The Beginnings of the Teaching of Modern Subjects in England*. London: Isaac Pitman, 1909.

———. "Dr. Joseph Webbe and Language Teaching (1622)." *Modern Language Notes* 26 (1911): 40–46.

———. *The English Grammar Schools to 1660: Their Curriculum and Practice*. Cambridge: Cambridge University Press, 1908.

Watson, Robert N. *Ben Jonson's Parodic Strategy: Literary Imperialism in the Comedies*. Cambridge, MA: Harvard University Press, 1987.

Webbe, Joseph. *A Petition to the High Court of Parliament*. London, 1623.

Wells, Samuel. *A Collection of the Laws Which Form the Constitution of the Bedford Level Corporation*. London: R. Pheney, 1828.

White, Robert. "*Cupid's Banishment*: A Masque Presented to Her Majesty by Young Gentlewomen of the Ladies Hall, Deptford, May 4, 1617." Edited by C. E. McGee. *Renaissance Drama*, n.s. 19 (1988): 226–64.

[Wilford, John]. *Memorials and Characters*. London: J. Wilford, 1741.

Willcock, John. *The Great Marquess* . . . Edinburgh: Oliphant, Anderson & Ferrier, 1903.

Wilmot, E. P. Eardley and E. C. Steatfeild. *Charterhouse: Old and New*. London: John C. Nimmo, 1895.

Wilson, Arthur. *Life and Reign of King James, the First*. In *A Complete History of England*, edited by White Kennet. 3 vols. London: 1706, 2:661–792.

Wilson, Thomas. *Discourse Upon Usury*. Edited by R. H. Tawney. New York: Augustus M. Kelley, 1965.

Wind, Edgar. *Pagan Mysteries in the Renaissance*. Rev. ed. New York: Norton, 1968.

Winstanley, William. *England's Worthies*. London, 1660.

Wotton, Sir Henry. *The Life and Letters of Sir Henry Wotton*. Edited by Logan Pearsall Smith. 2 vols. Oxford: Clarendon Press, 1907.

Index